ONCE A LEEDS FAN
Always a Leeds fan

ONCE A LEEDS FAN
Always a Leeds fan

HEIDI HAIGH

Cover photos

Top left and bottom left: *Jamie, Michelle and Heidi*

Top right: *Carl Shutt, Chris Fairclough, Michelle, David Batty at the back. Gary Speed and Mel Sterland with Jamie at the front*

Bottom right: *Jamie, Heidi pregnant with Charlotte and Michelle*

First published 2014 by DB Publishing, an imprint of JMD Media Ltd, Nottingham, United Kingdom.

ISBN 9781780913995

Printed and bound by Copytech (UK) Limited, Peterborough.

Contents

Foreword by Glynn Snodin   9

Prologue   12

What is a loyal fan?   16

Leeds over the Years   25

Memories from the Seventies   37

Season 1973–74 – Champions and Record Breakers   53

Season 1974–75 – Record 70 matches   67

Costs and statistics for seven years 1971–78!   87

FA Cup and League Cup memories   107

Memorable matches   124

Matches abroad   137

The Leeds United Supporters Club – Selby branch   154

Memories by Leeds fan Phil Beeton   169

Football Recollections by Andy Johnson   183

Memories from Leeds fans   194

Loyal Supporters   212

Fun times   231

This book is dedicated to my family
My husband Phillip (Captain),
children Jamie, Michelle, Charlotte (RIP), Danielle and Emily
and my granddaughters Hannah, Laura and Alexis.
Thank you for putting up with my dedication to Leeds United and for
being fellow Leeds United supporters.

Foreword

by Glynn Snodin

I sat and watched the 1972 FA Cup Final against Arsenal and supported Leeds United as they were the northern team. Leeds won the match which was absolutely fantastic and I became a Leeds United fan. Although I watched them regularly on the television at the time, I was unable to go to many matches as my dad was a miner so there was no money to go to watch the matches live. When we did go, it was a once in a blue moon treat and coming from Rotherham meant that it wasn't easy to get to Leeds in those days. I was also playing football on a Saturday morning for the school team, then playing Saturday afternoons and Sundays for other teams. I wanted to become a Billy Bremner, Eddie Gray, Johnny Giles or Allan Clarke as I idolised those Leeds United players.

Becoming a Leeds United fan is like a drug and you are drawn to it even more so once you have been there as a player and it just gets you. The great Leeds United side under Don Revie played under those supporters too. Leeds United supporters are worldwide; they are all over, everywhere you go you see badges in cars and fans wearing Leeds shirts, they are so passionate and it was great to play under them. When you ran out onto the pitch as a player, the crowd gave us a 12th man and also made you want to give that extra bit for the fans. I had a great gaffer in Billy Bremner and then Howard Wilkinson. They were great days and were one of the best experiences I ever had of playing in front of those fans.

I didn't have any celebrations in my head before I scored a goal at the Kop end, so I just ran and jumped on to the fence to celebrate with the fans. I was so excited that the Leeds salute just came out, especially when everyone else started doing this in return and I just thought wow! This created a great relationship with the Leeds fans that remains to this day. I would run out at matches as we were warming up and they would sing my name and as soon as they sang it the second time I would do the salute. This really fired me up for the match and ensured I gave my all for the fans. If I see a Leeds fan when driving, I would pip the horn and do the salute or have photos taken doing the salute. I feel proud and honoured when asked to do this with the best football fans in the world!

A great experience for me was the promotion day against Bristol Rovers in 2010 when I was Assistant Manager to Simon Grayson at Leeds. There was a 38,000 crowd at Elland Road and I have never heard a noise like it when Johnny Howson scored the equaliser for Leeds, then this was surpassed when Jermaine Beckford got the winner to promote Leeds back to the Championship. It was a fantastic experience as I said a thank you for putting me here in this crowd to be a part of it. Everyone had played their part by putting everything into getting promoted that season.

My son Connor wasn't really into Leeds and I persuaded him to come to a match with me. At the next match he said that he really wanted to go again as he had enjoyed it. Now he travels to both home and away matches with Greeny and Gareth and many other mighty fans and has got the Leeds bug. Connor loves the build up to matches, sometimes stays out for the weekend with friends and loves the club. I still watch Leeds on the television when I get the opportunity and even if things aren't going right on the pitch, I can still hear the Leeds fans singing. As the saying goes "ups and downs" Leeds fans keep going regardless. This is the best club I have been to with Simon Grayson, another Leeds fan too.

Another time I went to Middlesbrough when Leeds won 2–0 with my son Connor and sat in with the fans behind the goal. At half time I said I was going down for a drink and Connor told me that I shouldn't even attempt it. Well I did go down and found that I couldn't move on the concourse for thousands of Leeds fans, singing and throwing beer around. I was wearing a suit and tie and ended up joining in with the fans and never got my drink.

I returned to Connor wet through but thoroughly happy as I had loved the experience.

I came to Elland Road when scouting for Charlton Athletic and saw Leeds beat Liverpool 4–3. Howard Wilkinson was in the box with me and I jumped up when Leeds got back to 3–3. When the fourth went in, I was jumping up and down like mad and doing the Leeds salute again and as the title of this book says, Once a Leeds fan, always a Leeds fan, I couldn't agree more!

Prologue

My first book *Follow Me and Leeds United* was based on a diary I kept in the seventies when I didn't miss a Leeds United match home or away for seven years. I had the privilege of seeing the great Don Revie side and also went abroad to see them play. Following on from that book is this new one called *Once a Leeds fan, always a Leeds fan*! Once I started following Leeds United it became a way of life, along with the camaraderie and long lasting friendships that have survived for just under 50 years. The unique bond between these supporters means that whatever roller coasters of emotions we are put through following our team, we stay loyal and true. Whether you go to every match or not, you will always be Leeds, supporting them through thick and thin. Being a Leeds United supporter is never easy though, but I wouldn't support anyone else!

This book starts in the seventies and includes times of following Leeds up to the present day. Although there have been some bad times, there have been some fantastic times along the way. The Leeds United team during the seventies were one of the most successful of the era and they are the reason why I am still the Leeds United supporter that I am to this day. Although they didn't win the amount of trophies that they should have done, they still played some fantastic football. There are still stories to tell people about what it was like for the ordinary fan to try and support their team. In the seventies all we wanted to do was to go to matches following our team, but the violence that followed us around impacted on this many times. The eighties was also a time with lots of football violence, but it was also a time when the Leeds fans who had taken a battering in the seventies, had grown up and started fighting back. The names of people in this book are fans who I have met through all my years of following Leeds and include many who were named in my first book. I have also managed to get some other Leeds fans to share their own experiences as a supporter over the years.

Just before my first child Jamie was born in September 1980, I still went to Elland Road to see Leeds. I was heavily pregnant and although I had no problems with my immediate friends, I received some looks of disgust from some lads for being at the football. Nowadays seeing pregnant women at football matches is seen as a more common occurrence. This includes my elder daughter Michelle who attended the Nottingham Forest match on 21 April 2014 along with my two granddaughters Hannah and Laura. Michelle was 37 weeks pregnant and we joked with her that she would give birth at Elland Road! As it was, baby Alexis waited until three weeks later to make her appearance but Michelle did get their seats in the Kop to be near us, just in case! All my children have been brought up to support Leeds from an early age and still support them now. My eldest child Jamie attended his first match in 1982 when he was 18 months old. I took him onto the terraces in the Kop whilst pregnant with my second child Michelle. It shows how the crowds were down as Leeds were battling relegation, because I was able to stand in my usual place at the top of the Kop with my friends. There was plenty space around us too. My daughter Michelle attended her first match at eight months old and again I took her onto the Kop with me. I used to put her in a baby carrier and stand at the top again. Once both children got a bit older, I used to stand near the front of the Kop with them where they were able to run about more.

Later, my other daughters attended their first matches at an early age, Charlotte at six days old and Danielle and Emily both at five weeks old. Danielle had her photo taken with the First Division Championship trophy at three weeks old plus Emily had a season ticket before she was born! Danielle and Emily are both current season ticket holders with me in the Kop.

Again, I am including many photographs of this time following Leeds, as I feel it is important to share these memories. My first book evoked a lot of memories of that time to many fans and in writing the same, I found it took me back to these places. Once the book was published, I have had fans contact me who I haven't seen in over thirty years! It was great seeing them again and it felt like only yesterday, but it was great reminiscing about these times. Even though I was scared stiff going to many of the matches, talking about these times with other fans doesn't seem half as bad now!

I look back fondly at the fact that in the seventies, it was because of following Leeds United, that I had the chance to travel the world. I went to cup rounds and finals in Switzerland, Belgium, Spain, Greece and France; friendlies in Denmark, Holland and Belgium. I travelled all over the UK from as far up to Dundee in Scotland and down to Plymouth in Devon, from Ipswich and Norwich in East Anglia, to Carlisle on the West Coast. I am sure the only reason I travelled to London was because of Leeds United, as I never went there any other time unless we were picking relatives up from Heathrow Airport.

My travels all over the world have continued throughout my years of following Leeds United. In September 1995 my husband Phillip and I flew to Monaco for the day. November 2001 we used the chance to have a rare family holiday by going to Disneyland, Paris on our way to see Leeds in Troyes, France. I also had another day trip to Deportivo in Spain in April 2001 but missed out on the trip to Valencia due to having an operation. I'm sure they lost because I wasn't there! It certainly is a good Geography lesson going to football matches, including all the football grounds around the United Kingdom (UK).

By going to matches, as well as giving me skills that I never realised I had over the years; I also became Secretary of the Selby Branch of the Leeds United Supporters Club arranging transport and tickets. It was also through the Supporters Club that I met my husband Phillip when he was running the Halifax branch. The people who run the Supporters Club branches are people I have known for many years and are very loyal fans. They do this on a voluntary basis through their love of Leeds United, sometimes at great cost to themselves. Again, this book tells of the fans I have met along the way, as well as where I have travelled, because whoever you support, without these loyal fans the football clubs would be nothing!

My grateful thanks to the Leeds fans who have contributed to this book; Dave Cocker, Twiggster from Denmark, Hayden Evans, Captain, Karl Shepherd, Steve Waterhouse, Mark Dovey, Counte of Monte Fisto, Phil Beeton, Andy Johnson, Ashley Tabony, Neale Sheldon, Lee Hession, Andrew Butterwick, Terje On Tour Hansen, Arnie Pirie, Keith Gaunt, Brian Austin, Marc Bracha, Gary Sleat, Michelle Kite and leedsrSlickers. I also wish to thank Glynn Snodin for writing the foreword to this book.

My friends Sue and Carole have decided to write their own books and I wish them luck and look forward to reading their accounts of interesting times following Leeds United. This is my second book and I am also co-authoring another book with Andrew Dalton called *The Good, The Bad and The Ugly of Leeds United* that will be published in 2014. This joint book is based on the eighties and I am grateful for the opportunity of being involved in this.

Chapter One

What is a loyal fan?

I am a long standing fan of Leeds United so feel that I am allowed my feelings on what describes a loyal fan. There have been many arguments amongst the Leeds fans on the social media sites in recent times with differing views on this. I also remember plenty of arguments amongst my friends and me during the seventies, because I would always stick up for our fans no matter what.

A loyal fan in my eyes constitutes them still following their club over many years, through the ups and downs, the good and bad times. Leeds United in my opinion, have the most loyal fans in the world. What many fans seem to argue about is the fact that you cannot be a fan/supporter if you don't go to matches. I look at it this way that at times circumstances change for people. It could be that they attended all home matches in the seventies or earlier; it could be that they were ever present home and away or even just going to specific matches. Sometimes they stop going for a number of years and then restart. Sometimes cost is an issue and stops fans from attending matches in the flesh. Some fans live many miles away in foreign countries and get to as many matches as they can over their lifetime. Leeds fans are based all over the UK too and it is a fact that the majority of the Leeds support comes from outside the city. There are a hard core of fans from Leeds too, but it doesn't matter where they live or how many times they get to Leeds matches, they are all part of our support. These people are still loyal fans in my eyes because no matter what has happened over the years, they still show their loyalty to their club and as the title of this book says, this means to Leeds United.

Over the years, it got to the stage where the lack of football has got in the way of a good day out. The one thing that kept everyone going was the camaraderie amongst the Leeds fans who were able to enjoy themselves despite the lack of ambition on the football pitch. This is what I feel is special about our fans, having met thousands over the years and who are still as loyal to Leeds today as they were at least 40 years ago. We have a worldwide fan base including some Norwegian fans who have been attending matches regularly at Elland Road since the seventies, along with many others from Ireland and America. A group of Norwegian fans come over every year to play the Kippax Branch at football in a Viking Fest. I went to one recently and it was a great day out and it is lovely to see the loyalty that these fans show to Leeds United.

Leeds United have had a rollercoaster ride over the last 10 years, with the fans' loyalty tested to the extremes, but they have remained with them steadfastly. They are the most loyal fans in the country having sold out their away tickets on a regular basis. Most matches at the moment are being televised at silly kick-off times because the viewing figures they get are enormous. It feels like we should have our own TV channel with that many fixtures televised. Football matches kicking off at 3.00 pm on a Saturday are a rarity now for Leeds fans with many kicking off at 12.15 pm. These silly times, mean fans have to set off to far away televised matches sometimes as early as 2.00 am! Admittedly some of these departure times mean they get to pubs early enough for a pre-match drink, but still the loyalty these fans show is fantastic. Despite this, the Leeds supporters still attend the matches in great numbers, especially away from home. Their away support is regularly the highest in the Championship and many times higher than some Premiership clubs' fans.

My own support of Leeds United started in 1965 and I attended my first match in 1967. My first run of seven years without missing a match home or away started in 1971. Having left school and started working, this meant that I was earning my own money. With my friend Sue and I making a pact to go and see as many Leeds matches as possible without missing one, this gave us a challenge. It was something that I managed to do, whereas Sue found she had to miss some as she was still at school.

Once bitten by the bug as any true fan will tell you, it is impossible to give it up. At the start of my time following the club, the great Leeds United side under manager Don Revie were one of the most successful teams of the era. The pull to watch them was very great and some of the football from Leeds was the best I have ever seen. Billy Bremner always was and always will be my hero and I credit his 100% effort every match, for instilling in me the loyalty and determination I needed to follow my team. Having been interviewed again recently on BBC Radio Leeds about my first book *Follow Me and Leeds United*, I was asked why I didn't give up going to matches after getting beaten up in a friendly match at Doncaster Rovers by eight girls in 1973? Also by getting abused both verbally and physically by male supporters at matches, why did I continue to go? I said that it was because I was doing something I loved by following my team and why should I give it up because of other people? There were many frightening times in the seventies but once you had got home safely, had a cry and a sleep, you found things never seemed as bad as they had been at the time.

The other thing that kept you going was the other Leeds fans that you met. There were a group of regular fans who travelled together everywhere and the only time you saw them was at the football matches. Over the years, many of these fans changed and you made friends with more and more people, but the core fans remained the same and have done to this day. There was no internet in those days or mobile phones and you arranged to meet people at matches just by talking to them. Now, with contacts made at matches, you can keep in touch via the internet on message boards, Facebook, Twitter, Websites and by mobile phones. The networking is great and shows what a worldwide fan base Leeds have. Some of my contacts now are in Scandinavia, America and Australia plus many other places.

One Leeds supporter Phil Beeton has just been crowned the Supporter of the Year at the Football League Awards 2014. Phil who is a member of the Griffin Branch of the Leeds United Supporters Club has just attended his 2,000th consecutive match at Bournemouth. That is a fantastic achievement and well deserved. I got to know his wife Chris first when she became part of the group of Leeds fans in the seventies, who travelled to every match on Wallace Arnold coaches. I can remember Phil starting to become part of our group of friends and I attended their wedding. Phil has also been responsible for organising travel and tickets for many Leeds fans to matches here in this country and abroad. I have spoken to him about his memories which are written later on in this book.

There are also many more fans who deserve accolades for their support of Leeds and recognition of their services to other fans. These include Keith Gaunt who runs the Fullerton Park Branch and Mick Hewitt who runs the South Kirkby Branch of the Leeds United Supporters Club. Another lad also called Mick Hewitt who ran the Vine Branch is another one who should be mentioned. There are many more fans that are just as deserving and I think they do a fantastic job and are the best. Another fan from the Fullerton Park Supporters Club, Ian English, has just received the Peter Lorimer's fan of the year award at the End of Season Awards dinner. Ian uses a wheelchair and deserves recognition for overcoming difficulties to attend matches on a regular basis.

In the seventies I travelled to some away matches with Abbey Coachways, a coach company from the village of Carlton where I lived. They would only run to some of the nearer matches although they did go as far as Nottingham and Wolverhampton. The owner of the coach was a big Leeds United fan, Brian Baker and the coach ran to all the home matches. As my friend Sue lived in Riccall which was near York, we then started to travel with York Pullman coaches. When we travelled to home matches with Abbey Coachways, the car park was always full of coaches from different areas of the country. It was when Sue and I decided that we were going to travel to Southampton that we found out that the only way to get there was to travel from Leeds with Wallace Arnold coaches.

By travelling with any of these coaches though, it meant that you got to know fans who travelled regularly to the matches. There will have been some fans who only followed the team for a short while, some admittedly only going when Leeds were doing really well and winning. Many of the fans we met at that time though are still going to matches to this day and there have been long lasting friendships made. The bond between the fans is something that cannot be taken away and is what makes Leeds United fans unique in my opinion. If you took football out of the conversation, there wouldn't have been anything left to talk about and I love reminiscing about the times of following Leeds. That includes the bad times as well as the good!

Despite crowds going really low in the eighties at Elland Road, the loyalty of the fans away from home was immense. Before membership cards were brought in due to football hooliganism, you could just turn up on the day, jump on a coach and pay your way into the ground with cash at the turnstiles. Some fans would just decide on the day that they would go to the match after all and just turn up, so there was no pre-booking match tickets and travel. The only reason we pre-booked with Wallace Arnold, was to make sure we got a ticket and that we always travelled on number one coach. It was towards the end of the seventies that Leeds fans started taking more coaches to the matches, once the football specials were stopped. In the eighties a group of Leeds supporters took the service train to matches and became known as the Service Crew. That was no different to what my friends and I had done in the seventies although we were trying to avoid any trouble, whereas the Service Crew became known for being involved in trouble at matches.

The last few years as a Leeds United supporter have really been a roller coaster of emotions for everyone. There have also been plenty of matches where the team haven't turned up, but the fans have. We can have a fantastic day out with our fellow supporters only for the lack of football to spoil it. Our loyalty though has never ceased to amaze me and the *Once a Leeds fan, always a Leeds fan* title could not be more apt. The Chumbawamba song with the words "I get knocked down... but I get up again... you're never gonna keep me down!!!!" has also never been more apt a saying for Leeds fans (if I remember correctly, they were Leeds fans that sung this song). It feels like this has happened to us so many times, but it is also showing what fanatics we have as fans. However many times we get 'kicked in the teeth' we keep going back for more.

When Leeds were relegated at Derby County in 2007 to what I still class as the old Third Division (League One), Leeds fans still managed to have a laugh and act with dignity. They kept singing that we would be on the pitch when there was no intention whatsoever, but seeing how the Derby stewards and coppers reacted was quite funny. Leeds were automatically docked 10 points on entering voluntary administration which meant we were relegated. What we didn't expect was getting another 15 points docked at the start of the next season for not using the correct procedures for exiting administration.

The day I heard about the –15 points, was also the day that I started to post on the Leeds United message board, The Rivals, on the internet. I was absolutely seething and this feeling was shared with every other Leeds fan that I came across at the time. It felt like it was a Leeds against everyone else scenario but what it did do, was galvanise the support so that it was us against the world! The good thing about this was that it brought the support closer together and how we celebrated when we got back to zero points. It also meant that I was able to go to some new football grounds that I hadn't been to before with Leeds. I didn't manage to get to all the away matches but I got to quite a few and it was a great time again following Leeds regardless of the circumstances. The sad thing is that without having those extra points docked, we would have been promoted at the end of the season.

The internet has changed how football supporters keep in touch these days. It has also been a fantastic way of networking and promoting my first book *Follow Me and Leeds United*. I never thought I was good at anything until I started to use ICT. I was initially scared stiff that a computer would blow up in my face if I pressed the wrong button, especially when my children were so competent with them. I enrolled on a course where I found out that I had a flair for ICT and passed many exams. Once I realised I was good at something and that I did have some skills that I have developed over the years, I have designed and created my own website *www.followmeandleedsunited.co.uk* and use both Facebook *Follow Me and Leeds United* and Twitter *@FollowMeAndLUFC*. Not bad for someone who left school with one GCE and two CSEs! It also is a major change to when I first started following Leeds and going to matches, because now there are mobile phones with cameras/videos embedded in them for recording things as they happen. I still like to take lots of photos which I use as a networking tool too. Talking about photos, I think I have only taken a few and then when I come to upload them I realise that I have actually taken more like 50+ and recently 100+, oops! The one thing that comes across though is that lots of our fans enjoy seeing the photos from the matches, especially if they cannot get to them. It also keeps our worldwide fan base in touch with what is happening at the grounds and makes them feel part of it still. They also recognise people from over the years and once again, this spreads the name of Leeds United around the world. The first message board I frequented was the Rivals and I met up with *leedsRSlickers, Clearlysighted, BillyisGod, Hooter* plus a few more in the Peacock garden. It was nice to put some faces to names and we are all still in contact now. The latter were involved in the Leeds United Supporters Trust who put out a vision statement about what they wanted to see from the club moving forwards. I agreed with the statement and joined the Trust on that basis. I am also a Leeds United Supporters Club member too, having started out with the Postal Branch, then the Selby Branch and now I am a member of the Ripon Branch. My children and grandchildren are also all Supporters Club members. Whatever happens, I will never relinquish my membership of the Supporters Club. I travel to away matches with the Fullerton Park Branch of the Leeds United Supporters Club with my friend Sue who is an away season ticket holder. My children also come on the coach if they have tickets, although sometimes they make other travel arrangements.

The one thing that has really changed in football is the money that has now come into the sport. Sky TV has meant that football has changed beyond all recognition since I started following Leeds. Footballers are now on obscene salaries and paid more in one week than some of us will earn in a lifetime! Admittedly, if they are offered the huge financial incentives as part of their contracts, they are not going to say no! I do feel that this has had a detrimental effect on the way footballers play now, with some never showing their true worth. There is also too much player power where they only think about themselves and not their paying customers. Also the loyalty that players have towards their clubs is not the same as it was in the seventies. It is time to go back to making players earn their pay by paying win bonuses rather than large salaries in my opinion. I feel that too many players do not put enough effort into their play and are out of touch with the supporters of their club. Even if we lose I can accept it if they put 100% effort in. Unfortunately too many players do not live up to expectations and cannot take criticism. That is an opinion shared amongst many Leeds fans who have had to put up with lack lustre football and bad ownership problems at Elland Road for many years. Too many players cannot cope with the pressures of playing at Elland Road, when all we want is for a player to play for the shirt and give us 100% effort. Regardless of this, the support Leeds fans have shown their club is extraordinary, remarkable and shown true loyalty in times of strife!

It is now looking likely that the 'TOMA – Take over my A**e' the name given to the ownership issues by someone on the WACCOE message board, has been completed. Massimo Cellino has been given the go ahead to become a Director of Leeds United. Not without its issues along the way, but I will leave the writing about this to others. They will be able to explain what has happened at Leeds in a much better way than I would be able to do. What I will say though, is that the stress this has put our loyal fans under has been horrendous. Personally, I feel it has affected me pretty badly. I want stability at our great club and want to move forwards without all the issues in the background. At the moment though, there are still severe financial problems going on at the club which are a complete mess. We as supporters can only hope that this time the club gets sorted out from top to bottom in the right way, so that we can focus once again on the most important factor at Elland Road, the Football! I also look forward to our fan base not being divided anymore, as they were throughout the Bates era and during the last eight months. I know that you will never get everyone to agree to the same thing as there will always be differing opinions, but despite this I am hopeful that we will all soon be Marching on Together again!

Chapter 2

Leeds over the Years

I realise the years have sped past since I attended my first match, but it feels unbelievable when I realise I have supported them for just short of 50 years! I have no idea how many matches I have attended during that time but have probably only missed a handful of home matches since 1971. My record number of matches that I went to in one season was 1974–75 when I saw 70 matches. I don't think footballers now would be able to cope with that number of matches in a season. When I think of some of the pitches that Leeds played on in the seventies, many resembled a beach rather than a football pitch. The times they played on snowy, frozen pitches where they still managed to play football and show some fantastic skills, make footballers today seem very lightweight. Also the ball they played with was so much heavier in those days, which makes the football they played in those circumstances, stand out even more! Seeing any matches now of those earlier times of following Leeds makes me feel really nostalgic but I am so glad that I had the chance to be there. It is the Leeds United team of the late sixties, early seventies who have made me the Leeds fan that I am today. They showed what being loyal to your team is all about and is what has kept me following them all these years.

Leeds had fantastic success during the Revie years although they never won the trophies they should have, many times due to dubious refereeing decisions. This was evidenced by the European Cup Winners Cup Final in Salonika in 1973 where it was alleged that the referee was bribed and also the European Cup Final with Jimmy Armfield in 1975 with the alleged bribery of the referee. Although Leeds not playing well on a regular basis was starting to happen more and more when Armfield was in charge, the Leeds fans were still all shouting their support for him. It was always going to take time with the rebuilding of the team, after the majority of players from the Revie era came to the end of their careers at the club. After Jimmy Armfield was sacked I was disgusted as Leeds were still one of the top clubs in the country but that wasn't good enough for the board. It was also about this time that I stopped writing about what happened at matches in my diary. For a few years I also stopped going to away matches around 1979–80 although I still went to all the home matches. First of all I stopped going because of all the trouble at the away matches, as I couldn't cope with the fear and stress of getting to and from matches safely. I then had my first two children in 1980 and 1982 which impacted on going to away matches for a while. This was when I feel the decline became very rapid and there were turbulent times ahead for Leeds. Jock Stein was appointed manager but he only lasted a short time, refusing to sign a contract at Leeds and then accepted the position as manager of Scotland. Jimmy Adamson then became the manager of Leeds after Maurice Lindley initially took over as caretaker manager and things started off quite well in his first season after Leeds had got off to a bad start. Things got worse the following season when the worst football I had seen Leeds play came under his tenure, along with the lowest crowds seen at Elland Road. After Adamson was sacked Allan Clarke one of Don Revie's team took over, but even he couldn't stop the decline and subsequently it took Leeds a long while to get out and back to the top flight after relegation.

The decline also saw hooliganism start to get really bad and Elland Road became a cauldron of hate for visiting teams. Although the crowds went down dramatically, I think at one match there were only approximately 8,000 fans there, the atmosphere was brilliant. Visiting teams used to hate coming to Leeds because they were 'intimidated' by the atmosphere. Both the Gelderd End (Kop) and the South Stand generated this atmosphere and this is something that was a great thing to be part of. All the grounds had fences across the fronts of the stand and Elland Road became a ground that opposition clubs didn't like to visit. Although the quality of the football had disappeared this was a time in the early eighties, despite all the hooliganism that went on, that Leeds

United fans showed their loyalty and passion for supporting their club. It was also a time when we were made to have a red card to be able to travel to away matches. Due to all the trouble Leeds fans had been involved in, the authorities together with the club decided that away matches should become all ticket. The tickets would only be sold to members, season ticket holders and Supporters Club members and the personal details together with home addresses of the fans would be kept on a database for reference.

Once I started going back to away matches in the eighties it was like I had never been away. Hooliganism was rife but I actually felt safer in these times than I did when I travelled away in the seventies. There were some good times during these years though because the Leeds fans stuck together wherever they went. The abuse from lads had diminished from what it was like in the seventies and there was a lot a respect from many of them instead. Because we started getting coppers escorting us to and from the grounds, I stopped panicking that the opposition fans would attack me. After the violence in the seventies when many of our fans had taken a beating, they had started fighting back. Even though I still wore my colours, I didn't feel that violence followed me around as it had done in the past.

Leeds had been relegated from the old First Division when Allan Clarke was manager in 1982. Leeds had to travel to West Bromwich Albion (WBA) in a relegation battle, where unfortunately they lost 2–0 giving WBA the chance to survive the drop. Near the end of the match Leeds fans had started rocking the safety fences at the front of the terraces which eventually gave way after a good 10 minutes. This meant the coppers charged the Leeds fans with batons, the fans retaliated with missiles and trouble carried on until after the final whistle. WBA still had a further match to play against Stoke City another Midlands team, which gave them both an advantage with Leeds having already played their last match of the season. We knew there wouldn't be any favours heading our way, especially due to the trouble with the Leeds fans at WBA prior to this. It proved to be when Stoke won 3–0 at The Hawthorns therefore relegating Leeds to the Second Division. It was a foregone conclusion that they wouldn't do Leeds any favours and it certainly looked like WBA had lain down and died to ensure Stoke ended up safe, thus ending our First Division reign. Allan Clarke ended up being sacked as Leeds manager during the close season in 1982.

Eddie Gray another of Don Revie's team was appointed the new Leeds player/manager in the summer of 1982. Eddie Gray started to introduce some of the youth into the Leeds United team including John Sheridan, Tommy Wright and Denis Irwin, as part of rebuilding the squad. It was a good time to start with the youngsters as many of the current squad were coming to the end of their careers or had been on high salaries, which couldn't be sustained by the club who were having financial difficulties. I also thought that we started to play some attractive football during this time when these youngsters started playing for us. I had started going back to some away matches during Eddie's reign as manager and one that stands out for me was a pre-season friendly at Falkirk in 1983. I travelled up by car with a friend of mine Mike; along with both my children Jamie aged three and Michelle aged one. I can remember walking along the street pushing a double buggy with them both in and then hearing someone stood outside a pub shout my name as we passed by. There were loads of Leeds fans there and many I knew, but for some reason I didn't expect to see so many. Following Leeds over the years I should have known, but obviously with not being to many away matches for the previous couple of years, I had forgotten what it was like. Despite relegation to the Second Division, the loyalty of the Leeds fans was overwhelming.

When I arrived at the turnstiles with the children I thought it would be a good idea to go in the seats with them rather than go on the terraces. The turnstile operator said that I could go into the stand and not have to pay for Jamie and Michelle. I folded the buggy up and managed to get into the stand with a bit of difficulty, but was able to sit at the front of the stand with them both. It was a lovely sunny day and great to be back watching Leeds again. The match ended up with a 2–2 draw with Frank Gray the brother of manager Eddie, given a torrid time by Kevin McAllister who was making his debut for Falkirk. McAllister was a raw 19-year-old winger, a local lad who went on to become the club's player of the Millennium. Frank Gray couldn't catch the lad and got completely ripped apart by the player who became a firm fan's favourite for Falkirk.

I was devastated when a couple of months into the 1985–86 season Eddie Gray was sacked after a bad start by Leeds. Fans demonstrated in the West Stand because we wanted Eddie to stay as manager. We knew it was a time for rebuilding the squad with some of the youth in the team starting to develop and gain more physical strength. It was something that was going to take time, but unfortunately the Leeds United board saw it differently. The board wanted immediate results and weren't prepared to wait, although the vote wasn't unanimous to get rid of Eddie, as one of the directors resigned in protest at the decision.

Leeds then appointed Billy Bremner as manager which we felt at the time was to quieten the fans down, although the appointment was welcomed. As I idolised Billy when he was a Leeds United player I had no doubts about his commitment and loyalty to the club. At the time Leeds were having severe financial difficulties which ended up with Elland Road being sold to the council. The first season he was manager, Billy sold many of the youngsters that Eddie Gray had brought into the team as he felt their loyalty to Eddie would be detrimental to how they played for him. It wasn't until the following season that his team so nearly made it back to the big time. Leeds having got to the FA Cup semi-final in 1987 against Coventry, eventually lost 3–2 in extra-time. If only Brendan Ormsby could have either put the ball out for a corner or dummied the ball to let it go out for a goal-kick. Instead he was robbed of the ball by the Coventry player to enable them to score, but I do feel we could have won the match if it hadn't have been for that mistake. We also had the heartbreak of the play offs against Charlton. I felt Peter Shirtliff who was a Charlton player was lucky to stay on the pitch after a bad foul. He ended up scoring two late goals to win the match for Charlton. I was devastated that we didn't succeed under Billy as he had come so close to getting Leeds promoted and Leeds were very unlucky not to do it. The day that Leeds sacked Billy Bremner in September 1988, was a real low for me and many other Leeds fans; I was devastated as he was and still is my hero. I was down at Elland Road when he came to say goodbye to the players and there was a picture on TV of me in the crowd. He said goodbye to the fans who were there too, shaking hands with many of them. When I heard that Billy Bremner had died of a heart attack after a bout of pneumonia on 7 December 1997, I was so upset that a part of Leeds United was now gone. I had to go and pay my respects to the greatest player on earth, for giving me the best moments of my life in following Leeds. I had to go to his funeral and was in the crowd outside the church with loads of other Leeds fans to pay my respects to a Leeds United legend. I could also be seen in the crowd on the TV as I was wearing a bright blue coat. As much as I disliked Alex Ferguson the manager of man utd (as with my previous book this is a swear word and has to be in lower case), I was very pleased to see him turn up at the church for Billy.

When Howard Wilkinson, the next manager to be appointed took over, eventually the good times came back when Leeds won promotion to the First Division and then won the First Division title. Howard's first thing was to take down all the photos of Don Revie's players as he felt that Leeds were 'living in the past!' In his first season he brought in Gordon Strachan into the midfield and Chris Fairclough into the defence. It wasn't until the following season that Leeds started to give the fans some hope that things were going to improve. Vinnie Jones was signed from Wimbledon and had come with a reputation as a hard man. Vinnie soon ended up as a cult hero for many Leeds fans and even had a tattoo on his ankle saying 'Leeds United – Division Two Champions 1990'. Another signing was Lee Chapman who was to score the winning goal at Bournemouth at the end of the 1989–90 season to send us back into the First Division.

Promoted back to the First Division, the Leeds team had a fantastic midfield consisting of David Batty, Gordon Strachan, Gary McAllister and Gary Speed. This season was very good for Leeds considering it was our first one back up amongst the elite and ended up finishing fourth in 1990–91. It also included our epic FA Cup run with Arsenal that went to three replays, more about this is mentioned later in the book. The following season was to take Leeds back to the big time when they were crowned League Champions at the end of the 1991–92 season. Leeds had only four defeats in the league all season with their first loss in October against Crystal Palace away from home and also had a memorable 6–1 win away at Sheffield Wednesday with Dorigo, a Chapman hat trick, Whitlow and Rod Wallace scoring for Leeds. Leeds topped the table at the end of the season with 82 points and left man utd as runners up with 78 points. It was also the last time anyone would be Champions of the First Division as the Premier League that is known today, was created. So Leeds United are the last Champions to ever win the old First Division.

Unfortunately we didn't manage to maintain this momentum and the season after in 1992–93 ended up 17th and close to a relegation battle. In 1993–94 after a better season Leeds ended up 5th in the table, 1994–95 – 5th again and in 1995–96 – 13th. Unfortunately after an indifferent start, Howard was sacked in 1996 with George Graham brought in to steady the ship. Graham oversaw a number of losses so his goal was to sort out the defence and enable us to keep clean sheets. He managed this and although it made some of the matches seem quite boring at the time, at least we weren't losing and managed to pick up the points. Again he was another manager that found his second season reap the rewards as Leeds ended up in fourth position and secured their return to Europe in the UEFA Cup. Once George Graham went back to London to manage Spurs in 1998 David O'Leary who had been his assistant was promoted to manager after he left.

David O'Leary was very lucky that there were some up and coming youngsters at Leeds when he took over. Alan Smith was one of those youngsters and I can remember him coming onto the pitch at Liverpool and scoring a goal on his debut to put Leeds ahead (I think it was his first touch of the ball as well). Jonathan Woodgate, Lee Bowyer, Stephen McPhail and Ian Harte were other youngsters and Leeds ended up with an exciting team. With a good defence left over from George Graham and the introduction of the youngsters everything seemed to come together. Leeds were becoming a favourite even amongst other fans and we had some good times once again on the pitch. At the end of the 1998–99 season Leeds finished fourth in the Premier League and qualified for the UEFA cup. In 1999–00 Leeds finished third and qualified for the European Cup. These finishes in the league meant a return to European football which resulted in many exciting matches both abroad and at home. David O'Leary was to start the rot by spending loads of money on players along with the blessing of Peter Ridsdale the Leeds Chairman at the time. Once the bubble burst, off the field events overshadowed the club; these included the tragic murders of two Leeds fans in Turkey who were killed the night before the match in Istanbul by Galatasary fans. Woodgate and Bowyer were also involved in an incident in Leeds where they went to court for an alleged assault on a student, when things went from bad to worse. The rot was setting in and many a time the overpaid prima donnas who should have had pride in pulling the Leeds shirt on and playing out of their skins every match, didn't turn up and perform. Eventually Leeds were relegated from the Premier League in 2004 and were going into freefall financially.

The one manager who I think contributed to Leeds United's downfall more than anyone was Terry Venables (vegetables was the pet name given to him by some of us fans). He was appointed in July 2002 after O'Leary was sacked in the close season of 2002. He dropped Olivier Dacourt who played in midfield and replaced him with Paul Okon who wasn't fit to lace his boots as a footballer. It showed to me how out of touch Venables was, especially when he had a public fall out with Dacourt and said he would drive Dacourt to Italy himself as he had been linked with a loan move to AS Roma. That was a massive body blow as Dacourt was a very good player for us. Leeds were also starting to go through severe financial problems too and to ease things there were more player sales, which in turn resulted in further problems on the pitch. It ended up with Leeds battling relegation and Venables sacked in March 2003. Leeds managed to secure their Premier League survival with a 3–2 win away at Arsenal with Peter Reid now managing the club. Venables sacking also coincided with Peter Ridsdale the Leeds Chairman leaving the club at the same time. He effectively gambled with the future of Leeds by selling off future gate receipts, but the figures were based on Leeds qualifying for the Champions League again. Unfortunately this didn't happen and Leeds started to implode having debts of over 100 million.

Leeds went through a number of barren years after being relegated from the Premiership in 2004, Peter Reid had been sacked earlier in the season and Eddie Gray was given the role of caretaker manager but could not prevent us going down. We then got further relegated to League One in 2007. We did get to the play-off Finals against Watford at Cardiff in 2006 (Championship) and Doncaster at Wembley in 2008 (League One) but failed at both hurdles. Simon Grayson became manager in 2008 and he brought in as his assistant manager Glynn Snodin, both of them having played for Leeds in the past. This started to be a time when Leeds played some attractive football once again and managed to put up some good fights against Premiership teams that we met in cup matches, including a memorable one against man utd at Old Trafford. It was also a time when Leeds got automatic promotion back into the Championship in 2010 on the last day of the season. Fantastic scenes of celebrations were seen at Elland Road once again, especially when we thought it wasn't going to happen when Leeds were reduced to ten men when Gradel was sent off. The final score was 2–1 to Leeds after Johnny Howson equalised for Leeds before Jermaine Beckford scored the winner. The following season we were in or around the play off places and there was hope again that we could be promoted back to the Premiership. When Leeds started stuttering with results in 2012 rumours started flying around that Grayson would be sacked. I was one of the fans who didn't want him to be sacked as I didn't feel we would be better off in the long run. I wanted stability and sacking and changing managers as much as Leeds had done didn't work in my opinion. It always meant that there would be more players out of favour with a new manager and you were left to get rid of players that should no longer be there. As it was Bates did sack him and brought in Neil Warnock. He was another one who could talk the talk, but I was very sceptical that he would be right for Leeds, as he was only going to be there for a short while.

This takes us to where we are today, Brian McDermott the manager having left the club by mutual consent with a new owner Massimo Cellino at Leeds still with GFH Capital holding a percentage of the club and previous to them Ken Bates. It has felt like Leeds have been rotten to the core as a club for years and there is a lot to sort out. The only thing that has been shining out as usual has been the long suffering Leeds United fans. They have stuck with them through thick and thin with tremendous support. In the programme for the Blackpool match on 12 April 2014 is an article called I am Leeds and today I am the proud Leeds fan with her story published. With only a few matches left till the end of the season, Leeds at last got a win and beat Blackpool at home with two goals scored by Luke Murphy. Getting the three points hopefully settled the team down, avoided another relegation battle and gave us chance to move on as a club again, starting from next season.

Billy Bremner, Paul Reaney and Don Revie at the Irish Centre with Heidi and Karin, the photograph is autographed on the back by the team

Photo Yorkshire Evening Post – Chelsea 12 August 1972 – Joan, Maureen, Esther, Heidi, Chris, Colleen

Left: League Championship trophy 1974 Heidi with Mark
Right: Amsterdam preseason tour 1976 – Leeds fans on
the pitch at Ajax's ground

Left: Paris – European Cup Final 28 May 1975 – Leeds fans
Right: Jimmy Armfield's house 1975 – Andy, Carole, Jimmy and Linda

Chapter 3

Memories from the Seventies

Memories below are taken from extracts from the diary I kept in the seventies and refer to people I met along the way. I have met thousands of Leeds fans over the years and some of the names I mention are of Leeds fans who still go to matches to this day.

---

9 March 1968 against Bristol City which Leeds won 2–0 with goals from Jones and Lorimer.

I can remember Sue and me standing at the front of the Kop for this FA Cup tie and Gary Sprake got sent off. Jones and Lorimer had put Leeds into the lead, but all hell let loose near the end of the match when Garland a Bristol player brought Billy down. The referee went to book Garland who was then punched in the face by Gary, after Garland had spat in his face. Billy Bremner always was and always will be the greatest and a favourite player of myself and Sue, but Gary was another favourite at the time. The referee promptly sent Gary off so Sue swore at the referee calling him a b******d. At that time the coppers used to sit all around the outside of the hoardings at the front of the stands. One turned round and said: "I don't think your mother would like to hear you say things like that!" We were shocked to have a copper tell us off and didn't really say much for the rest of the match. It was down to one of the coppers near us, that Gary only received a fine in the end and wasn't banned as he had seen the spitting incident.

---

8 November 1975 saw the visit of Newcastle to Elland Road. Leeds won the match comfortably with a 3–0 win with goals from McKenzie (2) and Yorath.

A great match at Elland Road was against Newcastle. The Kop was in brilliant form at this match as we sang for over five minutes non-stop singing hello,

hello, we are the Armfield boys. I'm not sure if this was the match where we sang it and drowned out the Geordies singing the Blaydon races. It sounded great and I had to laugh in the end because our fans didn't stop singing it and this shut them up. As I was going back up the Kop at half time I hit Pete and he shouted: "hey copper arrest her and fine her £1,000 she's hitting me" and the copper laughed. After the match I went back to the Supporters Club for a drink. I saw Alan Jackson and Sandy playing table football so went over to have a word with them. I've no idea what we talked about but in response to something Alan said, I hit him and spilt his drink! He said: "she's not been in five minutes and she's causing trouble", but he wasn't mad at me luckily. Looking back at my memoirs I certainly hit a lot of Leeds fans, oops!

On 15 November 1975 we travelled to Middlesbrough for a 0–0 draw.

I travelled on a Wallace Arnold coach to Middlesbrough with my friends. I sat next to little Ian, Gary was in front of us and Sue, Carole and Violet sat on the back seat with Geoff and his friend. Bob Vasey and Kevin Sharp were sat in front of Linda. We sang a lot on the way up, which carried on when we got to Middlesbrough as all the coaches arrived together. Therefore all the Leeds fans went in a gang to the ground singing as we went, which was great as we normally didn't go up to the ground together, especially wearing our colours. As we passed a copper he said that lot won't come back. We crossed the road and the Howdle twins started singing Heidi give us a song, not that they got one! We got to the ground, went for some programmes and were ahead of the rest of the Leeds fans, when some Boro fans immediately called us names. Linda heard the Leeds fans coming round the corner so told them to say it again but they ran. We then got around the corner to see the Boro fans coming towards us because they had heard the Leeds fans coming, but stopped short of us.

We managed to get into the ground okay after this and I don't think there was much trouble outside, as for once there were a lot of coppers around. We were standing on the open terraces with no cover when it started raining. We stood in the corner of the ground amongst the Leeds fans where the home fans were also housed, singing and shouting. A group of Leeds fans decided to move to the right of us but we stayed where we were. At the start of the match some Boro fans came to the left of us and were soon surrounded by the Leeds fans, but the coppers intervened to stop them being attacked. One of the lads from Advance coach came to stand with us plus his mates and told us that they had had a knife pulled on them outside. He said his dad drove the Advance coaches and asked me why I didn't go back on it because it picked up in Goole and the surrounding area. They were going to ask me at both the Derby and Birmingham matches to see if I wanted to travel to away matches with them. During the second half we got absolutely soaked as the heavens opened even more. At about 4.30 pm we were going to the exits when a fight broke out and all the Boro fans started coming in. Because this was a ground renowned for violence from the Boro fans, we wanted to get back to the coaches safely hence leaving before the end of the match. We decided to go to the other entrance but Boro fans were hanging around that one too, so I said not to go that way. One Boro fan said we'll show you the way out and kick you out. We returned to the other entrance and found out that only six Boro fans had come into the ground and had got kicked to hell by the Leeds fans.

We didn't wear our colours back to the coach because you had to go half way round the ground and pass their end. We stayed close to this man and his little boy wearing Boro scarves till we got past their end with Karen and Linda in front of us. These two Boro fans said that we were from Leeds and asked us how we had come so I retorted that we had walked. He said he would walk us back home as he thought lasses from Leeds were great. He certainly wasn't getting the chance and no way were we going to trust him. All of a sudden we saw about seven lads spread across the path in front of us. Sue and I panicked thinking they were Boro fans going to prevent us getting back to the coach. It turned out to be the Advance coach lot and we told them they had nearly scared us both to death. Got back on the coach okay and saw a load of Boro fans go past. I thought we were going to get some windows put through but luckily on this occasion, we didn't. Some lads knocked on the window and asked me to go to the door but I didn't know who they were so stayed put. They said they were Leeds but I didn't trust them. One of the lads on our coach had been nutted and kicked and had his head split open. Ian said a Boro fan said to him that he was too young to go knacking Leeds fans and it was a good job he didn't know Ian was one. Gary said that he hit a Boro fan and shouted he's from Leeds and loads of Boro fans piled into their own fan.

---

25 September 1976 Leeds travelled to Middlesbrough for a match where they were defeated 1–0.

When we arrived at Middlesbrough, we found the Pontefract coach arrived at the same time as us. The Worksop and Doncaster lads arrived just after them so we all walked down to the ground together and didn't see any trouble. We got to the ground and some Boro were down the side streets but they wouldn't come out as the Leeds special lot arrived at the same time as us. Inside the ground we had to walk through some Boro fans stood at the side near the fence to get to the toilets, although coppers prevented the rest of the Leeds fans from going near them. We heard a scuffle whilst I was in the loos and two Boro fans tried getting a Leeds fan but a copper stopped them. We went over to stand next to Linda, Steve and the Leicester lads who spoke when they saw me. Saw a lad from Harrogate and he said Douggie was looking for me as he'd taken some prints off my photos and had his negatives from Holland. I also saw Mick from Selby and he said they'd just been got in town by some Boro fans. There wasn't much trouble in the ground although loads of Boro in the corner near us were arrested. At about 4.30 pm we decided to go and we got out of a side door with a lot of our lot and managed to get past their end before the gates opened. Once again at Boro we were leaving the match early to avoid any trouble. Gadge and one percent walked back with us and we found our coach was locked so we couldn't get on it. Carole, Karen and I went back to the shop then and saw the rest of the Leeds fans coming back wearing their scarves with the coppers escorting them. There had been some trouble and I saw two lads with blood on them, but Leeds fans had stuck together this year.

---

24 April 1976 came the last league match at QPR where Leeds lost 2–0.

I got a lift into Selby at 6.30 am with Jonathan and Nicky from Rawcliffe and caught the 7.25 am train with Sue who we met at the train station. Linda, Steve and Paul were waiting for us in Leeds station and others at the Corn Exchange before we went down for the coach. Sue sat with Alan, Carole with Paul and Ian sat next to me. At the services there were queues for the ladies on our side so Linda, Carole and I crossed over to the other side of the motorway where Linda decorated the loos with a pen. Was just going to go back to the other side when four coaches of Aldershot fans pulled in going to Halifax so we watched them come in and loads of Leeds fans came over too. Some Aldershot fans didn't dare come in at first, but we went down and started talking to some. They asked who I supported and then asked about the QPR match when we had won the league. This lad said he had been there and that there was loads of trouble after the match. He asked how many of us were going to QPR and we said they had only sent us 1,000 tickets, but loads more would go. He had heard that loads of our fans were going to their match, so said that if we were taking so many to QPR it can't be true about Leeds fans going to Halifax. Got back on the coach and I sat next to Paul.

On arriving at QPR at 12.45 pm we walked down to the ground but didn't wear our coats as it was warm enough. I had five scarves on and was wearing my Leeds jumper and shirt, Sue had her shirt and three scarves on and Carole had seven scarves, her banner and shirt on. Our scarves were normally worn around our wrists with one around our neck. We went into the pub next to the ground to use the loos and were pointed in the direction of some downstairs ones. We tried "fighting" our way across the pub to get to the loos but couldn't find them so we decided to go back out the front way. On our way out we saw Mick from Selby and he told us that there had been loads of trouble at the pub all morning. The Goole lot were also there and one lad told me that Sally from London was drunk. Just as we got outside we heard the Leeds fans starting to sing first, then the QPR fans started and we knew there was going to be some trouble in there. Three coppers went in the door we had just come out of as we heard glasses smashing. Some Leeds fans came running out of the front entrance and the QPR fans out of the side. Then the QPR fans shouted: 'charge' and started chasing the Leeds fans, so we dived to the side of the road, grabbing hold of the fence as they ran past us. Leeds fans stopped, turned and chased the QPR fans and then the QPR fans chased the Leeds fans again, before Leeds fans smashed some windows at the nearby White City. Eventually things quietened down as we went to queue up with loads of other Leeds fans to go into the ground. At the turnstiles we were told we had to go in the other side, so we went round the ground with loads of Leeds fans including loads of Cockney Whites. Some Millwall fans joined with Leeds and some with QPR (often when their club were playing away from home they would go to other matches in London).

In the ground we saw the Ossett lads, Billy and Mark. We went and stood over the tunnel as more and more Leeds fans came in, meaning we got crushed and could hardly move. We were swaying like mad when the coppers came in to the crowd of us. I got separated from the others then and was stood in front of the cameras next to Sean, Pete Underwood, Karen and Violet. At the end of the match I moved over to find Sue just as some QPR fans decided to invade the pitch from their end and some came over to the Leeds fans for a fight. Pete, Ian and some more ran on to the pitch but the coppers sent them back onto the terraces, then escorted out them of the ground to prevent any further trouble.

29 December 1976 came the last match of the year and saw us travel to Roker Park to see Leeds take on Sunderland and win 1–0 with a goal from Jordan.

We went into town, met Ian and Gadge then went to the Corn Exchange to get our money back from the QPR match that had been postponed on 18 December. For this one, we were travelling by car instead of by coach. We then went to the Viaduct where Gary Edwards wasn't pleased to see Karen dressed as usual with her yellow Leeds shirt and dress with patches on, as they weren't wearing any colours for this one. I was starting to get nervous about this match as this was another ground where we could expect trouble from opposition fans. We left Leeds at about 2.30 pm but when we went to get the car, we found it blocked in by a van. The lads tried bouncing the van out of the way and Ian accidentally pulled the bumper off before the lad turned up and moved it. Gary and Tony were in the front with Karen, Carole, Ian and I in the back, which meant Ian had to sit on my knee as he was the smallest. We got to Sunderland at 5.00 pm and went into the club shop and were told all the seats were sold out. We stood talking to them in there and they were great. We then went to see if we could get in the Roker Club and they said no. A Sunderland fan went past and said to Ian: "who the f****** hell do you think you're looking at you c***". Karen started mouthing it so I said "don't!" as I was scared of trouble starting and that nearly caused an argument. We went back to the shop and I said to Ian not to stick with us and he said where could he go? He bought a Sunderland scarf when that lad came back and said he'd kick Ian's head in. Whilst we were there looking at badges Mac and his mate came in and we said we were going to the Black Cats Club if we could get in. When we got there nobody was on the door so we went in. Two lads from Bradford were already in the club and one fellow gave me a Rangers programme. Carole went to the loo and this lad said: "a Leeds bird has gone into the loo shall we follow her?" I went a bit later but was scared stiff of being followed. When I came back a fellow said you're going to lose.

We went to go into the ground and met Douggie outside and had a chat before going inside. Saw Chris and Phil and stood talking to them, then some more of our fans who travelled with Wallies arrived and stood with us. There were some Leeds fans in a gang in the same end and they chanted and sang even when the Sunderland fans went for them, with some stood shouting during the whole match. Mac came in and asked why we hadn't gone in the Roker Club and we said we couldn't get in although he had managed to. When two fellas stood in front of us and blocked our view Phil wanted to smack them. At half time we went to the loos and got called Leeds twats by some Sunderland fans. My nervousness about potential trouble took over at the end of the match, when Carole panicked me by saying Sunderland fans were coming into the stand. My heart missed a beat as I immediately thought they were coming to get us especially when Karen got called names by some of their fans. Luckily no one came near us, so I calmed down. I saw a lad with fair hair who I recognised and he smiled. As we went down the steps to go out of the stand I felt someone nudging me; it was Mac and he asked if we were going in the club and I said yes the Black Cats. We managed to get back into the club once more and go and warm up in front of the fire as it had been a freezing -13 degrees! A group of us all sat together and stayed there for a while before setting off back to Leeds where Gary dropped us off at Karens.

---

1 January 1977 Everton were due to play at Elland Road – the match ended up being postponed because of a waterlogged pitch.
On this day I went into the club and they said there was to be a pitch inspection at 12.45 pm but they expected the match to be called off. There were some Everton fans already in the club who had travelled to the match. This did happen, so Carole, Karen and I stayed at the club until 1.45 pm but at this point I decided to go home. I had stayed over in Leeds on New Year's Eve so had to go and collect my suitcase from Karen's bedsit before going to the train station. Once there, I saw Gadge and his gang who came to talk to me and

they told me they were going to go after the Everton fans who had travelled to the match. I was ringing home from the pay phone to let my parents know I was on my way back when all these kids came up to me and started asking questions. My suitcase was covered in stickers that I had got from my travels abroad to watch Leeds. They asked if I'd been to Ajax, Paris and if I went to all the matches, whilst another lad asked if I'd been to a match today. As I bought my train ticket a fellow said I was being looked at from all directions. I sat with Gadge and some others in the buffet and when they left, I decided to go and check the train times when I saw some Everton fans coming in. They came into the buffet and I realised that they were the ones who'd been in the club earlier. I said to one that I thought they'd gone ages back and he said no they'd been boozing. One said: "I know you; you were in the club and had that banner, can I buy it off you?" Carole had made me a Scotland/Yorkshire banner so I said no chance it was my Christmas present. I then met Mick, Colin and two others from Selby so stayed with them before going on to the platform. On our way there someone poked me in the back and said hello; it was one of the Harehills.

***

On Monday 3 January 1977, we travelled to Highbury to see Leeds play Arsenal in a 1–1 draw with Clarke scoring the Leeds goal.

My brother-in-law Terry gave me a lift into Leeds on this day, so I got there at approximately 8.00 am. I saw Gadge and Ian so I went and sat in the café with them. Carole arrived first before Karen and some others from the Viaduct pub, who then got seats on our coach. There were two Wallace Arnold coaches travelling to this match. When both coaches stopped at the services, the Howdle twins and a lad from Bradford from the other coach came to talk to us. We got to Arsenal for 2.00 pm and Carole and I went to queue in the unreserved seats where there were only a few tickets left and we got in at about 2.45 pm. In the same stand were the Supporters Club lot and a lad from Harrogate. Carole and I thought we'd end up in a scrap with these stupid birds in front of us. They didn't wear any football colours but kept giving us mucky looks just because we were shouting for Leeds.

At the end of the match I kept my scarf on and Carole and I walked down by the tube station to the coaches. Karen was already on the coach as she'd left the ground early but none of us had had any trouble. Some lads on our coach hadn't been so lucky and had run into some trouble from the Arsenal fans. All of a sudden all these Arsenal fans appeared around the coach and they looked a right rough lot. Once everyone had got back onto the coach we all started talking; Gadge and Ian told us they had been in the North Bank and some others told us they had got a copper escort back. All of a sudden someone came up and grabbed me, it was Collar. He was telling us about Sal. She walks into the pub and said I hate these f*****g Arsenal w*****s and all sorts like that and when one asked for her Leeds scarf, she told him where to go. Because she had a southern accent too, the Arsenal fans just looked at her and didn't do anything. Collar also said that after the match, he had been looking for the coaches and was walking in the middle of the Arsenal fans. He said: "mind your backs please" and walked right through them. They were saying: "where are the Leeds coaches?" and asked Collar if he knew where they were. Collar said: "I hope so; I want a lift back with them!" The Arsenal fans said: "there's one", but were so stunned they didn't touch him. He made us laugh all the way back to Leeds telling us different stories.

On Saturday 22 January 1977 we travelled to West Bromwich Albion – The Hawthorns, where Eddie Gray and McQueen were the scorers for Leeds in a 2–1 victory.

Carole and I travelled with Wallace Arnold coaches and when we arrived at West Bromwich met Karen who had travelled with the Viaduct coach to the match. Once both coaches had arrived we went straight into the ground through the boys' entrance for 50p. Although I was 21 at this point I had no problems getting in. There was loads of trouble inside the ground and we could see some Leeds fans were running them ragged in their end; it was the Harehills lot. Whilst we were stood near the entrance we saw some West Bromwich fans coming into our stand. As we went on to the terraces the same ones raced up to the coppers and asked to go back out of the stand. We all went mad when we scored then all the lads went off scrapping with Sal leading them into the West Bromwich fans. The Leeds fans were fantastic and were singing we love you Leeds over and over again, United are back and jingle bells.

At the end of the match we all came out of the ground singing and were very happy, especially as Leeds came away with the victory. On our way back to the coaches I saw Alan J. and he asked if I'd got that cutting from the paper. He said: "you don't remember me do you?" and I said: "of course I do, you're p****d as were all the Harehills". When we were stopped outside the ground they got off their coach, went into an off licence and all went back with two bottles of booze each even though they were already paralytic. Carole, Karen and I didn't go back on the same coaches that we had arrived on, as we had been invited to Shrewsbury after the match and went back on their coach (Fishers) to Shrewsbury.

Saturday 12 February 1977 saw us travel to the Baseball ground at Derby for a 1–0 win with Jordan scoring for Leeds.

When we got in to the ground the Leeds fans were singing you'll never walk alone and they looked fantastic as everyone had their scarves up. We were all down the pop side with more Leeds fans being stood where the stand extended past the corner flag. Our fans started singing "who the f*** is Leighton James" (a Derby player at the time), to the tune of we'll support you ever more; we had to laugh at that. After meeting Karen and Cockney Sal, Carole left us to go down to the front of the stand whilst Karen and I went to the back (Carole was stood in the end where trouble later occurred). Schulz (little Barnsley) got arrested as he kept going in the Derby end along with the Harehills mob who kept fighting with the Derby fans. Carole was talking to another lad from

Barnsley who asked where I was, the one who was famous and had a banner. At 4.30 pm Karen and I were making our way to the end to see Carole when we scored and we all went mad. Got to Carole and Fiona and a lad I knew nudged me. Saw one from Bradford and he said hello when I stood waving my banner with Karen. Derby got an indirect free kick and I turned away saying: "don't let them score" and Scouse said: "it's alright they won't score".

At the end of the match we all went out singing and running down the road. Carole said she'd seen every nutter she could that day, loads who she hadn't seen for ages. To get back to the coaches there was a short cut down a very narrow ginnel which was fine, if there were only a small number of fans. I couldn't believe it when the coppers sent the thousands of Leeds fans in this direction, to all go down that stupid ginnel again. I saw Ski Slope from Wrexham just as a copper grabbed him, so the Leeds fans all shoved the copper away, got him away before another copper came up waving a baton at them. I looked up to see that we had reached the entrance to the ginnel and Carole and I wanted to get out and wait, but we couldn't because of the pressure of the crowd. We got crushed to hell and trapped against the wall and thought we were all going to end up on the floor, it was terrible!

Tuesday 8 March 1977 saw a trip to London for a match at QPR which ended in a 0–0 draw

I had the day off work so caught the 9.00 am bus to Selby then the 10.20 am train to Leeds. Carole met me in the station and first of all we went down to the ground to get a Wolves ticket for Janet. Keith Parkinson (a Leeds United reserve player) was on the bus and he started talking to us. We caught the bus straight back to town after buying a Joe Jordan Rosette for 60p. We then went to Kennedy's record shop for our '*United we stand*' record as this was sung by Leeds fans at Sutton United and Carole and I liked it. When we arrived for the coach, Gary Edwards was there along with Wack, Brod and Gary Noble. Karen arrived at 12.35 pm and we thought she wasn't coming. We stopped at Worksop for three quarters of an hour to pick some lads up and stayed at the pub there. After leaving there, we stopped at Scratchwood services before arriving at QPR for 6.45 pm. There were no fans at all going up to the ground so we weren't expecting many of our fans there. It cost £1 to get in the ground which was daylight robbery! We got in and then went to look for Cheesy and Craig who were with a few from the Wallies coach. Saw Sal, Phil and Ski Slope from Wrexham before Tony, Mac and the rest of them arrived who said that there were only 14 on the coach from Shrewsbury. Collar was there also and Paul (a soldier who Carole knew). It turned out that there were quite a lot of Leeds fans in the stand but mostly Cockney Whites as I found out, when someone grabbed me from behind and found it was Stan (Cockney White). At half time, I was on my way to the loo when Chris from Harehills grabbed my arm and asked how I'd gotten there. The ladies loos we'd gone into before the match had all the fellas going in so I did an about turn and went to another one. I was disgusted with the lads for using our loos. Later I was stood with Dale, then two Cockney kids came up arguing and I gave them a drink of orange. Some of the Shrewsbury lot said was I causing trouble, to which I replied, that they were just my size! Karen, Carole and I went back into the stand just as the match had restarted and we stood at the back with Cheesy before Sal joined us. She sang when the reds went up to lift the FA Cup it wasn't there, it wasn't there! About five minutes from the end QPR fans came in behind us and I thought they'd charge us, as I started shaking with fear. The Leeds fans moved out so Carole and I decided that we'd move to the exit. On seeing us moving, Mac and some others shouted part-timers to us.

As the final whistle blew we went straight out and got nearly back to the White City Stadium when all of a sudden the coppers turned these kids back and Carole and I found ourselves in the middle of all these QPR fans (skinheads with boots – loads of kids). I immediately thought we were going to have another Newcastle, (a match where we'd been chased by lads with knives). I just kept on walking; I had three Leeds scarves on and my adrenaline took over. If anybody was going to ask for my scarf I was going to tell them to f*** off but luckily no one said anything. We got back to the coach park and met Brod and Gary at the coaches. We then stood by the fence arguing with some QPR fans and Carole was mouthing at them, it was so funny. They said we'd not taken as many fans as usual and Carole's retort was that it only needed 20 of us to take them on. On the way back we stopped at Scratchwood services again and then went on to Leicester Forest. For the second week running we broke down (outside Rotherham). They'd never broken down in 135 outings and for the two weeks I'd travelled with them they have, so I said I wouldn't go with them again because I'd jinxed them.

Saturday 26 November 1977 saw us travel to Upton Park, West Ham which Leeds won 1–0 with a goal scored by Hankin.

We hired a car from Carole's dad's garage for this one. We went to pick up Bob first, then Ian and found out that Mick Binks was coming with as well. It ended up with six of us in the car as we still had to pick up Mick from Ossett as well. We pulled in at Leicester Forest behind the Three Legs coach and saw Gary Noble, Gary Edwards, Jock, Carl, Barry Mortimer, John and the Howdle twins.

We went straight for a cup of tea and whilst there we saw the man utd coach from Coventry pull in that we'd passed earlier so all the Leeds fans went out. One lad went across the grass and offered to take all the man utd fans on but they wouldn't. Then all the Leeds fans went over the grass towards their coach and they were all mouthing at each other before their coach pulled out, as another man utd coach pulled in. About five Leeds lads were stood outside the shop and we saw some man utd fans were in there. One of the man utd fans came out of the shop with his scarf on and a Leeds lad went up to him, saying "give us your scarf". The man utd fan asked if he could keep his badge – mufc midland red and the Leeds lad said okay. With that the man utd fan took his scarf off and handed it over. I couldn't believe my eyes and carried on back to the car. Back on the motorway as we got near to London the York Pullman coach was keeping up with us as well and the lads on the back seat kept waving. The man utd coach passed us again and I let it stay in front, because I wasn't going to stop at Scratchwood services if they were. I also thought they were going to throw something out of the top window at us so stayed well out of their reach.

We parked up as near to the ground as we could as Carole was limping because she'd had her toenail taken off and was using a walking stick. We weren't going in our usual place behind the goal but walked past it and went to the far side terraces instead. We got right to the front of the stand and during the match I didn't shout for Leeds (only in my head). I saw a lad from Bradford and he said it's not what you call a big following of Leeds fans, as there were only small pockets of our fans scattered around this part of the ground that we could see. No one was wearing their colours either to avoid letting the West Ham fans know they were Leeds, so as to avoid any potential trouble. There were some right ignorant West Ham fans where we were stood giving the Leeds players a lot of stick. Tony Currie had been playing for only three minutes of the match when he had to take a throw in next to us and he asked if he could sit down on the wall because he was f****d. At half time I went for a cup of tea and saw Ian and told him we were going straight to the car after the match. As I left Ian a lad shouted where has your scarf gone, so I turned around and there were three lads there, one smiled (I think they were off the Pullman coach). I went back into the ground and stood near the end whilst I drank my tea and saw a lad from the Three Legs who turned to his mate and said there's Heidi there. Three lads and a lass stood nearby (two lads with West Ham scarves on) started talking, laughing and turning round and then I recognised one of them as a Leeds fan. As I went back to join Mick and Carole, he said that we were winning 1–0 but I didn't believe him. With that Ray Hankin knocked one in with his head and Mick said: "we are now". Trying to stop yourself from jumping up in the air when your team puts the ball in the net is not easy, especially when you don't want the opposition fans to know who you are!

After the match we followed the Leeds coaches out of London when the team coach came up alongside of us and the driver waved, then the Pullman coach pulled up behind us. We pulled into Toddington services to find some more Leeds fans were in from the Three Legs and a Wallies coach. We hadn't seen any of them in the ground, but saw Little Dave, Stewart, Gary E and N and Barry M so went for a chat. Saw both Jimmys, two Leeds lads who'd hitched from Stoke and then Douggie Kaye knocked on the window to catch my attention. Mick drove the car from there till Leicester Forest and when we pulled in we saw a man utd coach was in, but all their fans were getting chucked out of the services. We took our scarves off and parked the car. Some Leeds fans were in the services including Sheena so went to see her and she told us that she'd walked into two man utd birds and sent them flying. As we went upstairs I told Ian and Mick to behave as they were mucking about, then said I felt sick when I saw this man utd bird come in. Mick and Ian were going on about her as I walked away with my cup of tea and tried going past a copper. He looked at me saying anymore swearing and you'll be out and straight to the cop station. Well seeing as I hadn't even been swearin … I just didn't bother to say anything to him. We stopped off in Wakefield for a drink with Mick before heading for Leeds. Went into the Mitre pub and I thought I could hear the Blaydon races being sung, which meant Newcastle were in town as they tended to stop off here on their way back from away matches. This was indeed the case as we headed into the pub. There were some Newcastle fans in and one started talking to Ian, Mick and Bob saying thousands are coming to Leeds.

Chapter 4

Season 1973–74
Champions and Record Breakers

29 match unbeaten run on our way to winning the First Division – League Champions.

This season was to be one of the best seasons of watching Leeds and I was there to share the glories. The last time Leeds United won the league in 1969, they did this with breaking a record of only getting beaten twice during the whole season. They also went on to become record breakers again on their way to the league title at the end of the 1973–74 season. This time they would play 29 matches from the start of the season without getting beaten in the league and this was also a fantastic time to watch Leeds when at the end of the season they won the league to become Champions once again.

The season started with a home friendly against Bradford City on 11 August – my birthday – where Leeds ended up winners by 2–0 with McQueen scoring both of our goals. The next match was an evening friendly at Belle Vue, the home of Doncaster Rovers and a 2–0 win from Leeds with goals by Jones and Cherry. This was the match where I was beaten up by eight girls just for supporting my team. This is covered in more detail in my previous book. The semi-final of the West Riding Cup on 18 August 1973 took place at Huddersfield where Jones and Lorimer scored to give us a 2–1 win, with the final at Elland Road against Halifax Town taking place three days later. Leeds won 2–1 with Lorimer and Jones scoring and this meant we won the Cup!!

August

The first league match of the season was on 25 August 1973 at home to Everton and we won 3–1 with goals from Bremner, Giles and Jones. Don Revie was a very superstitious man and it was hard not to become that way yourself. Throughout our unbeaten run my Leeds scarf remained unwashed, because to wash it would have meant us losing a match!

Tuesday 28 August 1973 saw us travel to London on Wallace Arnold coaches to see us play at Arsenal. Whenever we travelled to London in our early days of following Leeds the coach would only take us as far as Kings Cross. As far as I am aware, this was to prevent any damage to the coaches from opposition fans, who would throw things at them if they saw they were carrying Leeds supporters. We had to find our own way to and from the ground which meant travelling by tube to Highbury. We won 2–1 with goals from Lorimer and Madeley. Gary Edwards came with his mate Gary Noble and they became part of a group of Leeds fans following Leeds everywhere.

September

Our second visit to London in a week took place on the following Saturday 1 September 1973 when we played Tottenham Hotspur. This time we had one of our regular coach drivers on Wallace Arnold coaches and because of this Len drove us straight to the ground instead of dropping us off at Kings Cross. We sat in the unreserved seats above the Spurs fans. Clarke got carried off in this match that we won 3–0 with Bremner getting two and Clarke getting one before he went off injured.

We hammered Wolverhampton Wanderers 4–1 at Elland Road on 5 September 1973, with Lorimer getting two – one a penalty and Jones and Bremner getting the others. We were now playing mostly two matches a week with a second home match against Birmingham City on 8 September. Lorimer scored a hat trick in a 3–0 win. I went on the Snaith train to this one and I was starting to get recognised as a regular and a lad from Knottingley started calling me Leeds. This was also the match where I lost my lucky Greek necklace that I bought in Salonika and even though I contacted the ground it was never found unfortunately.

The following midweek match on 11 September 1973 was a night match at Wolverhampton. Although we didn't have any trouble ourselves, there were gangs of Wolves fans in the same end as us looking for Leeds fans. No one on our coach had any trouble and we came away with the points and another win, this time 2–0 with Jones and Clarke scoring the goals.

The next away match was Southampton on 15 September 1973. Our first coach broke down as well as the second one meaning we eventually arrived at the ground at 4.30 pm and saw some fans were already leaving the match. Clarke had scored twice in a 2–1 win and even though we were late getting there, they still let us in due to the gates being already opened to let the crowd out. We then went to a pub near the ground as we had to wait until 7.30 pm before a relief coach came to take us back to Leeds.

Onto 22 September 1973 we played man utd at home in a 0–0 draw where they played very defensively. Looking back it's no wonder really because at the end of this season they got relegated and we won the league. One of my friends got hit by a man utd fan in the station who was quickly arrested for it. There were approximately 10,000 of them and they seemed to be everywhere. I received a £2.60 refund from Wallace Arnold due to the coach breaking down on the way to Southampton.

29 September 1973 saw us go on the long trip to Norwich with loads of Leeds fans travelling to this one. The only stops along the way were at the services. We had pulled into the services and were queuing for something to eat when another coachload of Leeds fans pulled in. The next thing they queued up too and started eating things from the shelves and by the time they got to the tills, they only paid for a small amount of things or didn't pay anything at all! It was no wonder that the coppers wouldn't let us stop on the way back. We had a good win 1–0 with a goal by Giles.

October

I was very upset today 3 October 1973 because one of my favourite players Gary Sprake was transferred to Birmingham City. I know Gary made some mistakes at critical times for example, against Chelsea in the 1970 FA Cup Final when he let the ball slip through his hands, but I still thought he was a good goalie. Leeds also went on to win Stromgodset 6–1 at home that day with goals from Clarke (2), Jones (2), Bates and Gray.

Today 6 October 1973 I went on the train from Snaith to Leeds and travelled in with a lot of fans from this area. This involved a two mile walk to Snaith which I didn't mind doing as I was going to see my team play. Leeds were due to play Stoke which ended in a 1–1 draw with Jones scoring our goal. As I was waiting in the station for Sue and a friend, I saw one of the lads off the train who always called me Leeds.

I stayed in Leeds that night and went down to Elland Road the next morning to see the team training. They were getting prepared for the trip to Ipswich the following day. I was over the moon when both Billy and Les Cocker spoke to me and I told the team coach driver that I was also going to the match. It was another early morning start for the trip to Ipswich on 8 October 1973 and I had to put up with a lot of teasing on the coach. Collar was making comments about the fact that I wore dungarees to matches. I started off with a few Leeds patches at the top of my dungarees on the pocket, which meant you could hide your colours if necessary. It got to the stage where I had the patches down the front of each leg as well and I still have some of the patches to this day. The Ipswich match wasn't a good one for us as we came away with a 2–0 deficit and this was our first defeat of the season, although it was a League Cup match. Ipswich tended to be a bogey team for us over the years that followed for some reason.

On 13 October 1973 we went to Leicester away at Filbert Street for a 2–2 draw with Jones and Bremner scoring for Leeds. Loads of Leeds fans went to this match but before we left Leeds there was some trouble where our fans got the better of some man utd fans. Also the Manchester City special pulled in to the station whilst we were still there, but apart from lots of shouting nothing happened. 20 October 1973 and Liverpool were the visitors to Elland Road with Jones being our scorer in a 1–0 win to Leeds.

The UEFA Cup first round first leg took place at Elland Road against Hibernian on 24 October 1973. This was a 0–0 draw and there were thousands of Hibs fans in attendance. The second leg followed a fortnight later in Scotland.

The next match took us to Maine Road for the match against Manchester City on 28 October 1973. This was always going to be a nasty affair for Leeds fans as their fans would always cause trouble for us. There were lots of ginnels around the stadium which you had to use to get back to the coaches, but were horrible to negotiate as an away fan. Although the match ended up with a 1–0 win for Leeds with Bates being the scorer, some friends got attacked and one had his Celtic scarf nicked.

November

West Ham United at home on 3 November 1973 was a great match with Leeds winning it by four goals to one. Bates, Jones (2) and Clarke were the scorers for Leeds.

The second leg of the UEFA cup took us to Hibernian the following Wednesday 7 November 1973. I was able to plan my holidays from work around the football matches and took half a day or a full day off to ensure I could go to everyone. This leg also ended in a 0–0 draw at the end of 90 minutes and went into extra-time and still there was no score. The leg had to be decided and it was going to a penalty shoot-out. Billy Bremner was to score the decisive penalty for Leeds to win 5–4 and go through to the next round. It was an exciting finale to the match, sending the few Leeds fans who had made the long trip home very happy. For this one I arrived home after the match at 6.30 am the following morning and then went straight to work at 8.30 am.

10 November 1973 took us on a trip to Burnley and a 0–0 draw. This was another match with lots of Leeds fans there and I heard of a gang of approximately 50 Burnley fans getting done by Leeds fans. The next match took place a week later on 17 November 1973. This was getting to be a rarity as I was getting used to two matches a week and it certainly made the time go past quickly. This was a home match against Coventry and a 3–0 win for Leeds with Clarke, Jordan and Bremner scoring.

The following week we travelled to Derby County on 24 November 1973 for a 0–0 draw. I felt that there wouldn't be a threat from Derby fans at this match, but unfortunately for some of us it didn't turn out that way. The coaches were parked on a car park a short walk away from the ground. I remember walking up the road and across a bridge and eventually we turned onto the road down to the Baseball ground. A group of lads started coming down the street after us singing united and away the Leeds; songs we didn't sing. I said these aren't our fans although they were wearing Leeds scarves. All of a sudden all six of us were surrounded, they shouted Derby, attacked the lads with us and then ran off. It was all over in a couple of minutes but really scared me. After the match it was a different kettle of fish as they met their match when Derby fans were chased off by Leeds. Once back on the coaches there were no more problems apart from a great mob of Derby who appeared and just walked around the perimeter of the coach park.

The next round of the UEFA cup took place at Elland Road on 28 November 1973 against Vitoria Setubal. We won 1–0 with Cherry scoring but Lorimer also missed a penalty. It was snowing and freezing cold but I didn't wear a coat. This wasn't normally a problem inside the ground at home matches, as when so many people were crammed together on the terraces you kept fairly warm. Also, you had to be in the ground by 1.00 pm for 3.00 pm kick-offs otherwise you couldn't get up to the back of the Kop. The trouble was when you were travelling before and after the match as you certainly felt the cold then!!

December

QPR came to Leeds on 1 December 1973 and the match ended in a 2–2 draw with Bremner and Jones scoring. Before home matches we had got into the habit of calling in at Terry Cooper's sports shop that was not far from Briggate. We used to pass it when walking down to the ground, always calling in to say hello and Terry always had time to chat to the fans. I caught the bus back to the station after the match but somehow I ended up on a QPR special. Not that it mattered really because although I was covered in Leeds regalia the QPR fans were fine with me.

The Christmas period was going to be very hectic as there were going to be a number of away matches. The first being a trip to Ipswich Town on 8 December 1973. Another win, this time Yorath, Jones and Clarke were the scorers in a 3–0 scoreline. It was also another match with loads of Leeds fans there. The next match was Chelsea away on 15 December 1973. A number of us hired our own coach and were staying in London until midnight. This was to enable us to spend some time drinking in London after the match. There were a lot of Leeds fans there and we won the match 2–1 with Jordan and Jones scoring our goals. During the match, we were behind the goal to the left of the stand when all of a sudden, Chelsea fans charged at us all. It was a quick hide your scarf situation, but luckily by doing this quickly we managed to stay incognito.

On 22 December we played Norwich at home and won with a goal by Yorath. Boxing Day took us to Newcastle and another win with a rare goal by Madeley. The trip wasn't as bad as last year for intimidation from their fans and we didn't see any fights. When we got back to the coach park, three lads said loudly "shall we get them?" but didn't touch us thankfully.

We had a visit to Birmingham City on 29 December with Jordan scoring late on to keep our unbeaten run in a 1–1 draw. Earlier in the year the Provisional Irish Republican Army (IRA) had started a bombing campaign in England with the most recent bombings being five days earlier. During the match there was a bomb scare announcement that came over the tannoy asking people to evacuate the stands and said the gates had been opened. I have no recollection of the match being stopped in the meantime. We were stood down the side of the ground and everyone just said we were staying put and not going anywhere. It certainly wasn't going to stop us from watching the match. As it was nothing materialised so we made the right decision. The Birmingham fans went on the rampage after the final whistle with three Leeds coaches being smashed in before we got back to them. Our coach was okay but another one had a puncture and others had no windows. We eventually left there at 8.30 pm.

January

New Year's Day 1974 saw a 1–1 home draw against Spurs with Jones getting our goal. Then on the 5 January came the FA Cup 3rd round at Wolverhampton. We drew 1–1 and Lorimer scored from the penalty spot. A lad I knew got kicked and another got hit on the head. Luckily our windows didn't go through but other coaches weren't so lucky. On 9 January 1974 was the FA Cup 3rd round replay against Wolverhampton at Elland Road. Leeds progressed through to the next round of the FA Cup courtesy of a goal scored by Jones. Following on from this match, 12 January saw another home win against Southampton ending 2–1 with Jones and Jordan the scorers.

On 19 January we were at Goodison Park the home of Everton for a 0–0 draw. When we arrived we were met by Liverpool fans who were telling us to go in the Gladys Street end. We bought tickets to sit in the steep seats in the stand at the side. By going in the seats we avoided any problems but Helen was on the terraces and ended up being kicked. We also had the coach windows smashed on leaving the ground.

The FA Cup fourth round meant a trip to Peterborough on 26 January 1974. Whilst we were waiting for the coaches at the Calls the photographer from the *Evening Post* took a photo of Sue and I which ended up on the front page of the paper. Leeds took 8,000 fans to this fixture and there was lots of fighting and our fans smashed a hut. Leeds won 4–1 with Lorimer, Jordan (2) and Yorath being our scorers.

February

Starting a new month, 2 February 1974 saw us play Chelsea at home which ended in a 1–1 draw with Cherry the scorer for Leeds. Before the match we had to go to the *Evening Post* building on Wellington Street to get a copy of our photo from the Peterborough match. The second home match in a week took on another London club, Arsenal on 5 February 1974 where Leeds ran out 3–1 winners with an own goal by Simpson and Jordan got two.

Sue and I travelled to Manchester on Friday evening with Arthur a friend of the family, prior to the match against man utd on 9 February 1974. Arthur lived with his family in Urmston which was in walking distance of Old Trafford and we were going to stay the night there. We got to the ground early and bought tickets for the seats in the scoreboard end. This was a fantastic day because Leeds won the match 2–0 with Jones and Jordan scoring our goals in front of the highest home attendance of just over 60,000. It was a very uncomfortable walk back after the match though, because we felt sure that everyone knew we were Leeds fans. We felt that we stood out like a sore thumb as only Sue and I didn't have any colours on, but also we must have had silly grins on our faces knowing we had won. Luckily we managed to get back to Urmston in one piece where we went mad, jumping around and celebrated the win.

The next match was Bristol City away in the FA Cup 5th round on 16 February 1974. Bremner scored in a 1–1 draw which meant a replay was to follow at Elland Road. We were in Leeds for 5.30 am ready for the long trip down. There were loads of Leeds fans there and we ended up sharing the stand with Bristol fans. When we got off the coach we were recognised by some Leeds lads who had seen our picture in the paper. On the way home we stopped at the services and there were also some Newcastle fans in. They were after my scarf and badges which of course they weren't going to get, but at least it was good natured banter for a change. We got back to Leeds for 9.30 pm which was an excellent time and enabled me to catch the last train back to Selby.

The Bristol City return leg took place on 19 February 1974 and we ended up getting beaten 1–0. It was almost unheard of for Leeds to lose, especially at home. I was that upset that I sat down in the Kop and started crying only to have a lad tell me off and call me stupid. I was that mad then that I could have hit him, instead I told him where to go. Again as it was a cup match this meant our unbeaten league run remained intact. In my early days of supporting Leeds it was rare to drop a point at home and at least I had the privilege of being there. This is something that we had to get used to over time when Leeds have had more downs than ups, but it teaches you to be a good loser!

The day our unbeaten run was ended!

23 February 1974 we went to Stoke City where we were to lose our 29 match unbeaten league run from the start of the season. We started the match well but ended up losing 3–2 with Bremner and Clarke getting our goals. There were loads of our fans there and lots of fighting going on during the match. On the way home though there was lots of singing on the coach and it was a great atmosphere even though we had lost. My scarf could now be washed as we had lost and I didn't need to be superstitious anymore. As I said previously, Don Revie was a very superstitious man and this caught on with many Leeds fans being the same. Basically my thoughts were that if I had washed my scarf earlier we would have lost more matches.

A 1-1 score draw on 26 February 1974 with Leicester City at Elland Road saw Peter Lorimer score from the penalty spot. I got to Elland Road at 2.00 pm for this one and managed to get a lift home after the match.

March

The second of three home matches in a row on 2 March 1974 saw another 1–1 score draw although this time against Newcastle United, with Clarke scoring our goal. They brought loads of fans with them again. The third match on 9 March 1974 was against Manchester City in a 1–0 win with Lorimer winning the match for us with another penalty.

On 16 March 1974 we travelled to Liverpool where Leeds lost 1–0. We travelled with Fallas coaches to the match but unfortunately the coach broke down near Manchester. The coach driver managed to get it going again but then we broke down again completely about ten miles outside Liverpool. We managed to hitch a lift to the ground with a Liverpool fan which was a good job, as we got into the ground five minutes before the turnstiles shut as it was full. Afterwards we walked back to the coaches with some other Leeds lasses. Some scousers were trying to chat us up, saying that we should miss the coach and they would show us the way to the station. No way! I'm not sure if it was our original coach that took us back to Leeds or not, but at least we didn't get stranded in Liverpool thank goodness.

The next match on 23 March 1974 saw a heavy defeat at home against Burnley, where we lost 4–1 with Clarke scoring our goal. It was a rubbish match and some Leeds fans tried invading the pitch to try and stop it and nearly 'pulled my arm off' in the process.

We were in London again on 30 March to face West Ham United. We were waiting in Leeds train station getting ready to catch the train to London, when we were approached by a Leeds fan asking if we wanted to go direct to the ground by coach. As most coaches stopped at Kings Cross and you had to find your own way to the ground, we decided to travel with him by coach. On arrival, a West Ham fan wanted us to go into the ground with him but when we refused he started threatening us verbally. Luckily we didn't have any more bother but the match ended in a 3–1 defeat for Leeds with Clarke again scoring our only goal. On the way back we stopped in Leicester where some City fans tried persuading us to go to a disco with them but we refused.

April

Our next home match against Derby County on 6 April 1974 saw me taking my cassette recorder into the Kop and taping the crowd singing and chanting. We won this match 2–0 with Lorimer and Bremner scoring our goals. At least this put us back on a winning streak again after our bad run of defeats. I replayed the cassette on the way back to the station which caught the interest of many of our fans.

The next match was Coventry away on 13 April 1974. When we got to Coventry all the Leeds fans decided that we were going to take the Coventry end. We just queued up and paid to go in their end and the coppers didn't even try to stop us. I can't remember much trouble though. I went on the football special to this match and the ground seemed miles away from the station. Going back after the match I was in the last few stragglers getting on the train. The match was a 0–0 draw.

The Easter period saw us due to play two matches in two days which was something that happened regularly over the seasons. We played Sheffield United at home on 15 April 1974. It was a match where we were robbed as the referee kept disallowing goals that we had scored and the Leeds fans were going mad as it ended 0–0. We played Sheffield United again the next day 16 April 1974 but this time at Bramall Lane with the Leeds fans taking their end called The Shoreham. There were loads of Leeds fans there and we just queued up and went in, meaning the Sheffield fans disappeared as soon as they saw us. We won the match 2–0 with Lorimer getting both goals.

Our last home match of the season on 20 April was against Ipswich Town with a large crowd of just over 44,000. It was packed tight in the Kop and the atmosphere was fantastic. We thought we had won the league that day as we ran out 3–2 winners with Clarke, Bremner and Lorimer goals, but it was going down to the last match. We had to come out of the match ten minutes early because the tickets for the last away match of the season at QPR were going on sale straight after the match. What a mistake that was and Leeds soon realised they couldn't put them on sale. It was absolute mayhem in the West Stand car park and we were all getting crushed. A message soon came out that no tickets were going on sale today but would be on sale in the morning. We queued up from midnight to ensure we were amongst the first fans to receive our tickets.

So on to the last match of the season on 27 April 1974 at QPR where we won the league. Clarke scored our goal in the 1–0 win and it was a fantastic end to the season. Leeds fans went on to the pitch at the end and some ran at the QPR fans who quickly scattered. Carole and Margaret had taken some champagne with them and were toasting the League Champions at the end of the match. We stayed in London until midnight, got back to Leeds at 4.20 am and stayed on Leeds station until 6.00 am. Then we went down to Elland Road to get tickets for Billy Bremner's Testimonial match.

This was a fantastic way to end Don Revie's reign as manager of Leeds by winning the League Championship. I also felt this was a bad time for Leeds because Don Revie announced he was leaving Leeds to manage the England team. I didn't want him to go as he was part of Leeds but I could understand that he didn't want to be the one who broke the Leeds team up, as some of the players were nearing the end of their careers. It was a special time as a Leeds supporter to see them win the title in style. We ran down to City Square after Billy's testimonial match against Sunderland at Elland Road on 6 May 1974 which was 0–0, to see Leeds parading the trophy. But it was also a sad time as it meant things were going to change and the success of the era was drawing to a close.

Although the season was at an end we still had a few more football matches to attend. We played Huddersfield Town in a match at Leeds Road and lost 2–0 which could have been a West Riding Cup match. On 3 May 1974, 12 of us went up on the train to Middlesbrough for a testimonial for one of their players. We had to change trains at Darlington both going and coming back. We went in a pub before the match and met some very hostile people up there. To say we hadn't played them before, we weren't really expecting that.

The match ended up a 4–4 draw. On 18 May 1974 Carole, Sue, Margaret and I travel up to Scotland by train to see Billy and the boys take on England at Hampden Park.

The season had now come to an end and I had spent £122.18 on going to see Leeds, 64p going to see York City play Huddersfield at Bootham Crescent and £6.42 going to the Scotland v England match making a total of £129.24 on football for the season. I had also attended 61 football matches in total.

My final match of the season was a trip to the World Cup in Frankfurt which I won through selling Leeds United lottery tickets and one was a winner. It meant that the person who I sold it to won a free trip as well as me. I flew to the Scotland v Brazil match in Frankfurt from Luton and wore my Leeds things as normal. Billy Bremner's testimonial celebrations were still going on through the close season and I went to the Irish Centre in Leeds. My mum took a photo of me getting Billy's autograph when he was sat with Don Revie and Paul Reaney. My mum won an autographed football so I was ecstatic and my sister Karin won a tie.

Chapter 5

Season 1974–75 – Record 70 matches

The record number of football matches I saw was 70 during the 1974–75 season and was my best ever for attending matches in one season. The record of 70 matches included friendlies, testimonials, league and cup matches and European match ties. It is a record I am very proud of and it was a privilege that I had the opportunity to do this. Don Revie had now left Leeds to manage the England team and Jimmy Armfield was now manager of Leeds. Although I was sad to see the Don go as he had managed the most successful team of the era; I welcomed Jimmy as manager to Leeds. He was a gentleman and very well thought of in the game. With the Leeds team going through a transition and results in the league that were not as good as they had been in the past, Leeds still achieved the ultimate dream at the end of the season by getting to the European Cup Final in Paris in 1975. I received a letter from Leeds telling me that I would not receive a ticket for the final, but should be pleased as it was being shown live on television. As a loyal fan who had been to every match that season, that was like a smack in the face. After only getting 8,000 tickets for the final, I appreciated the fact that it was going to be a mad scramble for tickets, but there was no way I wasn't going to it. By hook or by crook I would be there and it was annoying to say the least when 'fans' were being shown on the television that couldn't get tickets. By going to all the matches you got to know the regular fans and those being shown had never been seen at any of the matches by me. Luckily for me, Carole my friend managed to get two tickets as she was also a season ticket holder and meant I was able to go. The days of playing 70 matches in a season have long gone for Leeds, but maybe this will be something they can aspire to in the future. Fingers crossed.

The season started on 8 August 1974 with a match at Huddersfield with Leeds winning 2–1 with goals from Giles and Bates. Sue and I went and I also took my nephew Mark who was nearly two years old with me and I remember asking her to watch Mark whilst I went down the steep steps to the toilets. He was watching for me as I came back up the steps and that's when I realised how many of them there were. Going back to the station afterwards I was carrying Mark in my arms as he had fallen asleep and a copper said that obviously Mark was a troublemaker. At the station we jumped on the special train back to Leeds. Around this time I managed to get my hands on the League Trophy that Leeds had won the previous season which was on show in the Pools Office next to Fullerton Park. I had my photo taken with it and Mark also sat next to it on the counter and had his photo taken. He had to be brought up as a Leeds fan and what a way to start.

The day before my birthday, 10 August 1974, took us to Wembley to see Leeds play in the Charity Shield against Liverpool and I stood with Gary Edwards and some of the Kippax lads. The score at the end of the match was 1–1 with Cherry scoring our goal and Billy got sent off for fighting with Kevin Keegan. Leeds lost the match overall on penalties.

The first league match of the season took us to Stoke on 17 August 1974 where Leeds lost 3–0. We went to Birmingham going and Liverpool coming back on the coach as the driver didn't know where he was going. Leeds fans had once again turned out in great numbers for this match. I got a lift in from work to the next match, QPR at home on 21 August 1974, when my sister Karin, husband Terry and nephew Mark went as well. It wasn't a good match for them to go to as we went down to a 1–0 defeat. I stood with the Kippax lads at the back of the Kop whilst Karin and family went to the front.

24 August 1974 was another home match against Birmingham City where again I took my cassette recorder with me to tape the Kop. There was a lot of trouble today with Birmingham fans taking a battering. We won the match 1–0 with a goal from Clarke.

On 27 August 1974 we travelled to London to the QPR match. I travelled with Wallace Arnold coaches (nicknamed Wallies Trollies) where we got taken to the ground instead of being dropped off at Kings Cross station and having to find our own way! By going to all the matches I was starting to recognise a lot of people and was forever talking to lots of Leeds fans. I stayed at my friend Christine's house in Harehills after the match and went home the next day.

The next trip was an away match at Maine Road to play Manchester City on 31 August 1974. We got beaten 2–1 with Clarke scoring our goal. It was also a bad match for trouble and was a very intimidating place to go. Many Leeds fans had gone into the seats for this one but found that the City fans had climbed over the small wall between the stands and infiltrated the Leeds fans. We had taken our colours off but knew they were looking for the Leeds fans as they crouched down and just stared at the crowd. Because you knew you supported the opposition, a different club to them, the fear they put into you was horrendous. It was a cheap match on 7 September, as I had received a complimentary ticket for being an agent for Leeds and selling bingo cards, plus it only cost me 16p on the train. It was Luton Town at home and ended as a 1–1 score draw with Clarke scoring our goal but it was a boring match. The selling of bingo cards was a means of raising some funds; I assume for the club but cannot really remember. As an agent you got a complimentary ticket for entry to the home matches plus you were also given a percentage commission based on the amount of tickets you had sold. I always saved my commission up and spent it in the club shop.

We had an away trip on 10 September to Leeds Road, Huddersfield for a League Cup tie which ended with a 1–1 draw and Clarke scoring for Leeds. I had left work early for this match and caught the train from Leeds to Huddersfield. When I got on the train a lad said that I was the jammy sod who had won a trip to Germany. It was a match where there were lots of Leeds fans who were prevented from meeting up with any town fans, due to them having an escort from the coppers.

On September 14 we went to Burnley on the football special. There were approximately 12 carriages to the special and again meant there were loads of Leeds fans there. I said I wanted a Burnley scarf and an obliging Leeds fan went and got one for me, but must have stolen one from someone in the crowd. Leeds fans from Hull and Snaith were on our train home to Selby. We lost the match 2–1 with Lorimer scoring our goal and being robbed by a 'stupid' referee. He made decisions not in our favour which cost us the match.

The next match took in our European Cup match at Elland Road against FC Zurich on 18 September 1974. It was a fantastic match with Leeds winning 4–1 with goals from Clarke (2), Lorimer a penalty and Jordan. I took my nephew Mark with me and he stood in the box at the back of the Kop where the coppers normally stood during the match.

Another great match followed at Elland Road when we entertained Sheffield United on 21 September 1974. We won 5–1 with goals from Clarke (2), McQueen, Lorimer and Yorath. Although Leeds were at home, some Sheffield fans attacked some of the lads I knew who came from near my village. Pete Dyson had his scarf nicked whilst Tony Carr got a beating. I was on the platform when the Sheffield special was taking them home and one of our fans threw a brick at the train as it was pulling out.

It wasn't a good match on 24 September when we played Huddersfield Town at home in a 1–1 draw. Clarke got our goal and to say it was September it was freezing cold! We went to Everton on 28 September 1974 the following week on a National coach. Leeds lost the match 3–2 with our goals scored by Clarke and Yorath. We sat in the stand for this one and I was talking to some Leeds fans who were in the stand below us. People were starting to recognise me and always made time to talk to me.

The first away match of our European adventure for this season saw us fly to Zurich on 2 October 1974 for the return leg with a 4–1 advantage from the home leg. We lost the match 2–1 with Clarke scoring for Leeds but went through to the next round 5–3 on aggregate. I swopped a scarf with a Zurich fan by the players' entrance as we waited for the team to arrive. Whilst we were stood there someone asked me if I was from Selby and it turned out that he worked at the funeral directors in the village where I was from. He was at the match with his son. Someone else also recognised me from Hampden Park and Germany when I had been to see Scotland play.

Back in England for the home match against Arsenal on 5 October 1974; we caught up with some of our fans including Collar and his mate to talk about our trip to Zurich. Once in the ground, I thought I was getting arrested when a copper grabbed me then threw me out of the way and grabbed a lad. I felt sorry for the lad but was certainly relieved that I was alright. We won the match 2–0 with McKenzie scoring both of the goals.

Huddersfield at home on 7 October 1974 ended with a 2–1 win for Leeds with Bates (given as an own goal by their player) and a Lorimer penalty. Some of the local lads from where I lived, Martin and Timmy, were stood with me. Three of the Leeds juniors were also watching the match in the Kop near where we were stood.

We went to Bury next on 9 October 1974 with Lorimer and Cherry scoring in a 2–1 win. As mentioned previously, England in 1974 saw many bombings by the IRA. Whilst we were in Leeds station beforehand, there was a bomb scare but luckily everything was okay and we were given the all clear. We then spoke to a few Leeds fans in the station before heading to Bury where Leeds fans took their end. On my way home on the train to Selby, I was in the unfortunate company of a load of man utd fans. I was the only Leeds fan on the train and as usual was wearing my colours which made me stand out. I was very nervous about being the only Leeds fan amongst them as I couldn't be certain that they wouldn't attack me, although on this occasion I was fine. After being physically assaulted at a Doncaster Rovers friendly match, I found this left me feeling scared and vulnerable when opposition fans were near me. Unfortunately these feelings have stayed with me for a lifetime.

We had a long trip on 12 October 1974 to East Anglia for the visit to Ipswich for a 0–0 draw. Getting to Leeds at 5.45 am, again I travelled with National coaches. We had a laugh on the coach and I took my camera with me, taking photos of some of the lads from Donny and Whitley. The third away trip in a row took us to Birmingham City on 15 October 1974 travelling with the National coaches again. The match ended up with us losing 1–0.

We had our first home match on 19 October 1974 for 12 days with the visit of Wolves. This was a 2–0 win for Leeds with Clarke and McKenzie getting the goals. Another away match followed as we travelled to Liverpool on 26 October 1974 which ended up with a 1–0 defeat for Leeds as Liverpool were jammy as usual. On the way back home on the train from Leeds we were accosted by Hull KR fans but they didn't hurt us.

There was a West Riding Cup semi-final match on 30 October at Elland Road against Huddersfield in front of a crowd of 1,116 fans. These cup matches only attracted small crowds hence the low attendance. We sat watching the match on the terraces and managed to get a request for a record to be played over the tannoy. Although we lost the match 2–1 with McNiven scoring the goal for Leeds, we had a right laugh talking with Phil and Steve from Bury. Saw some lads from Micklefield on the same train going back to Selby.

On 2 November 1974 we played Derby County at home. When I arrived at Leeds station I saw a Leeds fan from Derby who I recognised, although as usual I didn't know his name. The actual match was a defeat of 1–0 but Leeds didn't deserve to lose, in fact I used a word I won't repeat here to describe Derby.

The third home match in a row on 6 November 1974 was a great one in the European Cup second round, second leg against Ujpest Dozsa. Leeds won 3–0 with goals from McQueen, Bremner and Yorath. Straight away we decided we were going to the away leg in the next round. I saw a lad whose photo I had taken at Ipswich and John from Halifax stood near us on the Kop, who shouted jokingly that we were part timers.

On the 9 November 1974 we travelled to Coventry and again went on the football special. Leeds won the match 3–1 with goals from O'Hare, Hindley (own goal) and Bremner. The trek from the station to Coventry's ground was a very long one which meant we only got to the ground just before kick-off at

3.00 pm. The coppers were being very brutal with the Leeds fans although not me personally. When trying to get out of the ground after the match we got locked in, which meant it seemed to take forever to get back to the station and I thought we would miss the train.

Chester away in the league cup was a mid-week match on 13 November 1974. What a mud bath outside the ground! Massive puddles were everywhere and I managed to do my ankle in when I slipped, but luckily I didn't land in the puddles! When I got in the ground I saw the Donny lads who'd been fighting with the Chester fans then saw Trampas and his friends. Phil came up to me with his face covered in blood, having been smacked in the face by a Chester fan and somehow I ended up with blood on me. The Donny lads kept going fighting and one had his yellow scarf nicked so he wanted mine instead, which he didn't get. It was totally a bad night for Leeds as they ended up getting beaten 3–0. Also at the services on the way home, our coach was attacked by man utd fans who threw bottles and whatever else they could lay their hands on at it. When I got back to Leeds I got picked up by my dad. As he was driving me home he saw two lads with a broken-down car on the M62, so he stopped the car to help them and mended theirs.

On 16 November Middlesbrough were the visitors to Elland Road. I took Mark with me to this match. When we arrived there were loads of Boro fans there. I got Sue a present in the club shop and then accidentally left it on the counter, which meant I had to go back to get it. I had to go through a large group of Boro fans to get there where they all shouted at me, but nicely for once. We drew the match 2–2 with McKenzie getting both Leeds goals.

The trip to Carlisle on 23 November 1974 again meant we travelled on the football special. When we got off the special and were on the way to the ground, some shop windows were broken. I also had my can of coke taken off me by a copper. I thought it was a bad ground to be able to see from the terraces. Sue sprained her ankle so we had to go to the first aid which meant going out through the Carlisle fans end who commented on our arrival. Sue went back to the station in a Black Maria so we were asked by some of our lads why we had been arrested, ha ha! The match was a 2–1 win with Jordan and McKenzie scoring for Leeds. When we got off the special in Leeds there was a man utd fan in the station who was like a beacon to the Leeds fans, as all the lads turned back to go for him.

There was a boring match on 30 November at Elland Road against Chelsea, although we won 2–0 with goals from Cherry and Clarke. In the ground I was stood near the Wetherby and Donny lads. I had a laugh on the train into Leeds travelling with Pete Dyson. Coming back, there were no lights in the carriage and I sat with the lads from Whitley, Dale and Nev.

On 4 December we had the second visit of a London club to Elland Road within a week. This time was the visit of Tottenham which Leeds won 2–1 with goals by McKenzie and a penalty by Lorimer. When I got in the ground I saw a lad from Donny, Paul, who spoke to me. Also saw him again when coming out of the ground when he asked me who I supported.

The third London club in a row took us to West Ham on 7 December 1974. When we got off the coach at the ground, Sue and I nearly jumped six feet in the air when some West Ham fans jumped in front of us and shouted Leeds. Before the match we went into their club and even though we had our Leeds jumpers on, we were still asked who we supported! They wanted to know how much we had paid for the jumpers too. We went into the ground with Lindsay, Violet and two lads from Hull. We shouted and sang and it was a wonder we didn't get hit because we were amongst a load of West Ham fans. On the way out some West Ham lads told us to watch our scarves and told us they would be coming to Elland Road, to which I said I would look out for them (not really).

We were back at Elland Road on the 14 December 1974 for the home match against Stoke. McQueen, Lorimer and Yorath scored for Leeds in the 3–1 win. Before the match we went into Terry Cooper's shop on the bridge and I bought two new Leeds badges. I had started collecting badges and whenever there was a new one out I had to buy it. During the match Leeds fans were fighting with Stoke fans in the South Stand and the Stoke fans left ten minutes before the end of the match. We caught up with them at the park where they were surrounded by coppers. Because of our bad experience at Stoke, I thought it was a shame they hadn't been given a taste of their own medicine as loads of Leeds fans were walking slowly to wait for them. Our train pulled out at the same time as the Stoke special. Steve, Mart and Snowy tried nicking my scarves which were tied around my wrists as usual.

The next match took us to Newcastle on 21 December 1974 where Sue and I were supposed to collect some complimentary tickets that Mick Bates had got us. Due to arriving early and going into the Magpie pub just outside the ground, which was a favourite pub of the Newcastle fans, our group of Leeds fans had some trouble. When we were on our way out of the pub, the Newcastle fans waited for the last two lads who were behind us to go out of the door. A group of them then attacked our lads, kicking the hell out of them. Sue and I were so scared after this that we dare not go to the players' entrance to pick the tickets up. We also couldn't have cared less what the score was and probably were relieved that we lost the match 3–0.

Burnley were the visitors to Elland Road on Boxing Day 26 December 1974. The referee was terrible with the final score being a 2–2 draw with Jordan and Lorimer scoring for Leeds. Apparently Leeds fans attacked a Burnley fans' coach and "turned" it over. I stood with Fish and talked to the lads from Hull.

On 28 December 1974 we travelled to Leicester City where Leeds won 2–0 with goals from Frank Gray and McKenzie. We went on Wallace Arnold coaches where we had a good singsong on the way to the match. There were loads of Leeds fans again and we stood with the Hull lot. When we got back to Leeds we waited for the special train before catching our train back to Selby. Some lads said they had never made it to the match although they didn't say why. We had a laugh on the train with the Hull and Snaith lot.

Cardiff visited us on 4 January 1975 in the FA Cup with a resounding 4–1 win to Leeds with Eddie Gray, Clarke (2) and McKenzie scoring for Leeds. On

11 January 1975 West Ham were the visitors to Elland Road where Leeds won 2-1 with Clarke and McKenzie scoring. We were at Chelsea on 18 January where Leeds won 2-0 with McKenzie and Yorath scoring for Leeds. We got soaked standing in the rain for three hours and we were frozen. In the ground we stood with Leeds fans from Hull and Doncaster (Donny) and Steve from Hull told us he is coming abroad with us. When Leeds scored our fans ran to the back of the stand then Leeds fans ran back at the Chelsea fans. It cannot have been too bad where I was stood because I wore my scarf back to the coach. At the services I slipped and fell on my bum; oh dear, it's a good job I'm game for a laugh! I had an argument in Leeds station with some man utd fans and another lad and I told them where to go.

Wimbledon at home was on 25 January 1975 for an FA Cup tie and I took my sister Erica with me for her birthday treat. It was packed out in the Kop. Saw the Donny lads who told us they'd got smacked at Chelsea by West Ham fans and all the Leeds fans got done in. This match saw bad weather with terrible wind and rain. The match ended in a 0-0 draw. We set off on 28 January for the replay at Wimbledon where there was doubt about the match being played. Before setting off from Leeds someone had rung the ground to check the match was on and was told it was and we could set off. Unfortunately by the time we got to Worksop we found the match had been postponed. We weren't happy at all. We ended up going back to Leeds and watching the Leeds Juniors play a match at Elland Road instead.

Coventry at home on 1 February 1975 was another 0-0 draw. Saw the lads from Rotherham and was chatting with them. After the match, I walked back to the station to catch the train. On 8 February there was an away league match at Derby where I went on the football special again on my own and was another 0-0 draw. I saw some lads I knew and although I was offered a place to sit I stayed standing. On 10 February 1975 the rearranged match against Wimbledon took place at Selhurst Park, the home of Crystal Palace. We won the match 1-0 with a deflected own goal from Baysford. Again there were loads of Leeds fans there. There was another trip to Derby on 15 February only this time for an FA Cup tie. We were going on the special again but the match was called off prior to setting off due to bad weather. I saw the same lads I'd seen at Selhurst Park. The FA Cup match was rearranged on 18 February at Derby and I went on the football special, this time with Linda where we sat with the Hull and Bridlington lot. Leeds won the match 1–0 with another own goal this time from Nish. Saw some of the Leeds Juniors on the way back to the station who had also been to the match. Pete said he nearly got knifed but I don't know any more details.

There was an away match on 22 February at Middlesbrough where again we went on the football special, although this time we had a reception committee. When we got off the train we were followed by a large group of their fans to the ground albeit with a police escort. We eventually lost this escort when everyone started running and we ended up surrounded by Boro fans. They threatened us but didn't touch us and we managed to get to the ground okay. After the match we had to make our own way back to the station but managed to get back there in one piece without any further trouble. Leeds won the match 1–0 with a goal from Clarke.

On 25 February 1975 came the home match against Carlisle and a 3–1 win for Leeds with goals scored by Lorimer, Clarke and Gray. The lad from Donny asked if we were going to Anderlecht, which we were. He said that they would have lots of sweets on their coach and to go with them, but we had booked to go with Murgatroyd coaches from Harrogate. The Pools Office wanted some photos of us but I'm not sure what for.

On 2 March 1975 was the visit of Manchester City to Elland Road and a 2–2 draw with Lorimer the scorer of both Leeds goals. I saw loads of their fans surrounded by coppers for protection and also saw some of them getting attacked. In the ground I stood with a lad from Rotherham. The Manchester City fans were chased down Elland Road after the match.

The next round of the European Cup was a home tie against Anderlecht on 5 March 1975. Leeds were able to take a 3–0 lead into the second leg courtesy of goals by Jordan, McQueen and Lorimer. There was thick fog around which impacted on Abbey Coachways getting to the match on time and we missed kick-off by five minutes, eventually getting in at 7.35 pm. The thick fog impacted on the match too as you couldn't see past the half way line. Leeds fans in both the Kop and the South Stand were chanting to each other, to ask what was going on at the other end of the pitch.

There was the long trip on 8 March to Ipswich Town in the FA Cup 6th round which ended in a 0–0 draw which meant a replay for the following week. I got a lift into Leeds and then went on the special train taking my banner with me. On arrival some Ipswich fans commented that we were Gelderd Boot girls. Loads of Leeds fans came to meet the special when it arrived at Ipswich and I thought it was great to see so many of our fans there. The replay at Elland Road with Ipswich came on 11 March 1975. The Kop was packed as usual, the fans were swaying and there was a fantastic atmosphere. At one point I fell down the Kop when the crowd surged forward and scraped all my leg. I had never heard the Kop cheer so loudly, it was brilliant. When McKenzie scored the goal for Leeds in a 1–1 draw we went absolutely mental, getting hugged in the process of the celebrations. Everyone was jumping about for at least quarter of an hour and I was absolutely shattered. Because the match ended up with another draw this meant a second replay had to be arranged.

15 March 1975 there was a home match with Everton. I got a lift into Leeds with my mum and dad. The match wasn't a good one and ended in a 0–0 draw. I told some lads to stop criticising Terry and they said to watch it as I was getting mad. Saw some Everton fans with the coppers after the match and one of the lads I knew Les, got arrested for having a go at them. I managed to get a lift back from Selby and was told that loads of Everton fans got done.

On 19 March 1975 came the away leg of the European Cup with another trip abroad. We travelled to Anderlecht with Murgatroyd's coach from Harrogate, where we had had a great four days. Leeds were able to progress to the next round due to a goal by our inspirational captain Billy Bremner once again. It was a memorable night with loads of Leeds fans there creating a fantastic atmosphere. The only downside was getting soaked by the torrential downpour during the match. Getting soaked did not dampen our spirits though as the celebrations amongst us, went on late into the night. On our return to England three days later Leeds were playing Luton Town on 22 March 1975 so we were going straight there from Anderlecht. Leeds lost the match 2–1 with Jordan scoring our goal. We went straight back to Leeds after the match and it had been a fantastic trip with a great bunch of Leeds fans.

On 25 March 1975 was the next in our marathon of playing Ipswich Town in the FA Cup replays. This meant a visit to a neutral ground, Filbert Street the home of Leicester City. I went on an Abbey Coachways coach to this, which meant I didn't need to leave work so early. Snowy and some others decided to attack me on the coach and tied my scarves around my wrists. When we arrived at Leicester the coppers refused to let us into the ground because we were Leeds fans. Eventually we got in after going right around the ground. When going back to the coach we got shouted to by some lads I knew and saw loads had nicked Ipswich scarves. The match ended up with another 0–0 draw which meant a further replay was set for Thursday evening of the same week. This meant there were Saturday, Tuesday, Thursday and Saturday matches in one week. I think football players today would have a fit if they had four matches in a week. So to 27 March 1975, I got home from work to find out that Abbey Coachways had cancelled the coach due to a lack of interest with another replay. Luckily my sister Karin ran me through to Leeds to enable me to catch the football special train. I was talking to some lads who thought we'd get smacked in as there were not as many Leeds fans there this time. At the ground male coppers were searching the lads but couldn't search me because I was female. In the ground I stood with the Rotherham, Donny and Northampton lot. They asked if our photos had come out from Anderlecht which they had. When Leeds scored everyone was hugging each other but we ended up losing the match 3–2 with Clarke and Giles scoring for Leeds.

Newcastle were the visitors to Elland Road on 29 March 1975 and a 1–1 draw, with Clarke scoring for Leeds. We were walking down Lowfields Road and thought we were going to get attacked by some Newcastle fans but they ran in front of us and kicked some other Leeds fans. Going back to the station these Geordies chased some of our fans and Sue and I were bricking it and just stood there, but they left us alone and then luckily for us the coppers arrived.

On 31 March 1975 at the end of a busy month of football matches, saw the visit of Leicester City to Elland Road. The match was a 2–2 draw with Clarke and Giles scoring for Leeds. We visited Bramall Lane, the home of Sheffield United on 1 April for a 1–1 draw with a rare goal from Madeley. For this match I went on the service train rather than the football special trains.

Leeds lost at home on 5 April to Liverpool by 2 goals to 0. Before the end of the match some lads went scouser knacking (which meant they were going fighting) but the small group of Liverpool fans going back to the station were well escorted by the coppers so no Leeds fans could get near them.

The day dawned for the European Cup semi-final first leg against Barcelona on 9 April 1975 and I went in to Leeds early on the train. This meant working my dinner hour and leaving work to catch the train. We won the match 2–1 with Bremner and Clarke scoring for Leeds but Barcelona had a vital away goal which would count double for the second leg. As I was waiting to catch my train home I was talking to some Leeds lads from Kettering and Newcastle in the station.

Arsenal away on 12 April 1975 saw a group of us all meet at Doncaster station to get the service train to London. Leeds won the match 2–1 with goals from Clarke and Hunter. There was Kenny and Dave from Rotherham, the Hull lot with Steve, Pete and Violet plus Jonathan and Nicholas from Rawcliffe, as well as me. We had had some trouble in the ground and also at King Cross station when we were threatened by some Arsenal fans. Luckily no one got hurt though. We travelled back on the same train as the Leeds United team and were lucky enough, after trying for a second time, to get in to see the team and have a chat with them. As we got off the train at Doncaster on our return, there were loads of fans with black and white scarves in the station as we went to see the team off and they started singing. Whilst in the buffet waiting for our connecting train a load of man utd fans came off another train. Saw a lad Tony Morrill who I knew and I asked if he had actually been to a match. Some of the group caught the train to Selby whilst the rest went in to Leeds.

On 19 April 1975 came the home match against Ipswich, this time in the league. Leeds won 2–1 with Cherry and Harris scoring for Leeds. Stayed at Sue's house on Friday night and nearly missed the bus in Riccall. When we got on the train in Selby, all the Hull lot were on and they all shouted at us so we went and joined them. Arriving in Leeds we first went to Eastgate Market, then to Terry Cooper's shop and bought some Leeds patches. Then we walked back to the station and dumped our stuff in the lockers. We left our coats there because when you stood on the Kop it was so packed and hot that you didn't need a coat. We used to leave them in the pools office but had started leaving them at the station instead. We got soaked so went for a cup of tea and then stood talking to some lads from Selby. We got even wetter by walking to the ground from the city centre. Before the match we went into the supporters club and the Peacock. We were talking to the Kettering lads about the Arsenal match to see if they'd had any trouble but they were lucky and avoided it. I also agreed to fetch a programme back from Barcelona for one of them. We stayed in Leeds after the match and went round a few pubs before catching a later train home.

The European Cup semi-final second leg against Barcelona took place on 23 April. We drew the match 1–1 with Lorimer scoring for Leeds and McQueen being sent off, which reduced Leeds to ten men for a long time in the match. We flew to Spain on the pools office trip and were euphoric when Leeds won the match overall to get to the European Cup Final!

Leeds travelled to Wolverhampton Wanderers on 26 April 1975 which ended in a 1–1 draw with Frank Gray scoring for Leeds. Considering Leeds only had a couple of matches left before the European Cup Final due to be played in Paris on 28 May 1975, it was no surprise that there weren't many Leeds fans who travelled to this match. It was left to the die-hard Leeds fans to go to this, as everyone else seemed to be concentrating on going to Paris. The Leeds fans who did attend this match had a torrid time from the Wolves fans with loads of trouble.

The last league match of the season was a trip to White Hart Lane to play Tottenham on 28 April 1975. I went in early to Leeds, going to the ground first where I saw the team coach was just leaving and I was thrilled when Billy waved to me. This was another match with only a few Leeds fans going to it. We went on a National coach and on arrival went into the seats above the Tottenham fans in the Park Lane stand again. We must have been loud when we went in because they all turned round to look at us. It was a critical match for Tottenham and they needed to win so that they didn't get relegated. It also made us get very nervous and I thought that if Leeds won, then we wouldn't get out of the place alive! You always wanted Leeds to win but in a situation like this, it was a relief that we lost the match 4–2 with goals from Jordan and Lorimer. At least we were going to go home in one piece.

Norman Hunter's testimonial match was played on 5 May at Elland Road, which was Leeds v Don Revie's XI. We lost the match 3–2 with Bremner scoring both the Leeds goals. Met some Leeds fans from Wrexham and was talking to them in the station. On the train home showed the photos we took in Barcelona to Pete and the others from Hull. Our final match before the European Cup final was a testimonial at Walsall on 13 May 1975 for Nick Atthey which ended in a 3–3 draw and goals from Clarke, McKenzie and Jordan for Leeds. A very small group of five including me went from Leeds, but I wouldn't have even considered giving the match a miss.

Finally, 28 May 1975 is a date that will be long remembered by Leeds fans as the Final of the European Cup at Parc des Princes in Paris, Leeds versus Bayern Munich. It is also a date where Leeds United were robbed of their rightful place in the elite for winning the European Cup with the events of the day, mentioned in my previous book *Follow Me and Leeds United*. The referee, who had allegedly been bribed, disallowed Peter Lorimer's goal for Leeds. Beckenbauer who played for Bayern, went to the referee after he had pointed back to the centre spot signalling a goal. The referee then went to his linesman, changed his mind and gave a free-kick for the goal being offside. Things went downhill very rapidly after that with Leeds being defeated 2–0. Although these memories are etched in my mind forever, I am still grateful for having the privilege of being there.

Twiggster from Denmark said that he couldn't remember very much about the actual match as the events afterwards are ingrained in his memory forever! After the gendarmes cavalry charged us post match, I got separated from my mates then chased into a nearby park by THREE cops on horses and managed to hide in some bushes. The cops were batoning anyone wearing Leeds colours. A mate of mine and his missus got cracked skulls and concussion. I've been in some right rumbles at footy away matches, but have only ever been scared enough to hide my colours after this match. The cops were totally OTT and then Moroccan gangs were picking off the survivors, as some of their gang members got a beating and thrown in the river before the match, for trying to sell Leeds fans tickets at triple face value. I managed to get back to where our van was parked and luckily everyone was okay who had got back, but we were still missing two lads. They staggered up about an hour after me and one of them had been clobbered by a cop and had a bad pain in his shoulder. It turned out later that his collarbone was shattered beyond repair! There were no mobile phones back then, but the van had a CB radio and we found out that the French customs were being really heavy with Leeds fans at all the ports used to get back to England and many of our fans missed their ferries. We pooled our money and found we had enough for petrol to get to Zeebrugge and hopefully buy new boat tickets there. We did and had enough left over to get mightily drunk on the ferry to Hull! The barman on the boat was a Leeds fan, who kept sending us rounds on the house that were gratefully received. Except for that boat trip, it was the most horrible away day EVER.

Left: Heidi wearing Billy Bremner's shirt 1976
Right: Heidi in her bedroom

Left: Arsenal 6 December 1975 at the services on the way there
Right: Shrewsbury lot presenting clock to Paul Madeley at
Elland Road after QPR game

Left: Leeds fans at the disco
Right: Leeds fans on train to Selby after Ipswich FA Cup game
(Pete Underwood & Snowy)

Leeds fans (Ian, Gadge and others) at the services on the way to Ipswich

Eric, Sue, Nancy, Phillip Isherwood and Heidi Wembley 6.5.72

Chapter 6

Costs and statistics for seven years 1971–78!

In the seventies when I didn't miss a match home or away for seven years, I kept statistics for the whole time. When I first started going to every match once I left school in 1971 and had started working, I earned £8.00 a week. My earnings at that time enabled me to go and watch Leeds all over the country and most weeks it meant I was going to two matches a week. I was also paid weekly at that time so it was easy to manage my money. Pay day was on a Friday so if you had spent up, you didn't have to wait long to be paid again. I also gave my mum £2.00 a week board at the time. I feel that the comparison in costs to go to football matches nowadays was interesting and found that money in the seventies went a lot further than it does today.

Season 1971–72

Date	Opponents	Cost	Score	Scorers	Venue
21.8.71	Wolverhampton Wanderers	70p	0–0		Leeds Road
4.9.71	Crystal Palace	30p	2–0	Giles (penalty) Madeley	Leeds Road
18.9.71	Liverpool	45p	1–0	Lorimer	H
25.9.71	Huddersfield Town	57½p	1–2	Charlton	A
27.9.71	Derby County, FL Cup 2nd round replay	45p	2–0	Lorimer (2)	H
29.9.71	SK Lierse Belgium, UEFA Cup 2nd Round replay	45p	0–4		H
2.10.71	West Ham United	75p	0–0		H
9.10.71	Coventry City	£1.35	1–3	Own goal (og)	A
16.10.71	Manchester City	75p	3–0	Clarke Jones Lorimer	H
20.10.71	West Ham United, FL Cup 3rd Round replay Extra-time	75p	0–1		H
23.10.71	Everton (Got Jack's autograph)	75p	3–2	Cooper Charlton Lorimer	H

6.11.71	Leicester City	75p	2–1	Bremner Lorimer	H
20.11.71	Stoke City	75p	1–0	Lorimer	H
27.11.71	Nottingham Forest	95p	2–0	Lorimer Clarke	A
4.12.71	West Bromwich Albion	75p	3–0	Giles (2) Lorimer	H
11.12.71	Chelsea	£2.27	0–0		A
18.12.71	Crystal Palace	£2.31	1–1	Lorimer	A
21.12.71	Huddersfield Town semi-final Senior West Riding Cup	85p (paid for Erica)	3–2	Clarke (2) Lorimer	H
27.12.71	Derby County Got a Leeds United bag £1.20 and a scarf 80p	75p	3–0	Gray Lorimer (2)	H
1.1.72	Liverpool	90p	2–0	Clarke Jones	A
8.1.72	Ipswich Town	75p	2–2	Bremner Clarke	H
15.1.72	Bristol Rovers – FA Cup 3rd Round	75p	4–1	Giles (2) Lorimer (2)	H
22.1.72	Sheffield United – Brian Baker gave me my coach ticket back to me as twice I'd only gone back with them	45p	1–0	Clarke	H
29.1.72	Tottenham Hotspur	£2.10	0–1		A
5.2.72	Liverpool – FA Cup 4th Round	85p	0–0		A
9.2.72	Liverpool – FA Cup 4th Round replay kick-off 2.30 pm	£1.05	2–0	Clarke (2)	H
12.2.72	Everton	£1.82	0–0		A
19.2.72	man utd	75p	5–1	Jones (3) Clarke Lorimer	H
26.2.72	Cardiff City, FA Cup 5th Round	£1.80	2–0	Giles (2)	A
4.3.72	Southampton – Went to the top of the Kop with all the fans	£1.15	7–0	Lorimer (3) Clarke (2) Jones Charlton	H
11.3.72	Coventry City – Jack Charlton's 600th league appearance	75p	1–0	Charlton	H
18.3.72	Tottenham Hotspur – FA Cup 6th round – 60p for Kop	95p	2–1	Clarke Charlton	H

25.3.72	Arsenal	95p	3–0	Clarke Jones Lorimer	H
27.3.72	Nottingham Forest	75p	6–1	Lorimer (2) Clarke (2) Gray (2)	H
30.3.72	West Ham	£3.29	2–2	Gray (2)	A
1.4.72	Derby County	£1.37	0–2		A
5.4.72	Huddersfield Town	87p	3–1	Jones Lorimer Gray	H
8.4.72	Stoke City – Terry Cooper broke his leg and Nigel Davey broke his leg also in reserve game against West Bromwich	£1.66	3–0	Jones (2) Lorimer	A
15.4.72	Birmingham City – at Hillsborough FA Cup semi-final	£1.25	3–0	Jones (2) Lorimer	A
1.5.72	Chelsea	57p	2–0	Bremner Jones	H
6.5.72	Arsenal – FA Cup Final at Wembley. WE WON THE CUP!! Mick Jones dislocated his elbow	£3.15	1–0	Clarke	A
8.5.72	Wolverhampton Wanderers – at least 10,000 Leeds supporters were locked out	£1.47	1–2	Bremner	A
10.5.72	Went to Leeds to see them bring the cup home over 40,000 supporters were there				
12.5.72	Halifax Town – Final of the West Riding Senior Cup – WE WON THE CUP!! Peter Lorimer scored from the half-way line	85p	4–3	Lorimer (3) Jordan	H

Season 1972–73

Date	Opponents	Cost	Score	Scorers	Venue
31.7.72	Doncaster Rovers (friendly) – 25p to go in	82p	3–0	Bremner Giles (pen) Jordan	H
2.8.72	Bradford City (friendly) 25p to go in	68p	2–1	Jordan Lorimer	H

12.8.72	Chelsea. We had our photos on front page of Evening Post.	£2.65	0–4		A
15.8.72	Sheffield United – gave Dad 40p to fetch me from Doncaster. Single to Sheffield 65p. Single to Doncaster 22p. When going back to the station passed 6 lasses (Sheffield) who asked who I was for. I said I don't know and one called me a bloody b*****d	£1.85	2–0	Colquhoun og Giles (pen)	A
19.8.72	West Bromwich Albion – got a flag 35p and paid 35p for photo of us going to Chelsea	£1.07	2–0	Clarke Giles (pen)	A
23.8.72	Ipswich Town	90p	3–3	Jordan (2) Giles (pen)	H
26.8.72	Tottenham Hotspur	£2.95	0–0		A
30.8.72	Southampton	90p	1–0	Bremner	H
2.9.72	Norwich City	£1.12	2–0	Jordan Charlton	H
6.9.72	Burnley – League Cup 2nd Round	90p	4–0	Lorimer (2) Jones Cherry	H
9.9.72	Stoke City – Karin gave birth to Mark 8lb 5oz. Went on special	£2.08	2–2	Lorimer Clarke	A
16.9.72	Leicester City	£1.10	3–1	Clarke Jones Bates	H
23.9.72	Newcastle United	£2.12	2–3	Clarke Jones	A
27.9.72	Ankaragücü (Turkey)	90p	1–0	Jones	H
30.9.72	Liverpool	£1.10	1–2	Jones	H
4.10.72	Aston Villa – FL Cup Third Round – our coach windows smashed on way back. It took 8 bricks before the window next to me went. Another cracked	£2.24	1–1	Charlton	A
7.10.72	Derby County	£1.11	5–0	Giles (2) Clarke Bremner	H
11.10.72	Aston Villa – FL Cup Third round replay	90p	2–0	Own goal Jones	H

14.10.72	Everton	£2.48	2–1	Jones Jordan	A
21.10.72	Coventry City	91p	1–1	Charlton	H
28.10.72	Wolverhampton Wanderers	£2.35	2–0	Gray Lorimer	A
31.10.72	Liverpool – FL Cup 4th Round	£1.64	2–2	Jones Lorimer	A
4.11.72	Ipswich Town	£2.46	2–2	Charlton Lorimer	A
8.11.72	Carl Zeiss Jena – ECWC Second Round 2nd leg	55p	2–0	Cherry Jones	H
11.11.72	Sheffield United	£1.25	2–1	Clarke (2)	H
18.11.72	Crystal Palace	£2.67	2–2	Jones Giles	A
20.11.72	Went to Elland Road for replay against Liverpool and when we got there found the match was off				H
22.11.72	Liverpool – FL Cup Fourth round replay – got a lift in, they scored with 10 seconds to go	90p	0–1		H
25.11.72	Manchester City – all goals scored in last 20 minutes	£1.20	3–0	Cherry Lorimer Clarke	H
2.12.72	Arsenal	£2.65	1–2	Lorimer (pen)	A
9.12.72	West Ham United	£1.20	1–0	Jones	H
16.12.72	Birmingham City	£.1.25	4–0	Clarke (2) Jones Lorimer	H
23.12.72	man utd	£2.05	1–1	Clarke	A
24.12.72	Newcastle United	£1.12	1–0	Jordan	H
30.12.72	West Bromwich Albion – postponed because of flu				A
6.1.73	Tottenham Hotspur	£1.30	2–1	Jones Lorimer (pen)	H
13.1.73	Norwich City – FA Cup 3rd round	£2.67	1–1	Lorimer	A
17.1.73	Norwich City – FA Cup Third round replay	90p	1–1	Giles	H
20.1.73	Norwich City	£2.67	2–1	Jordan Clarke	A
27.1.73	Stoke City	£1.25	1–0	Clarke	H
29.1.73	Norwich City at Villa Park, FA Cup Third round 2nd replay	£1.88	5–0	Clarke (3) Jones Lorimer	A
3.2.73	Plymouth Argyle – FA Cup 4th round	£1.20	2–1	Clarke Bates	H

10.2.73	Leicester City	£2.19	1–2		A
17.2.73	Chelsea	£1.20	1–1	Jones	H
24.2.73	West Bromwich Albion – FA Cup Fifth round	£1.25	2–0	Clarke (2)	H
3.3.73	Derby County	£1.82	3–2	Lorimer (2 1 a pen) Clarke	A
7.3.73	Rapid Bucharest – ECWC Third round First leg	90p	5–0	Giles Lorimer (2) Clarke Jordan	H
10.3.73	Everton	£1.25	2–1	Clarke Lorimer	H
17.3.73	Derby County – FA Cup 6th round	£1.82	1–0	Lorimer	A
24.3.73	Wolverhampton Wanderers	£1.30	0–0		H
28.3.73	West Bromwich Albion	£2.16	1–1	Clarke	A
31.3.73	Manchester City	10p	0–1		A
2.4.73	Coventry City	£1.97	1–0	Reaney	A
7.4.73	Wolverhampton Wanderers – FA Cup semi-final at Maine Road	£1.95	1–0	Bremner	A
11.4.73	Hadjuk Split – ECWC Semi Final First leg – lost my voice through shouting at the ref – he sent Clarke off and was horrid. They kicked hell out of Leeds	95p	1–0	Clarke	H
14.4.73	West Ham United	£2.65	1–1	Clarke	A
18.4.73	man utd	£1.32	0–1		H
21.4.73	Crystal Palace	£1.25	4–0	Bremner F Gray Lorimer Clarke	H
23.4.73	Liverpool	£2.05	0–2		A
28.4.73	Southampton	£3.05	1–3	Hunter	A
30.4.73	Birmingham City	£2.00	1–2	Jordan	A
5.5.73	Sunderland – FA Cup Final	£3.15	0–1		A
16.5.73	AC Milan – ECWC Final in Salonika, Greece	£46.00 + £8.00 spending	0–1		A
61 matches attended total cost £148.97					

Season 1973–74

Date	Opponents	Cost	Score	Scorers	Venue
11.8.73	Bradford City (Friendly)	£1.52	2–0	McQueen	H
15.8.73	Doncaster Rovers (Friendly) – I got smacked in by 8 lasses, a Doncaster lad Graham saved us	36p	2–0	Jones Cherry	A
18.8.73	Huddersfield Town – semi-final West Riding Cup – came back on the special – it got wrecked, 2¼ hours to get back	£1.43	2–1	Jones Lorimer	A
21.8.73	Halifax Town – Final West Riding Cup – We won the Cup	63p	2–1	Lorimer Jones	H
25.8.73	Everton	£1.18	3–1	Bremner Giles Jones	H
28.8.73	Arsenal	£3.94	2–1	Lorimer Madeley	A
1.9.73	Tottenham Hotspur – Clarke got carried off	£3.57	3–0	Bremner (2) Clarke	A
5.9.73	Wolverhampton Wanderers	£1.15	4–1	Lorimer (2 – 1 a pen) Jones Bremner	H
8.9.73	Birmingham City	£1.18	3–0	Lorimer (3)	H
11.9.73	Wolverhampton Wanderers	£2.28	2–0	Clarke	A
15.9.73	Southampton	£3.18	2–1	Clarke (2)	A
22.9.73	man utd	£1.04	0–0		H
29.9.73	Norwich City	£2.54	1–0	Giles	A
3.10.73	Stromgodset	£1.15	6–1	Clarke (2) Jones (2) Bates Gray	H
6.10.73	Stoke City	£1.16	1–1	Jones	H
8.10.73	Ipswich Town	£2.51	0–2		A
13.10.73	Leicester	£2.31	2–2	Jones Bremner	A
20.10.73	Liverpool	£1.34	1–0	Jones	H
24.10.73	Hibernian –UEFA Cup First round First leg	£1.15	0–0		H
28.10.73	Manchester City	£2.03	1–0	Bates	A

3.11.73	West Ham United	£1.40	4–1	Bates Jones (2) Clarke	H
7.11.73	Hibernian –UEFA Cup Second round Second leg	£4.22	5–4	Penalties Lorimer Clarke Bates Frank Gray Bremner	A
10.11.73	Burnley	£1.90	0–0		A
17.11.73	Coventry City	£1.52	3–0	Clarke Jordan Bremner	H
24.11.73	Derby County	£2.05	0–0		A
28.11.73	Vitoria Setubal –UEFA Cup Third round First leg	£1.15	1–0	Cherry	H
1.12.73	Queens Park Rangers	£1.46	2–2	Bremner Jones	H
8.12.73	Ipswich Town	£2.78	3–0	Yorath Jones Clarke	A
15.12.73	Chelsea	£4.00	2–1	Jordan Jones	A
22.12.73	Norwich City	£1.52	1–0	Yorath	H
26.12.73	Newcastle United	£2.33	1–0	Madeley	A
29.12.73	Birmingham City – 3 coaches smashed in. Bomb scare but we all stayed put	£2.54	1–1	Jordan	A
1.1.74	Tottenham Hotspur	£1.61	1–1	Jones	H
5.1.74	Wolverhampton Wanderers – FA Cup 3rd Round	£2.50	1–1	Lorimer (pen)	A
9.1.74	Wolverhampton Wanderers FA Cup Third round replay	£1.39	1–0	Jones	H
12.1.74	Southampton	£1.42	2–1	Jones Jordan	H
19.1.74	Everton	£2.54	0–0		A
26.1.74	Peterborough United – FA Cup Fourth round – Sue and I had our picture on the front of the Evening Post. 8,000 Leeds fans	£2.10	4–1	Lorimer Jordan (2) Yorath	A
2.2.74	Chelsea	£1.46	1–1	Cherry	H
5.2.74	Arsenal – only 26,000 there	£1.82	3–1	Simpson og Jordan (2)	H

9.2.74	man utd	£1.00	2–0	Jones Jordan	A
16.2.74	Bristol City	£3.67	1–1	Bremner	A
19.2.74	Bristol City	£1.50	0–1		H
23.2.74	Stoke City – we got beaten after 29 matches unbeaten in the league	£2.19	2–3	Bremner Clarke	A
26.2.74	Leicester City	80p	1–1	Lorimer (pen)	H
2.3.74	Newcastle United	£1.48	1–1	Clarke	H
9.3.74	Manchester City	£1.57	1–0	Lorimer (pen)	H
16.3.74	Liverpool	£2.11	0–1		A
23.3.74	Burnley	£1.36	1–4	Clarke	H
30.3.74	West Ham United	£4.12	1–3	Clarke	A
6.4.74	Derby County	£1.36	2–0	Lorimer Bremner	H
13.4.74	Coventry City	£2.51	0–0		A
15.4.74	Sheffield United	£1.51	0–0		H
16.4.74	Sheffield United	£2.05	2–0	Lorimer (2)	A
20.4.74	Ipswich Town	£1.58	3–2		H
27.4.74	Queens Park Rangers – WE WON THE LEAGUE	£4.68	1–0	Clarke	A
	Huddersfield Town	£1.23	0–2		A
6.5.74	Sunderland – Billy's testimonial	£1.90	0–0		H
3.5.74	Middlesbrough – testimonial for B Kerr	£4.11	4–4		A
18.5.74	Scotland v England – Hampden Park	£6.42	2–0	Jordan Dalglish	
18.6.74	Scotland v Brazil in Frankfurt, Germany		0–0		
61 matches – total cost £129.24					

Season 1974–75

Date	Opponents	Cost	Score	Scorers	Venue
8.8.74	Huddersfield Town	£1.54	2–1	Giles Bates	A
10.8.74	Liverpool – Charity Shield at Wembley – lost on penalties when normally shared it 6 months a piece	£4.16	1–1	Cherry	A
17.8.74	Stoke City	£2.06	0–3		A

21.8.74	Queens Park Rangers	84p	0–1			H
24.8.74	Birmingham City	£1.50	1–0	Clarke		H
27.8.74	Queens Park Rangers	£4.04	1–1	Yorath		A
31.8.74	Manchester City	£1.73	1–2	Clarke		A
7.9.74	Luton Town	66p	1–1	Clarke		H
10.9.74	Huddersfield Town – League Cup	£1.97	1–1	Lorimer		A
14.9.74	Burnley	£2.49	1–2	Lorimer		A
18.9.74	FC Zurich	£1.24	4–1	Clarke (2) Lorimer (pen) Jordan		H
21.9.74	Sheffield United	74p	5–1	Clarke (2) McQueen Lorimer Yorath		H
24.9.74	Huddersfield Town	£1.12	1–1	Clarke		H
28.9.74	Everton	£2.62	2–3	Clarke Yorath		A
2.10.74	FC Zurich	£65.00 + £10 in Swiss francs	1–2	Clarke		A
5.10.74	Arsenal	75p	2–0	McKenzie		H
7.10.74	Huddersfield Town	£1.10	2–1	Bates (og by theirs) Lorimer (pen)		H
9.10.74	Bury	£1.94	2–1	Lorimer Cherry		A
12.10.74	Ipswich Town	£3.10	0–0			A
15.10.74	Birmingham City	£3.02	0–1			A
19.10.74	Wolverhampton Wanderers	74p	2–0	Clarke McKenzie		H
26.10.74	Liverpool	£2.10	0–1			A
30.10.74	Huddersfield Town – semi-final West Riding Cup	£1.14	1–2	McNiven		H
2.11.74	Derby County	59p	0–1			H
6.11.74	Ujpest Dozsa – European Cup	£1.12	3–0	McQueen Bremner Yorath		H
9.11.74	Coventry City	£3.25	3–1	O'Hare Hindley own goal Bremner		A
13.11.74	Chester – League Cup 4th Round	£2.21	0–3			A
16.11.74	Middlesbrough	£1.31	2–2	McKenzie		H

23.11.74	Carlisle	£2.74	2–1	Jordan McKenzie	A
30.11.74	Chelsea	74p	2–0	Cherry Clarke	H
4.12.74	Tottenham Hotspur	52p	2–1	McKenzie Lorimer (pen)	H
7.12.74	West Ham United	£3.78	1–2	McKenzie	A
14.12.74	Stoke City	74p	3–1	McQueen Lorimer Yorath	H
21.12.74	Newcastle United	£2.93	0–3		A
26.12.74	Burnley	77p	2–2	Jordan Lorimer	H
28.12.74	Leicester City	£2.39	2–0	Frank Gray McKenzie	A
4.1.75	Cardiff	£1.34	4–1	Eddie Gray Clarke (2) McKenzie	H
11.1.75	West Ham United	74p	2–1	Clarke McKenzie	H
18.1.75	Chelsea	£4.11	2–0	McKenzie Yorath	A
25.1.75	Wimbledon	£1.76	0–0		H
	Wimbledon postponed but had got as far as Worksop before we found out	£4.00			A
1.2.75	Coventry City	90p	0–0		H
8.2.75	Derby County	£2.89	0–0		A
10.2.75	Wimbledon (at Selhurst Park, Crystal Palace)	£6.09	1–0	Baysford own goal	A
15.2.75	Derby – was going on the special but called off – postponed				A
18.2.75	Derby	£1.27	1–0	Nish own goal	A
22.2.75	Middlesbrough	£2.74	1–0	Clarke	A
25.2.75	Carlisle	93p	3–1	Lorimer Clarke Gray	H
2.3.75	Manchester City	82p	2–2	Lorimer (2)	H
5.3.75	Anderlecht – European Cup	£1.12	3–0	Jordan McQueen Lorimer	H
8.3.75	Ipswich – FA Cup 6th round	£4.66	0–0		A
11.3.75	Ipswich – FA Cup Sixth round replay	70p	1–1	McKenzie	H
15.3.75	Everton	67p	0–0		H

19.3.75	Anderlecht – European Cup	£34.00	1–0	Bremner	A
22.3.75	Luton Town	£1.30	1–2	Jordan	A
25.3.75	Ipswich – FA Cup Sixth round Second replay at Filbert Street, Leicester	£1.35	0–0		A
27.3.75	Ipswich – FA Cup Sixth round Third replay at Filbert Street, Leicester	£2.80	2–3	Clarke Giles	A
29.3.75	Newcastle	£1.42	1–1	Clarke	H
31.3.75	Leicester	£5.63 (£2 booze and £2 lost in purse)	2–2	Clarke Giles	H
1.4.75	Sheffield United	£2.04	1–1	Madeley	A
5.4.75	Liverpool	82p	0–2		H
9.4.75	Barcelona	£1.86	2–1	Bremner Clarke	H
12.4.75	Arsenal	£9.00	2–1	Clarke Hunter	A
19.4.75	Ipswich	£1.84	2.1	Cherry Harris	H
23.4.75	Barcelona – semi-final of the European Cup	£82.05	1–1	Lorimer	A
26.4.75	Wolverhampton Wanderers	£4.50	1–1	Frank Gray	A
28.4.75	Tottenham Hotspur	£4.50	2–4	Jordan Lorimer	A
5.5.75	Leeds v Don Revie's XI – Norman Hunter's testimonial	£1.35	2–3	Bremner (2)	H
13.5.75	Walsall v Leeds – Nick Atthey testimonial	£5.87	3–3	Clarke McKenzie Jordan	A
28.5.75	Bayern Munich at Parc des Princes, Paris – Final of the European Cup – WE WERE ROBBED!!	£68.65	0–2		A
70 matches – total cost £400					

Season 1975–76

Date	Opponents	Cost	Score	Scorers	Venue
1.8.75	Scarborough	31p	1–0	Felix	A
5.8.75	Doncaster	£1.87	2–1	McNiven (2)	A
8.8.75	Halifax Town West Riding Cup semi-final	£1.72	4–2	Yorath Lorimer Cherry Clarke	H
16.8.75	Aston Villa	£8.00	2–1	Lorimer (2)	A
20.8.75	Norwich City	£8.00	1–1	Cherry	A
23.8.75	Ipswich Town	£1.36	1–0	Lorimer	H
26.8.75	Liverpool	96p	0–3		H
30.8.75	Sheffield United	£2.88	2–0	McKenzie Clarke	A
6.9.75	Wolverhampton Wanderers	92p	3–0	McQueen Clarke McKenzie	H
9.9.75	Ipswich Town – League Cup 2nd round	£1.60	3–2	McKenzie Lorimer Clarke	H
13.9.75	Stoke City	£3.25	2–3	Lorimer (2)	A
20.9.75	Tottenham Hotspur	£1.50	1–1		H
27.9.75	Burnley	£3.34	1–0	Cherry	A
4.10.75	QPR	£1.06	2–1	Clarke Lorimer	H
7.10.75	Notts County	£1.35	0–1		H
11.10.75	man utd	£1.56	1–2	Clarke	H
18.10.75	Birmingham City	£4.36	2–2	Cherry Hunter	A
22.10.75	West Bromwich Albion eleven – Johnny Giles Testimonial	£5.21	1–3	McKenzie	A
25.10.75	Coventry City	£1.60	2–0	Yorath Clarke	H
1.11.75	Derby County	£3.02	2–3	Cherry McKenzie	A
8.11.75	Newcastle United	£1.80	3–0	McKenzie (2) Yorath	H
15.11.75	Middlesbrough	£2.84	0–0		A
22.11.75	Birmingham City	£1.92	3–0	Bremner McKenzie (2)	H
29.11.75	Everton	£1.98	5–2	Lorimer (2) Clarke (2) Eddie Gray	H
6.12.75	Arsenal	£5.17	2–1	McKenzie (2)	A
13.12.75	Ipswich	£3.75	1–2	McKenzie	A

20.12.75	Aston Villa	£1.60	1–0	Clarke (his 100th league goal)	H
26.12.75	Manchester City	£2.25	1–0	Madeley	A
27.12.75	Leicester City	£1.56	4–0	Clarke McKenzie (2) Lorimer	H
3.1.76	Notts County Third Round FA Cup	£1.89	1–0	Clarke	A
10.1.76	Stoke City	£1.79	2–0	McKenzie Bremner	H
17.1.76	Wolverhampton Wanderers	£4.29	1–1	McAlle og	A
24.1.76	Crystal Palace – Fourth Round FA Cup	£2.09	0–1		H
31.1.76	Norwich City	£1.68	0–3		H
7.2.76	Liverpool	£2.93	0–2		A
11.2.76	Celtic Friendly	£10.52	3–1	Eddie Gray Clarke McNiven	A
21.2.76	Middlesbrough	£1.45	0–2		H
23.2.76	West Ham United	£5.33	1–1	McKenzie	A
28.2.76	Coventry City	£2.09	1–0	Frank Gray	A
2.3.76	Derby County	60p	1–1	Frank Gray	H
9.3.76	West Ham United	10p	1–1	Jordan	H
13.3.76	man utd	£3.55	2–3	Cherry Bremner	A
20.3.76	Everton	£4.54	3–1	Bremner Jordan Harris	A
27.3.76	Arsenal	£1.53	3–0	Clarke (2) Bremner	H
31.3.76	Newcastle United	£3.80	3–2	Newcastle og Cherry Harris	A
3.4.76	Burnley	£1.55	2–1	McKenzie Hampton	H
10.4.76	Tottenham Hotspur	£7.17	0–0		A
14.4.76	Sheffield United	60p	0–1		H
17.4.76	Manchester City	£1.68	2–1	McNiven Harris	H
20.4.76	Leicester City	80p	1–2	McKenzie	A
24.4.76	QPR	£5.45	0–2		A
26.4.76	Sunderland	£3.40	2–1	McNiven Clarke	A
1.5.76	Rangers v Hearts at Hampden Park	£6.60	3–1	Parlane (2) MacDonald	A

3.5.76	Newcastle United – Paul Reaney's testimonial	£1.00	4–5	Lorimer (2) Clarke Stevenson	H
15.5.76	Scotland v England at Hampden Park	£10.12	2–1	Dalglish	A
Total spent £158.28 – 55 matches					

Season 1976–77

Date	Opponents	Cost	Score	Scorers	Venue
6.8.76	Anderlecht – Olympic Stadium, Amsterdam	£75.48 total for both matches	2–3	Currie Harris	A
9.8.76	Borussia Mönchengladbach		3–3	Eddie Gray (2) Clarke	A
21.8.76	West Bromwich Albion	£1.19	2–2	Harris Clarke	H
24.8.76	Birmingham City	£5.73	0–0		A
28.8.76	Coventry City	£4.73	2–4	Frank Gray Currie	A
1.9.76	Stoke City – Second round League Cup	£4.55	1–2	Currie	A
4.9.76	Derby County	£1.80	2–0	Eddie Gray Cherry	H
11.9.76	Tottenham Hotspur	£6.58	0–1		A
18.9.76	Newcastle United	£2.07	2–2	McNiven Harris	H
25.9.76	Middlesbrough	£5.13	0–1		A
2.10.76	man utd	£3.18	0–2		H
6.10.76	West Ham United	£5.80	3–1	Eddie Gray Lorimer Harris	A
16.10.76	Norwich City	£5.38	2–1	Frank Fray Eddie Gray	A
23.10.76	Liverpool	£2.72	1–1	McNiven	G
30.10.76	Arsenal	£1.14	2–1	Cherry Jordan	H
6.11.76	Everton	£4.05	2–0	McQueen Jordan	A
10.11.76	Stoke City	75p	1–1	Lorimer	H
15.11.76	Huddersfield Town – West Riding Cup Final	£2.35	2–0	Hankin (2)	H
20.11.76	Ipswich Town	£6.65	1–1	McQueen	A

27.11.76	Leicester City	98p	2–2	Lorimer McNiven	H
4.12.76	Bristol City – abandoned at half time fog	£5.65	0–0		A
11.12.76	Aston Villa	£1.14	1–3	McNiven	H
18.12.76	QPR – postponed				A
27.12.76	Manchester City	£2.19	0–2		H
29.12.76	Sunderland	£2.66	1–0	Jordan	A
1.1.77	Everton – postponed waterlogged pitch	£1.39			H
3.1.77	Arsenal	£5.93	1–1	Clarke	A
8.1.77	Norwich City – Third Round FA Cup	£2.65	5–2	Clarke Reaney Jordan McQueen Hampton	H
22.1.77	West Bromwich Albion	£5.73	2–1	Eddie Gray McQueen	A
29.1.77	Birmingham City – Fourth Round FA Cup	£4.89	2–1	Jordan Clarke	A
2.2.77	Birmingham City	£1.99	1–0	McQueen	H
5.2.77	Coventry City	£1.90	1–2	Jordan	H
12.2.77	Derby County	£4.29	1–0	Jordan	A
19.2.77	Tottenham Hotspur	£2.03	2–1	Jordan Clarke	H
26.2.77	Manchester City – Fifth Round FA Cup	£2.28	1–0	Cherry	H
2.3.77	Newcastle		0–3		A
5.3.77	Middlesbrough	£2.36	2–1	McQueen (2)	H
8.3.77	QPR	£7.81	0–0		A
12.3.77	man utd	£7.42	0–1		A
19.3.77	Wolverhampton Wanderers FA Cup 6th Round	£4.69	1–0	Eddie Gray	A
23.3.77	Norwich City	£2.00	3–2	Reaney Hampton Jordan	H
26.3.77	Eire – Paul Madeley's Testimonial	£2.89	2–5	Harris Jordan	H
29.3.77	Halifax – Semi Final West Riding Cup	£2.79	4–3	Hankin Lorimer Harris Thomas	A
2.4.77	Liverpool	£6.37	1–3	McQueen	A
8.4.77	Manchester City	£3.11	1–2	Jordan	A
9.4.77	Sunderland	28p	1–1	Cherry	H
12.4.77	Stoke City	£3.76	1–2	Jordan	A

16.4.77	Ipswich Town	£1.94	2–1	McGhee Clarke	H
23.4.77	man utd – FA Cup Semi Final at Hillsborough	£4.24	1–2	Clarke	A
26.4.77	West Ham United	£2.10	1–1	Jordan	H
30.4.77	Bristol City	£1.94	2–0	Thomas Eddie Gray	H
4.5.77	Everton	£2.10	0–0		H
7.5.77	Aston Villa	£4.46	1–2	McNiven	A
10.5.77	Bristol City	£6.73	0–1		A
14.5.77	QPR	£1.54	0–1		H
16.5.77	Leicester City	£4.05	1–0	Frank Gray	A
28.5.77	Wales v Scotland – Racecourse Ground, Wrexham	£5.70	0–0		
1.6.77	Scotland v Northern Ireland at Hampden Park	£5.55	3–0	Dalglish (2) McQueen	
4.6.77	England v Scotland at Wembley	£7.65	2–1	McQueen	
	Other matches				
14.8.76	York v Barnsley at Bootham Crescent	£1.74	0–0		
9.10.76	Aston Villa v Rangers at Villa Park – match abandoned after 53 minutes for rioting	£7.12	0–2		
14.12.76	Goole Town v Wrexham at Victoria Pleasure Grounds, Goole	67p	0–1		
15.3.77	Barnsley v Don Revie XI All Stars at Oakwell, Barnsley	£1.45	6–3	Ray Hankin (3) David McCreery Brian Greenhoff Alan Woodward	
21.5.77	Liverpool v man utd – FA Cup Final at Wembley – Leeds United Pools Agent trip	£1.39	1–2	Case	
Total spent £288.93 – 61 matches					

Season 1977–78

Date	Opponents	Cost	Score	Scorers	Venue
3.8.77	Odense, Denmark	£73.20	4–1	Lorimer (2) Hankin McNiven	A
6.8.77	PSV Eindhoven, Holland	£60.00	3–1	Lorimer Hankin McNiven	A
9.8.77	Doncaster Rovers	95p	1–2	Felix	A
12.8.77	Racing White Daring Molenbeek, Belgium	£20.45	2–2	2 own goals	A
20.8.77	Newcastle United	£6.53	2–3	Hankin Lorimer	A
24.8.77	West Bromwich Albion	£1.65	2–2	Jordan McQueen	H
27.8.77	Birmingham City	£1.98	1–0	Hankin	H
31.8.77	Rochdale – League Cup 2nd round	£2.35	3–0	Jordan Cherry Harris	A
3.9.77	Coventry City	£4.91	2–2	Hankin McQueen	A
10.9.77	Ipswich Town	15p	2–1	Hankin (2)	H
17.9.77	Derby County	£4.68	2–2	Lorimer Graham	A
21.9.77	Scotland v Czechoslovakia at Hampden Park – World Cup Qualifying	£6.32	3–1	Jordan Hartford Dalglish	
24.9.77	man utd	£1.71	1–1	Hankin	H
1.10.77	Chelsea	£9.21	2–1	Lorimer Hankin	A
5.10.77	Aston Villa	£1.15	1–1	McQueen	H
8.10.77	Bristol City	£4.75	2–3	Hankin (2)	A
10.10.77	Bradford City – West Riding Cup Final	£2.45	5–2		A
12.10.77	Scotland v Wales at Anfield	£5.02	2–0	Masson Dalglish	
15.10.77	Liverpool	£1.85	1–2	Thomas	H
22.10.77	Middlesbrough	£5.03	1–2	Harris	A
26.10.77	Colchester – League Cup 3rd Round	£2.85	4–0	Jordan Graham Lorimer Hankin	H
29.10.77	Leicester	£4.23	0–0		A
5.11.77	Norwich City	£1.71	2–2	Lorimer (2)	H

9.11.77	Leeds v Scotland XI Peter Lorimer testimonial	£2.80	5–2		H
12.11.77	Manchester City	£4.55	3–2	Jordan Graham Hankin	A
19.11.77	Nottingham Forest	£1.71	1–0	Hankin	H
22.11.77	Leeds v Ajax Jubilee Match	£1.15	2–1	Jordan Clarke Currie own goal	H
26.11.77	West Ham United	£6.32	1–0	Hankin	A
30.11.77	Bolton League Cup 4th Round	£3.82	3–1	Graham Jordan Frank Gray	A
3.12.77	QPR	£1.98	3–0	Needham own goal Flynn Currie	H
10.12.77	Arsenal – in hospital having tonsils out		1–1	McQueen	A
13.12.77	Bradford City – semi-final West Riding Cup		2–0	McQueen	A
17.12.77	Manchester City	£2.56	2–0	McQueen Cherry	H
26.12.77	Wolverhampton Wanderers	£6.07	1–3	Jordan	A
27.12.77	Everton	£1.89	3–1	Hankin (2) Lorimer	H
31.12.77	West Bromwich Albion	£5.54	0–1		A
2.1.78	Newcastle United	£1.25	0–2		H
7.1.78	Manchester City – FA Cup 3rd Round	£1.90	1–2	Frank Gray (pen)	H
14.1.78	Birmingham City	£5.20	3–2	Arthur Graham Hat-trick (3)	A
18.1.78	Everton quarter-final League Cup	£3.15	4–1	Currie Lorimer (2) Eddie Gray	H
21.1.78	Coventry City	£2.65	2–0	Hankin Harris	H
30.1.78	All Stars 11 v man utd at Goole Town	60p	2–7	McNiven	
4.2.78	Ipswich Town	£5.20	1–0	Eddie Gray	A
8.2.78	Nottingham Forest – semi-final League Cup 1st Leg	£3.15	1–3	Eddie Gray	H
11.2.78	Derby County – postponed				H

15.2.78	Nottingham Forest – semi final League Cup Second Leg – got to Nottingham – match called off at 6.00 pm				A
18.2.78	man utd – postponed				A
22.2.78	Nottingham Forest – semi-final League Cup 2nd Leg	£2.75	2–4	Frank Gray Graham	A
25.2.78	Chelsea	£2.45	2–0	Frank Gray Currie	H
1.3.78	man utd	£2.87	1–0	Clarke	A
4.3.78	Bristol City	50p	0–2		H
11.3.78	Liverpool	£3.85	0–1		A
18.3.78	Middlesbrough	£2.15	5–0	Graham (2) Clarke Hankin Middlesbrough own goal	H
25.3.78	Everton		0–2		A
27.3.78	Wolverhampton Wanderers	£2.15	2–1	Graham Hankin	H
28.3.78	Leicester City	£2.40	5–1	Eddie Gray (3) Frank Gray Graham	H
1.4.78	Norwich City	£4.70	0–3		A
8.4.78	West Ham United	£1.60	1–2	Graham	H
12.4.78	Derby County	15p	2–0	Hankin Eddie Gray	H
15.4.78	Nottingham Forest	£5.45	1–1	Frank Gray (pen)	A
16.4.78	Rangers v Scottish Select at Ibrox	£6.00	5–0	Greig (2)	
17.4.78	Dundee – Peter Lorimer's Testimonial	50p	3–2	Lorimer	A
22.4.78	Arsenal	£2.20	1–3	Currie	H
26.4.78	Aston Villa – couldn't afford to go		1–3	Hankin	A
29.4.78	QPR	£7.00	0–0		A
Total cost – £337.39 – 59 matches					

Chapter 7

FA Cup and League Cup memories

Dave Cocker – Memories of the 1965 FA Cup Final against Liverpool and FA Cup run.

My dad, Les Cocker, was the trainer for Leeds United alongside Manager Don Revie. We travelled down on Friday afternoon on a Pullman train specially hired for the Leeds team and families. The train departed from Leeds Central station and on arrival in London the team and families went their separate ways. The team were staying at The Savoy and the families were staying at the Charing Cross Hotel. Mother was staying at The Savoy along with Elsie Revie but the players' wives weren't allowed to stay as they couldn't mix with the team the night before a match. At the Charing Cross Hotel there were a few kids of approximately 13 to 14 years old including me, Duncan Revie, Robert Collins and the son of the Earl of Harewood.

We spent the whole night before the match carrying on in the hotel. The fashion accessory at the time was a duffle bag with a cord over it. The in thing at football matches at this time was throwing toilet rolls in the crowd. We had an idea then that as we would be sat near the Royal Box, getting hold of some toilet rolls would be a good idea. We then proceeded to nick all the toilet rolls and stuff them into our duffle bags to take to the match. When Ron Yates was being presented with the FA Cup as Liverpool won, you can see a toilet roll whizz past his head thrown by yours truly!

Even though Leeds had been beaten, it was just nice to be there as nobody expected it. Leeds, having just gained promotion from the Second Division, ended up runners up in the league and FA Cup Finalists in their first season. It was gutting, but the best match for me had been the FA Cup semi-final replay at Nottingham Forest's ground against man utd on 31 March 1965. The first match had been played at Hillsborough, Sheffield Wednesday's ground and it was a very tight match although there had been a lot of hassle there. Bobby Collins had ragged Denis Law's shirt in that first leg and in a picture taken at the time, he looked punch drunk. The replay was set for the following Wednesday evening where Billy Bremner showed his quality once again, when he scored the winning goal in the last minute. He did it in so many matches, which saw dad swinging Don Revie round when the ball hit the back of the net! I think this was the biggest moment for the club, it was the making of us as a team and the start of things by getting to the FA Cup Final. The FA Cup during this time was a very special occasion and was the only match to be shown live on TV.

The replay at Forest was also the first time that I saw football violence. There had been nothing during the match, but afterwards as we were making our way back to the players-wives' coaches, even the wives were getting jumped on as well as me. man utd thought they had a God given right to win every match.

Going to the final in London was special but the trip back with no cup was annoying. Leeds did win the League Cup in 1968 with a Terry Cooper goal against Arsenal and we came back with that cup on the train.

In 1972 after Leeds had won the FA Cup against Arsenal with an Allan Clarke goal, I travelled back on the train with the rest of the families but without the players on, as they had gone straight to Wolverhampton for their next match. Leeds had to play their last match of the season two days after the Final so they didn't get a chance to celebrate their win. They ended up training in a park in Birmingham in their Leeds kits instead, preparing for the Wolverhampton match.

The train that had been hired for all the wives, juniors, reserves and families, saw me sat in the back Pullman carriage. There was a tab on the train with all the drinks being free. I had been persuaded by the others with me to go and ask Don for the FA Cup so I did and walked back with it to join the others. They helped me fill it with champagne and drank it from the cup, a special moment; we had the FA Cup in our hands. The carriage had approximately 18 people in it including some Leeds youngsters, Glan Letheren, Byron Stevenson and Sean O'Neil. Although it was a private train it stopped at Doncaster for what seemed like ages. The press were on the train too and it was one big party but sadly, no first team players were on it to share the celebrations. I think the delay was down to so many people turning out in Leeds so they had to stay in Donny till the coppers had time to sort the crowd out. When the train did leave Donny it never really got going. It was crawling north of Donny where people were stood in back gardens with banners as they knew the train was going past and I was hanging out of the window holding the FA Cup! By the time the train arrived back in Leeds I was absolutely rat arsed but was still carrying the cup. The press were going to take a photo of the wives with the cup and Christine Yorath said as I walked up with cup, "Where is the lid?" That's when I panicked and ran back to the train to look for it and luckily it had fallen under a table. Amazing! I was then able to go back with the cup and the lid so the girls could have their photo taken with it. Don and dad had come back to Leeds to do the press interviews and then set off straight back to Birmingham. On Sunday they were with the squad having a training session, arriving only a couple of hours after the players

---

My own memories of FA Cup runs.

I remember watching the 1970 FA Cup Final on the television and being gutted when Sprake made his error and Chelsea forced a replay as the match ended in a 2–2 draw after extra-time. Although the pitch was in a horrendous condition due to the Horse of the Year Show having being staged there the week previously, Eddie Gray had played magnificently. Leeds took the lead through Charlton before Chelsea equalised. When Jones scored to give Leeds the lead again we really thought it was going to be our year, but again Chelsea equalised. We had to go and pick my mum up from Doncaster station as she was coming home from a trip to Germany. I was happy to see my mum and because she arrived on one of the Leeds United special trains with all the fans, I was made up seeing all the Leeds fans on the train when it pulled into the station. Due to the state of the Wembley pitch after the FA Cup Final the replay was switched to Old Trafford. Sue and her dad went to the replay and it was only afterwards that I found out I could have gone as they had a spare ticket. Even though Leeds lost I would have loved to have gone to the match.

January in 1973 came a month where we played Norwich City four times. The first time going to Norwich was the third round of the FA Cup on 13 January. This ended up in a 1–1 draw with Lorimer scoring for Leeds. The Wallace Arnold coach had no heating on and I was frozen. Lots of Leeds fans went to this match. The replay was at Elland Road on 17 January which also ended up in a 1–1 draw with Giles scoring this time. There were already a lot from Hensall and Snaith on the coach when I got on. The following week on 20 January we went to Norwich again to play them in the league. This time there were very few Leeds fans that went and Norwich fans felt brave enough to come and surround us although nothing kicked off. On the coach home twins Helen and Sheila and a lad called Mick introduced themselves to me. Although Helen and Sheila stopped going to matches in the seventies I keep in touch with Christmas Cards. It would be nice to meet up with them again someday. I can't believe where the time has gone! The second replay in the FA Cup ended up being played at Villa Park on 29 January. When we arrived at Villa Park the Leeds fans stayed together in a large group and went up to the ground. I followed the group as they went up and down the small streets near the ground and some house windows were smashed before everyone went into the ground. We were in the Holte End and there were thousands of Leeds fans there, with a few Norwich fans near the front of the stand. This match was fantastic as Leeds hammered Norwich 5–0 with Clarke getting a hat trick and Jones and Lorimer scoring the others.

The FA Cup semi-final against Wolves at Maine Road in April 1973 ended up with us missing the first 20 minutes of the match because the coach had been stuck in traffic. For this one I had gone with Abbey Coachways as they were running transport that day. Luckily with us being late we weren't involved in any trouble but it meant I couldn't get a programme so was very peeved. The twins who had gone on Wallace Arnold coaches had arrived a lot earlier and there had been lots of trouble with running battles between Leeds and Wolves fans. The match was one of those fantastic memories with Billy Bremner scoring a memorable goal to take us to Wembley with a 1–0 victory, our second final within two years.

On 3 January 1976 we played the FA Cup third round away at Notts County. Leeds won 1–0 with a goal from Clarke. I met Carole off the 7.00 am bus from Selby and then we caught the 8.00 am bus to Goole and met Sue on it. We met the Advance coach at Rawcliffe and it was nice to see that we had a full coach. We got to Nottingham at 11.00 am and walked round the ground before we went to a packed out pub where a woman wanted us to serve behind the bar. Went to look for programmes and then went back to the pub and found a long queue of Leeds fans. You didn't see any county fans at all there were that many of us. The queue to get in was massive before they opened the gates. Saw Snowy and the Selby lot. When we got into the ground a lot of Leeds fans had managed to get into the side but the coppers wouldn't let us so we had to stand on the open end. When we walked past the front of the stand these lads shouted Heidi but I didn't know who they were. Saw the Rangers fan from Harrogate who'd been to Ibrox with us.

The FA Cup fourth round on 29 January 1977 took us to St Andrews, Birmingham with Jordan and Clarke scoring for Leeds in a 2–1 win. Sparky, a man utd fan was already on the 8.00 am bus to Selby when I caught the bus at Carlton, so I went straight upstairs to avoid him. Unfortunately once he saw me get on the bus he followed me upstairs. I had my 'I hate man u' badge on which he didn't like. Carole met me in Leeds station off the 8.43 am train and we had a trip to the little shop in the market and Wallies before we all went to a café. There were a few of us there Karen, John, Jock (Mick), Ian, little Paul and Gary Felton. We went to the Calls to catch the coach and saw some lads off the coaches who we knew and they asked which one we were on. It turned out we were all on number one coach. At the services, all the Leeds fans were standing singing we hate man u to a coachload at the other side. Coppers with dogs stopped them going over although a few managed to get over.

When we arrived at Birmingham there were loads of coaches in and all the Leeds fans arrived together. We all got off the coaches chanting and singing and going round as if we owned the place. We left the Leeds fans going into the end and Karen, Carole and I went round to the supporters club. Three lads had a go at us as we walked past them but we soon shut them up, by saying that they wouldn't come to Leeds and say that. Roy, Chris, Phil, Margaret and Graham were already in the club when we got in. We saw the Birmingham fella who wears loads of badges and said hello as we always speak to each other. He told Margaret he's known me and Carole for years and he'll see us in our club to buy us a drink the following Wednesday. We were due to play them again, but at Elland Road, although this time in the league. Leeds fans started singing as well as the Birmingham fans so I thought there was going to be some trouble but nothing happened. We had got tickets for the seats but Karen decided she wanted to go on the terraces with the majority of the Leeds fans so bought another ticket. Carole and I went in to the seats section in the ground but when I saw the Leeds fans at the far end of the ground they looked fantastic. I decided I wanted to join the Leeds fans on the terraces so I went and asked a copper if I could go over to join them in the other end. After checking that there was just me wanting to do this he said go on. So I walked past the Birmingham kop which was along the right hand side of the ground to the other end. I found Karen and we stood at the back near Collar, Jock and Ian. Sal was there too and she told us that she'd had her scarf pinched by man utd fans on the train last week and some West Brom fans had kicked her. Saw Billy, one of the Donny lads and Chinky along with loads we knew and loads we didn't. Mac had managed to sell Karen's seat ticket for £1.35 so she didn't lose out by getting a further ticket for the match. The singing from the Leeds fans was fantastic and we totally out sung the Birmingham fans. The coppers on the terraces were right swines though as they kept getting Leeds fans out for nothing, searching them and kicking them out. Saw Schulz who had a broken hand and one of Scunny's mates with blood pouring down his head, although he didn't even know he was bleeding. Graham from Kippax had been on a barrier when we scored and started celebrating but the coppers got him, dragged him out, hit him and ripped his programme.

At the end of the match it was terrible trying to get out as it was jam packed. Loz who I knew said: "it's a bit packed isn't it Heidi?" I nearly fell flat on my face going down the slope and if I would have done everyone would have landed on top of me. A little lad off the coaches told me to be careful as they were bricking us outside. He kept trying to get me to go over a spiked fence but I said no I'll go out the main way. Birmingham fans were bricking us and I got splattered with mud. Leeds fans were all running over to the coaches and a gang of Birmingham fans were coming the other way. Coppers were coming at us on horses and one nearly hit me with a baton and a dog nearly got me. Leeds fans started throwing bricks back and one just landed a foot in front of me and hit a car. I shouted: "watch who you're throwing things at you stupid sods" and a lad said: "you tell them love".

We had a word with Tony and Eddie before getting on the coach. Carole and I were talking to the lads sat behind us who said I was Queens of Wallies and another lad chanted *Daily Express* to us. They remembered Sue, Carole, Linda and I having our photos taken by the *Daily Express* in the West Stand Car Park at Elland Road and ever since they always shouted that to us. We didn't leave until 5.45 pm and the fumes from all the coaches nearly choked us. On my way to the station a lad stopped to talk who had hitched it to the match and he wanted to know how long it was since I'd missed a match. I said about five or six and he said the lads on the coach thought it was about 13 or 14. In the station I met Binks, another Hunslet lad and one of the Harehills (ginger hair). They told me that Leeds fans on the special had got chased all over Birmingham and the special had been smashed up.

We played Norwich at Elland Road in the FA Cup third round on 8 January 1977 which Leeds won 5–2 with our scorers being Clarke, Reaney, Jordan, McQueen and Hampton. The night before this match Carole had stayed at my house because we'd been to the Croda (who I worked for) dinner and dance. We caught the 9.00 am bus to Selby and went for a walk into town. We went in the sports shop near the traffic lights for a white number 9 for our blue Scotland shirts. As we were wearing lots of different Leeds and Scotland colours, the fella said we were the most colourful sight ever to go in there and said we've to call again. We then went back to the station for the 10.20 am train. We sat in the buffet whilst we were waiting and there were some more Leeds kids there too. On the train there were quite a few man utd on so we walked up and down the train twice with our Scotland banners on and they kept looking.

We met up with Karen at the ground where we pushed our way to the top whilst Carole stayed further down the Kop. It got very crowded where we were, but the atmosphere before the match was electric. I put my banner round me like a scarf to make sure I didn't lose it, as I had been wearing it like a cape. At half time as we were leading 5–1 you'd have thought we'd won the cup, what a fantastic match! During the second half Norwich got a goal back but that didn't change things and the atmosphere was magic. The FA Cup matches always have a special feel about them as there was the chance to go to the Final at Wembley. Afterwards when I got back to the station this lad said: "I wish you were my sister" and I had to show my banner to him. He said: "it should have Lancashire on rather than Yorkshire," but I said, "no chance!"

Wednesday 22 February 1978 saw the rearranged second leg of the League Cup semi-final at Nottingham Forest and we lost 4–2 with Frank Gray and Arthur Graham scoring for Leeds. I can't really remember when things started going downhill for Leeds. The signs were there when we had played Nottingham Forest at Elland Road in the first leg, which we lost 3–1 with Eddie

Gray scoring the Leeds goal. As far as I was concerned Leeds played pathetic and I went mad especially in the second half. I could have sat and cried then as I was so mad and said I wasn't going to see Leeds again as I wasn't going to waste my money. I was raging when I got back in the club and not in a good mood. Carole was the only one who hadn't given up. After the match I decided I wasn't going to bother watching the replay on the television in the Supporters Club and set off home. Going past Hunslet on the M1 I saw four Forest coaches stopped at the side of the road and reckoned they'd been bricked. Although fed up after this match I was still going to the second leg.

We got all the way to Nottingham to find out that the match had been called off at 6.00 pm. There were a lot of angry Leeds fans sent on their way back to Leeds. The date of the rearranged second leg came about and that again was in doubt due to fog and it was only confirmed at 3.00 pm that the match was on. I was travelling by car this time with Mick, Dave and Paul from Selby and they picked me up at home. This meant I didn't have to take any holidays from work. Got to Nottingham and we got lost trying to get to the ground but eventually parked outside the Magpie pub where we blocked a car in. I kept my scarf and badges on as we ran two miles to the ground as it was getting near kick-off. I kept up with Mick and Paul but Dave lagged behind us. Some Wallies coaches passed us so we weren't the only ones getting there late.

We eventually got to the ground and the coppers were saying three parts of the ground were shut because they were full. Therefore, I had to run around to the other end of the ground to get in before that side closed, I was so out of breath that I nearly fainted. Got to the turnstiles where the Nottingham Forest fans had just bust a gate down to get in. I was going to follow them in but there were Forest fans at the top shouting for Leeds fans to go in. Mick said to take my scarf off if we were going in that stand but we had second thoughts and decided to go round to the side where the Leeds fans would be instead. There were puddles and mud everywhere, but I ran straight through them as I thought it would be a waste of time going round them! We couldn't believe it when we got to the turnstiles for Leeds fans, as we found that there were no queues and the turnstiles were still open.

We got straight in and headed for the Trent End (the Forest end) as there were no ladies toilets in the side of the ground where we were. Luckily the match hadn't kicked off when we got back in the stand so we went down to the front where I had seen Alan Green and Silver. It turned out that there were quite a few Leeds fans around us that I knew Fiona, Douggie Kaye, Jock, Barry and some others. Mick spotted Carole so we went to join her. Saw Dave Williamson and he said he hadn't seen us for a while then Ian came to join us. Leeds got off to a great start and the first half was fantastic. We scored our first goal in the 15th minute with a cracking left footed shot from Frankie Gray who was outside the area at the time. Forest levelled the score within five minutes but Leeds scored again within a minute to put us back in front on the night. Arthur Graham robbed the ball off a Forest player in the penalty area and put the ball into the back of the net to send the travelling Leeds fans wild. Tony Currie hit the woodwork too with a fantastic shot just before half time which would have meant that we were level on aggregate if the ball would have gone in the net. Leeds went in at half-time leading 2–1 and there was hope that maybe we could win the match and get to Wembley. Unfortunately the second half didn't live up to the first and was crap, but at least they fought this time. Carole and I had a slanging match against the referee Clive Thomas as he was a disgrace and nearly walked the ball into the Forest net. I think the heavy pitch in the penalty area also contributed to Forest scoring, as the ball didn't clear very well as it got stuck in the mud a few times. The tie was probably lost at Elland Road as we gave them hope with the strong lead Forest took into the second leg.

Took my scarf and badges off at the end because I knew we'd got a two mile walk back to the car and didn't want to be spotted by Forest fans. Saw Tony from Walsall, Barry and Jock as we were going out and Barry asked where my scarf was. I said it was round my waist because we've got a long walk back to the car. As we came out of the ground and went up to the Trent End we got caught in the crowd and nearly ended up slipping down the embankment. In the end we walked along the muddy sides where there was still another road before the river. As soon as we got back to the relative safety of the car, we then let off steam. We were able to rant and rave about everything that had happened in the match, the final score and also the Forest fans. Our observations were that next to man utd, Forest had the biggest number of hooligans in all parts of the ground.

We set off in the car only to get lost again and we ended up in Carlton (Notts). Mick got out of the car at a chip shop to ask some lads the way as I got out to untangle the seat belt. They said they were Leeds fans so I went over to talk to them and then Dave and Paul jumped out too saying they wanted some chips. As we had all got out of the car, Mick went back and shut the door and told me to lock my side, so I did. Then Mick realised he'd left the keys in the ignition with the full lights on which meant we had a bit of breaking in to do. We managed to get my window down about half an inch with a fella helping us, but it was no good. Someone else came to help having got a metal coat hanger from a shop, but he still couldn't do it. Paul and I were going to try the cop station but Mick didn't want us to because he'd got a spanner on the back seat. He thought it would look bad if the cops saw it. Mick started to have another go and I was just walking off when he got the lock up and managed to open the door. Phew what a relief!

We got lost again and ended up in Arnold so we decided to stop at a pub. As we went in to the lounge, I thought nobody would know I'd been to a football match until I looked down and saw the state of my shoes, socks and trousers which were caked with mud and wet through. An elderly couple next to us heard us say we were Leeds fans and they were really nice when we spoke to them. We realised that there were some Forest fans in the next room. I'd had a pint of lager by this time and wanted to go in there to show them that I was a Leeds fan. Although I was giggly and acting about, I decided that it wouldn't be a good idea. As we were going out of the pub, Mick shouted 'up Leeds'. We got into the car as some Forest fans were coming out of the pub and shouted Leeds out of the window and waved our scarves at some more. You should have seen their faces and one stuck his fingers up at us. We eventually managed to find our way out of Nottingham and made our way home.

During the 1990–91 season we played Arsenal in a marathon FA Cup run before we were knocked out of the FA Cup. The first match on 27 January was a 0–0 draw at Highbury and the replay at Elland Road was the following week on 30 January. This match ended in a 1–1 draw after extra-time which meant a further replay. Chapman was the scorer of our goal. This was to be at Arsenal again on Wednesday 13 February which also ended up 0–0 after extra-time. I had travelled down with the Selby Branch of the Leeds United Supporters Club to this one with my children Jamie and Michelle. As I was pregnant with my third child at the time, we were able to stay at my mum's house in Carlton when we got back at 3.00 am. Leeds were finally beaten when the last replay on Saturday 16 February saw us lose 2–1 at Elland Road with Chapman again scoring our goal. It also cost a small fortune to go to all the matches in such a short space of time. Ironically when we next played Arsenal in the league on Sunday 17 March 1991 again at Highbury, I was in labour so couldn't go to the match. I gave birth to my daughter Charlotte at 10.25 am and her birth was announced live on Sky TV by Greavsie at half-time!! Charlotte also attended her first Leeds match against Crystal Palace the following Saturday at six days old and I still think she holds the record to this day. She went in the crèche in the South Stand whilst we watched the match and I have a picture of her in the cot, taken by Carol and Steve from Darlington. It's a case of start as you mean to go on, with the children supporting Leeds and going to the matches too. The club had also started putting advertising hoardings around the pitch and as our seats were on the front row, we had to stand up to see the match. Not a good idea when you are still suffering from high blood pressure and giving birth the previous week, oops! I wasn't going to miss another match if I could help it though, the things we do for Leeds!

January Third remember the date! – In 2010 the rivalry of past contests between Leeds and man utd meant that 9,000 Leeds fans went to this FA Cup tie at Old Trafford. As soon as the third round draw had been made, this whetted the appetites of the Leeds fans. We were in League One and man utd were in the Premiership, light years away from where we were at the time in footballing terms. Could we be the giant killers? Could we upset the odds by winning the tie, especially away from home? Personally, I had a good feeling about the tie and said we could win it. More often than not, away teams were beaten into submission at Old Trafford prior to the match taking place and going with the mentality that they wouldn't be able to win there. It used to annoy me greatly that teams would just lie down and die to give man utd the points rather than put up a fight. This time when Leeds headed there with Simon Grayson as manager, along with Glynn Snodin as his assistant, they knew what beating them at the "old toilet" (as some Leeds fans called it), would mean to the fans.

Memories from Sue, Keith and Ciaran were that nobody thought we would ever win there at this stage and they were just looking forward to the trip back there with Leeds. The atmosphere had been electric with Leeds fans in fantastic voice and enjoying their day out. Things were to get even better in the 19th minute when Beckford ran onto the ball after a fantastic cross from Johnny Howson. As he hit the ball towards the goal past the advancing goalkeeper, it was like watching this in slow motion. It took an eternity for the ball to crawl over the line and into the back of the net to put Leeds into the lead and send the travelling hordes of Leeds fans into rapturous celebrations! We were one up against man utd and there was no way we were going to let this slip. man utd did have their chances to get back into the match straight away when Leeds kicked the ball off the line, but we went in at half time one goal up.

The second half was certainly a battle, with strong tackles as Leeds had their heads up aiming for the glory of winning. There were some really bad tackles from man utd who were trying to intimidate Leeds, who counter attacked by giving as good as they got. However much pressure was put on Leeds though, they managed to sustain the attacks and were unlucky not to go further in front when Snodgrass hit the crossbar with a free-kick. It was a fantastic match with some great memories at the final whistle, to realise that we had actually done it. We had beaten man utd 1–0 at their home ground in the FA Cup! At the end of the match, Leeds fans were locked in the ground for a long time and the celebrations and singing carried on for ages. We didn't care how long we had to stay there and as the players came out for a cool down they received a hero's welcome with the first ones out being Kisnorbo and Casper. It's a date that will long be remembered as a Leeds fan and was also made into a song by Leeds fans and sung on the terraces afterwards. January Third remember the date, we beat the team that we f*****g hate, we knocked the scum out the FA Cup, we're Super Leeds and we're going up!

FA Cup Final 1972 – Twiggster from Denmark.

Having missed out on Wembley tickets two years earlier for the Final against Chelsea (we went to the fiasco that was the replay at Old Trafford), me and my mate Chris decided we were going to this one, even though we didn't have tickets. We'd saved enough money (we hoped) to get a ticket outside Wembley, on the day. Both of us were 19 years old and out of work and pretty skint, we found ourselves on the slip road to the M1 going south, early on the Friday afternoon before the match. Thumbs held expectantly high and hoping for a lift in the inclement weather.

After an hour with no luck finally a lorry driver stopped, having seen our Leeds scarves. He could only take us to Leicester Forest, but we were on our way! Archie his name was and an avid Leeds fan. He was a decent bloke who chatted LUFC constantly all the way to the services. He even gave us some of his lorry driver meal vouchers when he dropped us off, so we could get summat to eat there. He was finishing his shift at 6pm, then going back to Leeds and getting the train to the Final on the Saturday morning. He wished us luck and drove off. Chris and me used some of the vouchers to get sarnies and a mug of tea and then went to stand on the slip road back to the M1.

We stood there for an hour and a half with not one car stopping for us. Went back to the services and used the rest of the vouchers for more tea and some chocolate bars, before going back to the slip road where we stood there for another hour with no luck. It was now late afternoon and we were wondering if we'd even get near London that night, or even the next day. We were squatting down by now and demoralised and never noticed the Bentley that stopped 10 yards further on, until we heard the horn sound and a posh voice asking if we "wanted a lift or not?" A Bentley driver, offering us a lift!! He was a chauffeur on his way to Watford and wanted someone to talk to, on his way to pick up his boss. He'd seen our Leeds scarves and it turned out his dad knew John Charles and Major Buckley, so he felt obliged to help us! We were in heaven! In a warm Bentley, with a mega sound system (for the time) playing pirate radio, the driver offering us whisky and snacks from the mini bar in the car and constantly chatting about Leeds United, until he dropped us off at Watford Tube station! "You can get the tube direct to Wembley from here", he said and drove off. Leaving Chris and me gobsmacked and not a little drunk from the whisky! It was now 8.30 PM and we were almost there!

I dunno how we did it, but we got on a tube without buying tickets and bunked the ride to Wembley. Several other Leeds fans were on the train, beer was passed around and the singing began! The late homecoming commuters on the train all moved to another carriage! I don't think anyone of us lot had paid for their fare, as we all rushed together through the gate after we got off. The poor ticket collector must have been scared to death!

We just tagged along with the group, as we had no idea where we were going to sleep that night and hoping someone could suggest something. Walking around Wembley (with cops controlling our movements by now), we went around a few pubs with the group. Dunno who was buying the beer, but our glasses were always topped up. Come closing time, everyone disappeared off to their hostels or whatever, leaving us two rather drunk lads to our own devices. Chris went for a slash behind a wall and I heard him cheer. He came back with a box of eight beer cans! So we had beer for the night, but still nowhere to sleep. We wandered towards the stadium, looking for somewhere out of the way to pit down. All we had for protection were our ex-army greatcoats that were fashionable at the time and warm.

We got to the stadium around midnight. Being experienced pop festival goers and used to looking for shelter, we began trying the doors around the ground. All of them were locked. Suddenly one I tried opened! We hid across the pathway and waited five minutes or so, expecting an alarm to go off, or security to appear. Nothing – so we ran inside and closed the door! Pitch black, but with matches we made out a staircase going up. So we drunkenly groped our way up the stairs, until we arrived at a landing. Lots of doors, all locked. Again we found one open! We went inside and Chris found a light switch to turn on. We were in a cleaners' store room full of mops and brushes and the smell of cleaning chemicals was disgusting.

I saw a door across the room so we made for that and it was unlocked! Went through and the lights were already on. Cautiously we went inside (almost sober now, with anxiety!) and we were in a laundry room. It smelt better and was nice and warm! We set up a couple of makeshift beds, from boxes and clean towels and even found some cushions! My watch said 12:15 am, so we settled down to drink the beer Chris had found. Having a look around the room, I spotted a small fridge. As we were both starving, we quickly got that open, hoping for well – *anything* to eat. BINGO! Four wrapped ham and cheese sarnies, a couple of Mars bars and a few bags of crisps! We made short work of those (saving the Mars bars for breakfast) and I noticed an electric kettle by a sink. A quick look in the cupboard above the sink discovered teabags and sugar. We were set for what the morning could bring! We finished the beers and settled down to sleep.

We awoke to a terrible noise, like an invading army! I looked at my watch and it was 1pm!!! Fans were already inside the stadium! Leeds fans too, from the chants we could hear. We made a quick brew and scoffed our Mars bars, but we were scared we'd be too late to score any tickets once we got back outside. Ah well, we could use the money we had for tickets, watching in a pub. On the way back through the cleaning store room, I spotted another door. I carefully opened it and we looked through – onto the concourse inside Wembley, at the Leeds end!!! We were out there in a flash and mingling with Leeds fans. No seat allocations back then so we got on the terraces with everyone else. Slightly hung over, but buzzing! We were in!

The actual match needs no further comment – but post match, Chris and I still had the money we'd brought with us for tickets! Hungry again, we feasted on Jamaica patties and some pies and we actually found a few of the lads from the night before in a pub and repaid the drinks they'd bought us and did we ever celebrate! They even smuggled us onto their coach back to Leeds!!

I guess the powers that be looked down on Chris and me – and Leeds United, that day!!

Best away day of my life!

P.S. In case you were wondering. When we woke up in the laundry room at Wembley, we really needed to pee. We used a corner in the cleaning room, as it smelt so bad anyway!

ON ON ON!

Chapter 8

Memorable matches

Dave Cocker – Nottingham Forest v Leeds 24 August 1968 – Fire!!

I used to travel to away matches with Wallace Arnold coaches and the drivers always wanted me on their coach as I was able to get hold of tickets for the matches. I would normally sit in the jump seat at the front of the coach and then travel back with the Leeds United team either by train or coach.

I recall travelling to Nottingham Forest in August 1968 as it was my younger brother Ian's first away match at the age of 12. We travelled on a Wallace Arnold coach and on arrival went straight to the players' entrance to meet our dad, who had got the match tickets for us. Once inside the ground we went to find our seats above the terraces below. We sat down and our seats were just to the right, in the middle where the flames eventually started next to the directors' box. I had already sat there previously watching the FA Cup semi-final replay against man utd in 1965, with Billy Bremner scoring a last minute goal to send Leeds to the final at Wembley.

Approximately 30 minutes after the start of the match, we saw people beginning to stamp the floor of the wooden stand which was packed with supporters. We then started to see smoke and flames coming through the floor of the stand. No one seemed scared about what they could see though and carried on watching the match. As soon as the whistle went for half time, Ian and I ran to the exit only to find an inferno of flames in front of us! The Paddock below was rammed with standing supporters who had no idea of what was happening, until everyone started shouting 'fire!' Everyone started to get onto the pitch and Ian found he was lifted from the seats and passed over the heads of the standing supporters to the safety of the pitch below. Once we were both safe we went and stood by the dugouts. In the meantime, the Leeds

United players had gone down the tunnel into the dressing room. Eventually all the seating and Paddock spectators were assembled on the pitch where they stood and watched the fire taking hold in the stand. As we watched the flames get higher, we noticed the BBC reporters were still on the gantry at the top of the stand and at that moment quickly descended to escape the flames.

My thoughts turned to what was happening with the dressing room? One thing I do remember seeing as we were stood there waiting, was three balls used as spare ones during the match, on the floor in the dugout. We stayed as close to the Leeds dugout as we could and luckily that's where dad found us when he suddenly appeared. He was relieved to see that we were both safe then told us to go with him. We walked to the exit at the opposite end to the Trent end, out of ground, over the Trent Bridge to the Trent Bridge Hotel at the other side. As we looked back we could see enormous flames booming out. As we walked into the function bar overlooking the hotel, we found both teams still in their kits sat there having a beer! What happened next was the funniest thing, when the referee walked in with the ball under his arm flanked by his two linesmen. "What are you doing, I haven't postponed the game yet!" he cried. Everyone cracked out laughing as all we could see were 200 foot flames shooting out of the stand!!

As we were watching the flames we could see that the car park behind the stand was rammed full and the team coach was also parked there and going nowhere. Because of this, it meant that the fire brigade couldn't get anywhere near the ground and had to let the fire run its course, instead trying to spray water on it from afar. It also meant that the team coach got burnt out as they couldn't move it away from the flames.

Prior to this the Leeds United team were in the dressing room having a team talk by Don Revie. Norman Hunter always came out for the second half with his hair plastered down by splashing water on it or having a quick shower at half time. He'd gone in there and found the ceiling coming in so ran back to tell the others and was told to shut up as Don was talking. Once he made them realise there was a fire and it was serious, they went to get out of the dressing rooms. Faced with smoke to the left and flames to the right, they left everything and went back onto the pitch and into the car park. Terry Hibbitt had won 20 quid at bingo earlier which was a lot of money in those days. As he was stood outside he realised the money was still inside the dressing room and ran back in to get it. Instead of just grabbing his pants with the wallet in it and running out, he grabbed his pants, took out the wallet and then left his pants and ran out!

As there was now no coach to take them home, taxis were ordered to go to Leeds. A fleet of taxis arrived and dad got in one alongside me, Ian and Terry Yorath. Terry lived next door but one to us with Norman Hunter's mum, who he lodged with. The taxi driver said to us that he would have to go home first to tell his wife that he'll be gone for four hours. He drove us to a council estate in Nottingham then said: "do you fancy a quick cup of tea?" So out of the taxi we got with Terry still wearing his Leeds kit and dad wearing his tracksuit!

Other taxis going back to Leeds had Jack Charlton and Billy Bremner going to Oulton with possibly Mike O'Grady with them as he lived near Halton Moor. Another taxi took Norman Hunter, Gary Sprake, Terry Cooper and Paul Reaney. All the Leeds players were still wearing their kits as they travelled back home up the M1. Half way back along the motorway, we could see smoke rising up in the sky for the second time that day. As we got nearer, what did we find? Only that it was a taxi on fire and there stood on the hard shoulder of the motorway was none other than Norman and crew wearing their Leeds kits! A guy called Mac who sold ladies underwear and perfumes had gone to the match on his own. On seeing the players stood at the side of the motorway, he picked them up and they have been friends ever since.

The players had lost everything including their house and car keys. The following day as their cars were still parked up at Elland Road, my dad drove back down to Forest to see if anything was left as no one from Forest would give them any answers. On arrival at the City ground all that remained of the stand was a pile of ash. The only way that dad could tell where the dressing rooms had been was seeing a pile of Leeds United medical equipment. The stand had fallen in, there had been at least 20,000 supporters on the pitch and like a phoenix rising out of the ashes, dad found three footballs still in the dugout where they had been left!

It was a good job there were no fences otherwise thousands would have died. As it was no one died in the fire which was a miracle really, but they reckoned it was caused either by a dropped cigarette or a spark from a cable. Also an accumulation of rubbish that had dropped through the floor may have contributed to the fire spreading so quickly. Ironically the same possible causes caused a fire involving Bradford City in May 1985, but tragically 56 people died and over 250 supporters were injured. Terry Yorath was also caught up in this tragedy too as he was the manager of Bradford City at the time.

My own memories.

Barcelona in the semi-final of the European Cup on 23 April 1975 Second leg – score 1–1 with Lorimer scoring the Leeds goal (Leeds went through to the final in Paris 3–2 on aggregate having won the first leg at Elland Road 2–1 with goals from Bremner and Clarke).

I have just been reading one of my scrapbooks from the seventies that I still have in my possession having sold the rest of them. The newspaper cuttings include the home and away leg against Barcelona in the European Cup semi-final in 1975. The nostalgia these have created has taken me back to the Nou Camp in Barcelona for the second leg with the prize being the European Cup Final in Paris. Our skipper Billy Bremner had described this match 'as the last mountain he had to climb and was confident to send out a message that they were not going to surrender the 2–1 lead. They were not going to sit back and defend but would go and attack Barcelona'. Billy's comments in an article by Alan Thompson: "The atmosphere will not trouble us. It will be fatal to sit back and defend against Barcelona for the simple reason that their attack is the best part of their side. Their defence is vulnerable. We will go out to win. What's the point of trying to sit on one goal and face 90 minutes of possible torture?"

They were wise words from Billy Bremner because it is something that I totally agree with. The best form of defence is attack and by putting pressure on the opposition it keeps them on the back foot. The team for Leeds United was Stewart, Cherry, F. Gray, Bremner, McQueen, Hunter, Lorimer, Clarke, Jordan, Yorath and Madeley. Subs were Reaney, E. Gray, Harris, Hampton and Letheren. Johann Cruyff who would be playing in the Barcelona team commented back that Leeds were all talk and dismissed the fact that Leeds would go there and attack. He was confident that Leeds wouldn't score as Barcelona hadn't conceded any goals during their European Cup run.

Leeds did in fact score as early as the seventh minute. A long clearance from Stewart after Hunter had passed the ball back to him, gave Jordan the opportunity to out jump his marker and head the ball onto Lorimer. He proceeded to smash the ball into the net and wasn't called 90 miles an hour for nothing! The goal was enough to silence the Spaniards in the crowd and send the Leeds fans including myself into raptures. Sue and I both ended up in tears we were so happy. Leeds certainly took no prisoners on that memorable evening with the whole team performing heroically. Dave Stewart in goal had the match of his life and certainly ensured that Leeds got through to the Final in Paris. Joe Jordan had blood all down his shirt having been cut on his face during the first half, later having five stitches in his forehead. Leeds were reduced to 10 men after 70 minutes when McQueen was sent off after Barcelona had equalised just before the incident. My memories of the last 20 minutes were of sheer torture, especially as we were playing with 10 men. Sue and I couldn't watch the match and turned away as we couldn't bear to look. At that moment in time we found the Spaniards around us were telling us that Leeds would get through and not to worry. This proved to be the case and it was a euphoric moment when the final whistle went and we knew that we had got through to the Final on 28 May 1975. Out of the crowd of 120,000 there were approximately 1,000 Leeds fans and we certainly made ourselves heard. It was a shame we were in three different pockets and not altogether. We were stood behind the goal, there were some Leeds fans to the left of us and some more to the right of us. Fences divided the different areas but we were all on the bottom tier. Billy brought the team over to celebrate with the Leeds fans at the end of the match along with Jimmy Armfield who was the manager for us. It was certainly a memorable match; especially being there to share the emotions and is something that will stay with me forever. A very proud moment as a Leeds United supporter.

A memorable match but for the wrong reasons was Birmingham for the last match of the season on 11 May 1985 – Karen's 25th birthday. The day will always be remembered by me for the death of Ian Hambridge and the Bradford Fire Disaster.

There was still an outside chance of Leeds being promoted back to the First Division but no one expected the amount of Leeds fans (an estimated 8,000) who turned up at St Andrews for the match. We arrived early and I can remember Karen and myself sitting on the last barrier at the back of the stand. We heard just before kick-off that there were still thousands of Leeds fans outside trying to get in. Eventually they all got in without paying when the turnstiles were broken down.

I can't remember when the trouble started but Birmingham fans (together with Chelsea fans) invaded the pitch from the clock end and then things started getting thrown from the Leeds end. There had been some Leeds fans sat on top of the refreshment hut that was half way down the middle of the terraces and everything had been calm until there was a message over the tannoy telling the fans to get off it. It was like a red flag to a bull and meant that loads more descended onto the hut and started pulling it apart, proceeding to throw any piece of wood or item from the hut down onto the fans below or the pitch. It was absolute mayhem then with Leeds fans trying to get onto the pitch as well, some, who were down the right hand side to us, did go onto the pitch, so it was kicking of at both ends of the ground. Without the fences at the front of the stand, things would probably have been worse. We just stayed sat at the back of the stand whilst all the trouble was going on. I think the players were taken off the pitch and back to the dressing room by this time, as events were turning ugly, but I can't really remember.

Police horses ended up on the pitch and in the meantime I can remember Collar and the Kippax branch members at the other side of the fence trying to calm things down and clear the pitch. I can also remember Eddie Gray having things thrown at him too, how anyone who claimed to be a Leeds fan wouldn't know he was our manager at the time is beyond me. Eventually calm was restored and the match ended very late with Leeds losing 1–0. I can remember walking back to the long line of coaches and waving to Mick Smith as I passed one of them.

Once back on the coach, we started to hear the news from Bradford that a fire had swept through the wooden stand killing 56 people at Valley Parade. Bradford had been celebrating promotion one minute then watching a stand burn down the next. It was a very sobering moment when you realised that some fans had died at a football match. We then started to hear that there had also been a death and injuries at St Andrews! 15-year-old Ian Hambridge died when a wall collapsed on him at the end of the match, which was caused by the pressure of fans when they were forced down a narrow passageway by the coppers. We sent a letter of condolence to his parents but it would not have been much comfort for them, as they had the suffering of his death at a football match to cope with.

Bradford City at Odsal 20 September 1986 – Leeds lost 2–0

After the Bradford Fire Disaster they played some of their home matches at Odsal. Leeds were due to play there in 1986 and after the trouble at Birmingham, the fans had to have a membership card and matches were made all ticket for away grounds. Because the fans had been well behaved the authorities made the mistake of lifting the ban on Leeds fans with the match at Odsal being the first one. It was like an open invitation for everyone to come to the match and despite the club issuing a plea for the membership cards to be kept in place, the authorities went ahead with their decision and violence ensued. We were stood on the terracing at the side of the pitch when we saw smoke coming from the refreshment hut. A chip van near us on the terraces ended up on fire when Leeds fans got on top of it and started rocking it. Although I think the fire was an accident, the ones on the roof were culpable because the hot fat inside spilt over and the van went up in flames. It wasn't long after the Bradford fire disaster at Valley Parade and this caused a lot of bad flashbacks for the Bradford fans when they saw the van alight. Trouble started kicking off all over the place when the match was held up for a while as Leeds fans went onto the pitch to get away from the fire, then decided to charge the Bradford fans at the opposite side to us in the seats. The Bradford fans scattered and the stand emptied very quickly. Although the match was held up twice, we were told that the match would not be abandoned and would be played to the finish. We had stayed where we were on the open terrace and eventually the match was completed with Leeds having been beaten After this match had erupted in violence, Leeds United asked the powers that be to reinstate the all ticket matches and membership cards which are still in place to this day.

Bournemouth 5 May 1990 Leeds won 1–0 with a Chapman header and were promoted to the First Division.

Another match that sticks out as a memorable match was winning promotion from the Second Division and winning the title at Bournemouth in 1990. It was the last match of the season and there were only a limited number of tickets for this, so thousands of Leeds fans travelled down to it. Many had gone down without tickets and because it was also a Bank Holiday weekend, had made it a holiday. It was a gorgeous hot day and everything was set up to be a perfect ending to the season.

On arrival at Bournemouth there were thousands waiting in the car park, looking for any spare tickets. I had travelled down on a double decker luxury coach from Voyager International from Selby with the Supporters Club branch. The ticket distribution for this match had been made by giving tickets to our branch members who had attended the most matches that season. This was the fairest way of distributing the tickets as it meant the fans who had been the most loyal, were rewarded with a ticket for the match. Some of the lads wanted to go down themselves to make a weekend of it.

I decided to get into the match as soon as possible rather than hang about outside as things were starting to turn ugly. Leeds fans were being forced back by the coppers and then retaliated. Things were starting to get thrown and it wasn't an ideal place to be. I ensured I kept my ticket hidden until I got to the turnstiles as I didn't want anyone to snatch it out of my hand as they were like gold dust! Once inside the ground I sat in the seats down the side and the terraces behind the goal to my right was jam packed full with Leeds fans. Many fans were perched on some scaffolding at the back of the stand; rather them than me though!

We heard that some fans with genuine tickets who hadn't got in early had been refused entry into the ground. The coppers refused to let them in as they said the ground was full and many had got in with forged tickets. A terrible decision or just used as an excuse because trouble had been kicking off outside the ground between the coppers and the Leeds fans.

The team for this match was Day, Sterland, Beglin, Jones, Fairclough, Haddock, Strachan, Kamara, Chapman, Davison and Speed (Shutt, and Batty both coming on as substitutes). Howard Wilkinson the manager, had a decision to make because Bobby Davison had been injured the night before. Carl Shutt was due to replace him but because he got so nervous before a match, Wilkinson didn't tell him. He put Davison on for approximately five minutes before subbing him and bringing Carl Shutt on to replace him. He did the job that was required and Chapman scored a header to win the match for Leeds. Everyone went onto the pitch at the end of the match to celebrate our promotion back to the First Division.

We heard later from some of our fans who went down for the weekend that they all congregated on the beach. Everyone was drunk and generally they had been having a good time singing songs, paddling in the sea and building campfires. The coppers instead of just watching them, as they weren't doing any harm broke up the party, effectively causing problems that could have been avoided. Once they had dispersed the Leeds fans and they all went in different directions, we heard that some Leeds fans had been attacked by car loads of Chelsea fans. In my opinion, this set the scene for the troubles outside the ground on the day of the match as mentioned above.

Hayden Evans memories.

Hayden tells the story of his group of friends travelling to all the away matches during our promotion winning season in 1989 – 1990 ending at Bournemouth.

Things had changed whilst following Leeds, there were membership cards to get tickets, a greater Police presence at grounds, no alcohol and generally more restrictions in place which impacted on the day out. My group of friends, including me were all season ticket holders so we thought we would hire a luxury coach to take approximately 30 of us to the away matches. We hired a Wharfedale Pullman Executive coach for the journeys and enjoyed travelling to the matches eating bacon sarnies on the way down with beer stuffed under the seats.

One of the lads, Alan Ross, who blagged his way through everything - who has since died - decided that he would get some professional stickers done for the coach window. The sticker had 'Leeds United Directors' together with some Leeds badges on it. The funny thing though, it was nothing but a scam as none of us had any connections to the directors of the club!

We proceeded to stick this onto the front of the coach as we literally travelled to all the away matches that season in this way. Ross stood at the front of the coach wearing a fluorescent jacket to make us look official, so that as soon as we pulled up to the Police escorts he would put his thumb up to them. Unbelievably, it worked every time as a Police outrider would escort us to the ground ahead of all the rest of the Leeds fans who were still stuck on their coaches awaiting an escort! There was no messing about and we were always taken through the gates into the main stands by blagging our way in.

This worked well until the final match of the season at Bournemouth where it backfired big style! We had gone down for the weekend and decided to get to the ground and go straight in because we knew it had been mayhem in Bournemouth overnight. Ross gave the Police outrider a thumbs up once again and we were escorted straight into the large car park outside the ground. Unfortunately this time we came upon the scene of 3–4,000 Leeds fans without tickets having running battles with the Police, who were desperate to get tickets from the 'Leeds United directors!' They ambushed the coach chanting: "we want tickets" and it was a really bad situation to be in. Some of the lads, who were well known, ran to the front of the coach to point to their faces, hoping someone would recognise them and realise they were not the directors at all. At the same time some others were tearing the stickers off the windows! We got off with it in the end but it got pretty scary.

We had one good season with the coach and were amazed that no one had sussed us out, but found out that once Leeds were promoted it had run its course as the club had become aware of it. The lads also had a private room paid for at Elland Road which was full of the same lads. Against man utd it got very hairy and spilled out of the room. That was when Howard came and had a word with me saying that I couldn't be doing stuff like that as I was an agent and representing the players. After this things quietened down!

League Champions! Sheffield United - 26 April 1992.

What a day this turned out to be when Leeds won the First Division for the third time. Leeds still had a home match to play against Norwich but results from today's matches meant they were crowned champions once again. Our nearest rivals man utd had to play at Anfield against Liverpool in a later kick-off whilst ours kicked off at lunchtime. I travelled with the LUSC Selby Branch to the match and my first memories of the day were when the coach was proceeding slowly outside the ground getting ready to drop us off outside the stand. A Sheffield fan proceeded to get smacked on the back of the head by the wing mirror off the coach and he turned round to give us a mouthful of abuse. It was an accident but he must have been close to the edge of the path for it to happen in the first place.

I was heavily pregnant with my daughter Danielle who was born later in the year at the start of July and I was in the seats for this one. The only thing I hated about the seats was that they were so steep I felt dizzy if I stood up and had to cling on to the seats. This match was one of the most bizarre ones as Leeds won the match 3–2 with the way the goals were scored. Sheffield scored first and then Leeds nearly equalised when Dorigo's free-kick was dropped by the goal-keeper but luckily for him it went wide of the post for a corner. The equaliser came in injury time at the end of the first half from a quick free-kick from Gordon Strachan. The ball ended up with Wallace trying to lob the Sheffield goalie who crashed into his own defender leaving him on the floor and the ball sprang loose across the goalmouth to Gary Speed whose path was blocked by two defenders. Gary and a defender went for the ball together and the defender got there slightly ahead of Gary and hit it. The ball hit Gary, shot back across the goal, hit Rod Wallace and the ball went into the net right in front of the Leeds fans! It sent us all into raptures and kept our hopes up of winning the title that day.

Leeds started the second half strongly with Gary Speed hitting the woodwork. David Batty won a free-kick to the left of the pitch at the far end of the ground to us. McAllister sent the ball in and everyone missed it including the goalkeeper who misjudged the pace of the ball, only for Jon Newsome to head the ball into the net to send Leeds into the lead. Please let this be our day, as we went mad once more! Our hopes were dashed when Sheffield equalised from a corner, the ball was headed across the goalmouth and it looked like the chance had gone for Sheffield to score as it went past everyone. Unfortunately one of the Sheffield players got to the ball on the bye line passed it back low and the ball hit Chapman and ended up in the net. An own goal and an equaliser meant my heart dropped once more. The match went our way with another bizarre goal, Leeds kicked the ball out of defence, it was headed on by Chapman, nodded on by Cantona which Rod Wallace chased and put the defender under pressure. He kicked the ball back and another defender Gayle picked it up and didn't look under pressure although Cantona and Wallace were bearing down on him. He went to clear the ball, mishit the pass into the air and went to head it at the same time as the Sheffield goalie came out, only for Gayle to head the ball into the net for Leeds to take the lead once again. Another own goal but in our favour this time, surely it had to be our day now?

You need a bit of luck sometimes and this was one of those days where the luck went our way with the way, that the goals were scored. At the end of the match we were all celebrating as the end was in sight and hopefully by the end of the day the score at Anfield would go our way. The pressure was now on man utd to get a result whilst all the Leeds fans went out celebrating in the pubs whilst watching the match. The result at Anfield did indeed go our way with Liverpool winning 2–0 and the title was ours. What a fantastic feeling to be crowned First Division Champions once again. It had been a fantastic end to the season and the Leeds fans had once again played their part in following their team all over the country in their numbers.

Chapter 9

Matches abroad

Valetta (Malta) v Leeds 19 August 1979 – UEFA Cup First round Second leg Leeds won 4–0 with Hart and a hat-trick from Graham.

Captain (Phillip) from Halifax who would later become my husband, gave his account of travelling by himself to the match in Malta. He had bought an inter-rail ticket and made his way there dossing down wherever he could. Whilst in Sicily he had been sleeping in a beach hut when he was found by the owner who took pity on him. Captain was given a very sweet drink which tasted fine but afterwards he was made to suffer. Whatever it was, somehow it attracted the flies and he got bitten to smithereens.

By the time he arrived in Malta the day before the match, the authorities wanted to hospitalise him as they thought he had got chicken pox. Luckily he managed to persuade them otherwise and he got to the match okay. He met up with Simon from Reading and both were looking for somewhere to stay. They met a priest who had trained in Leeds and he showed them somewhere to go. There were some caves that hadn't been used for a long time so they made that their home for the first night, but on the second night they slept in a hotel. Phillip flew back home via Rome afterwards.

When Leeds started playing in Europe again Phillip and I started going back to the away legs. We both went to Monaco and Troyes as a family holiday but for the rest of the ones we attended it was a case of only one of us going. I went to Munich and Deportivo and Phillip went to the Stuttgart match including the replay at Barcelona and also went to Czechoslovakia.

AS Monaco v Leeds 12 September 1995, UEFA Cup First round, First leg, hat-trick by Tony Yeboah.

Phillip and I went to Monaco for the day to see Leeds play when we started attending a few foreign matches and it was great travelling abroad to a match in Europe again. My sister Erica had agreed to have all four of our children for a few days, so it meant that we could go to the match, I was very excited! We arrived at Leeds Bradford airport in good time for the trip and we were to fly on a jumbo jet from Iceland! It was a rare occurrence for a jumbo jet to take off from this airport due to the length of the runway.

Our departure was delayed but eventually we were sat on the plane ready for take-off. It had been about 15 years since I'd last flown and I found myself gripping the seat really hard on take-off. My fears were to be compounded when some Leeds fans started taking the mickey saying they could smell burning and we were going to crash! Most people laughed it off but I was petrified and kept expecting the plane to just drop out of the sky. I was starting to panic but once I realised the Leeds fans had been taking the mickey I calmed down.

We arrived at Nice airport and were taken into the centre of Nice by coach where we had a few hours to spare to explore, as they didn't want us in Monaco too early. It was a lovely place by the sea and the weather was fine. We met up with Steve, Carol and their son Graham from Darlington by the park and took some photos. Eventually we were allowed to board the coaches to Monaco. A lot of the Leeds fans headed straight for the bars, but Phillip and I went for a walk around the ground. We had been told there would be no tickets on sale for Leeds fans, only to see a ticket office open selling them! We walked around the marina and then I heard someone shout my name and found it was Tony from Wrexham who I hadn't seen in 15 years. It was great to catch up with him as it felt like only yesterday and we had a drink with him before heading back to the ground.

It was bedlam getting into the ground with the amount of Leeds fans arriving at the same time. Eventually we managed to get in and made our way up the steps onto the terraces. The Leeds stewards had travelled to this one and one of them who we got on really well with, was beaten up by some Leeds fans on the steps. There was no love lost between the fans and the stewards at that time.

We could see Brian our friend over to the left of us more or less behind the goal whilst we were stood at the side nearly opposite the goal. It was a fantastic match with lots of singing and Tony Yeboah scored a hat-trick. After he scored his third there had been a collision between the goalie and one of their defenders where they had clashed heads. The defender was down for a long time and everyone fell silent as we thought he had died as he wasn't moving. Eventually though he came round and was carried off the pitch on a stretcher to a round of applause from all the Leeds fans.

We were taken back to Nice airport for the plane home and everyone was very happy. We had a great time and I was really glad that I had been able to go back to Europe to see Leeds again!

---

6 April 2000 Galatasary v Leeds UEFA Cup semi-final, First leg

Phillip and I took it in turns going to the foreign matches as we couldn't afford for us both to go and the next match was my turn and it was Galatasary in Istanbul, Turkey. I was so scared about what I'd heard about them and their reputation that I decided not to go but Karen still went. Every Leeds fan knows the tragedy that occurred there and the horrendous events, when two innocent Leeds fans were murdered ahead of the match, Christopher Loftus and Kevin Speight.

I was just parking the car in the garage when radio reports started coming through about two Leeds fans being stabbed to death. I was shaken to the core as I ran into the house trying to find out more. I rang Karen's house and spoke to her son Wayne who confirmed that she had travelled to the match. I was so scared for her and the rest of the Leeds fans out there.

All the news reports started coming through on the television and I was distraught to see the events unfold. I also knew some of the lads who were being interviewed on the television. My heart went out to the families and friends of both Christopher and Kevin whose only crime was to go to Turkey to support their team. I couldn't believe it when the match was ordered to take place by the powers that be, or Leeds would forfeit their place. Leeds United themselves cancelled any further flights bringing Leeds fans over for the one day trip as it wasn't safe. That match should never have gone ahead and the Leeds fans who were there, all turned their backs at the start of the match as a display of unity and out of respect for the two Leeds fans. I can also never forget the sight of the Leeds players coming on to the pitch into the cauldron of hate where there would be no way they would win that match, which proved to be.

All Galatasary fans were banned from the return leg at Elland Road and there was a hostile atmosphere on the night. Leeds didn't get through to the Final, but all the football paled into insignificance as our thoughts were with the families of the two murdered Leeds fans. Leeds fans also hung scarves, flags, shirts and mementoes along the fences outside the West Stand and made around Billy Bremner's statue into a shrine. It was nice to see that fans of other clubs laid tributes too. It was also a poignant time for us as a family too, as the lads were murdered the day after the anniversary of our daughter Charlotte's death, so all will never be forgotten.

Munich 1860 v Leeds Champions League 2000 – 2001. First round qualifier, Second leg. 23 August 2000.

As soon as we drew Munich I said I would have to go to the away leg as my cousin Günter lived nearby. I got in touch with him and arranged to meet up. I was travelling on the day trip from Leeds and went on my own although I saw many people I knew throughout the trip. When we arrived at Munich I let the coaches all leave with the Leeds fans on them and stayed at the airport. The people in charge of our trip asked me if I'd be okay and I said yes although once they'd driven off I got a bit anxious. I saw this tall lad stood near me and I said something to him and it turned out to be my cousin's son Gerd! The last time I had seen him he was a little boy, how tall he was now. We went for something to eat and did some shopping, where I bought my vegetable knives that I always got from Germany. All of a sudden I thought there was no way I could take any knives with me to a football match, or to have on the plane, so I arranged for them to be sent home for me. We walked miles and I ended up with massive blisters on my heels as I'd been wearing new trainers. Eventually they dropped me off near the ground and I walked up there and had something to eat before finding the entrance to go in. Luckily for me I didn't have the knives on me as I had my bag searched and I just said in German that I had bought some things for my mum and they were fine with me.

As I was stood near the front of the stand, Chris Mozzer from Tadcaster came to talk to me and took some photos. Another lad also came to talk to me who remembered me. We went mad because as soon as we got back into the stand for the second half, Alan Smith put us ahead to lead 3-1 on aggregate having won the home leg 2-1 with Smith and Harte goals. This was the final score and we left the stadium very happy. I managed to meet up with some others off our trip so was able to find the coaches to get back to the airport and go home!

Deportivo La Coruña – European Cup quarter-final Second leg. 17 April 2001.

It was my turn to go to Europe again so I booked on this trip with my friends Sue and Karen together with Sonya my niece. I needed cheering up as I'd a few health problems at that time and was awaiting an operation. We flew again from Leeds/Bradford airport and I was so excited to be travelling abroad to see Leeds again. With the cushion of the win at Elland Road in the first leg we were in a good position to progress through to the next round.

When we arrived near the ground we found it was a short walk away from the sea front. We found a bar and a girl who was on her own asked if she could join us so we said yes. Met Shaun Mahoney from Bradford and had a chat and took a photo of him. We ended up going paddling in the sea and had a really good time. I was a bit wary of going in the bars next to the ground which were full of Leeds fans singing, as there were so many Police around and I didn't want anything to kick-off. We went into the ground well before kick-off and met up with Carole and her partner Ashley in there. The stand was very steep and we were in the corner quite high up. When the teams came out at the start of the match their fans threw lots of small pieces of paper into the air.

Leeds had won the first leg 3–0 with goals by Harte, Smith and Ferdinand so were in a good position to progress through to the next round. As it was we lost the match 2–0 and although I thought they could get a third goal I still felt sure that we would do it. As it was, Leeds came out winners 3–2 over both legs and I was dancing about when I came out of the ground saying how fantastic it had been. All of a sudden Yorkshire Television came over to me and asked for an interview and I just said that I knew we would do it. Later when I returned to work one of my colleagues Sue said that as soon as she heard my voice she knew it was me without looking at the screen of the TV!

For the semi-finals Leeds were drawn at home to Valencia first and away for the second leg. Both Phillip and I were going to go to both legs but in the end I was unable to go to the first leg as I had an operation the same day. I would have still got home and gone but was banned and was very disappointed not to be at the match and felt sure that drawing 0–0 was because I wasn't there. I had mentioned to the doctor carrying out my operation that I was flying to Spain in two weeks and was very upset when I came round from my operation to be told that I could not fly and also he could not rule out cancer (it was not the case though). I was more upset about missing the match and it ended up with Karen's son Wayne going in my place. I am positive because I was not there, that this was why we lost 3–0 and our chances of going to the European Cup Final again failed.

ESTAC Troyes v Leeds Europa League, Second round, Second leg. 2001-02. 1 November 2001.

As our holidays were always taken around following Leeds United, as soon as we heard this draw we decided we were going to Disneyland Paris and then on to the match. Sue was going to come with Phillip and me by car and we were taking Danielle and Emily with us. Michelle had an exam and was very disgruntled that she couldn't go. Getting tickets for the girls in the end was quite difficult as Leeds decided they were going to use loyalty for this. As they had both got season tickets and we said we were going on a family holiday, we managed to get their tickets in the end, having had to put an appeal in to Leeds to get them.

When we arrived at Disneyland I don't know who the bigger children were, Sue and me or Danielle and Emily! We also wore our Leeds shirts with pride before going on to Troyes. Phillip took a photo of Sue, Danielle, Emily and me wearing our Leeds shirts and this appeared later in the Leeds programme. The heading was Disneyland Whites and we were chuffed to bits to see that.

From Disneyland we travelled down to Troyes for the match which was in lock down because of the coppers. There was nowhere to eat or drink near the stadium and we ended up getting in the car and driving till we found a McDonalds about 15 minutes away.

When we got back to the ground the coppers were not letting anyone within reach of the stadium without checking that they had tickets. When we got through, they stopped me and both girls were distraught to see their mum getting searched by female riot coppers on entering the ground. I had to reassure them that I was okay once I got through. We met up with Carole and Ashley in the ground and then went up into the stand where we stood right above the tunnel. The end at the right behind the goal was packed tight with Leeds fans and we felt sure that anyone with tickets elsewhere had been put in with us. Emily screamed the place down when someone threw their beer in the air and it drenched her. She was only eight at the time.

At Elland Road in the first leg Leeds had won 4–2 with both Viduka and Bowyer getting a couple of goals each. Leeds ended up losing the return leg 3–2. Viduka and Robbie Keane were the scorers for Leeds as they won the tie 6–5 overall. Troyes scored their first goal which was a cracker from outside the area straight from a corner. Viduka equalised on the night so Leeds were still comfortably ahead on aggregate. Troyes scored their second from a long free-kick outside the area which rolled across the ground and into the net. I'm not sure if it was deflected but Martyn didn't move in the nets so it was a possibility. It was when they scored a third that we started to get a little anxious and were trying to work out the aggregate score. As it was such a high scoring match we lost count of whether we would go through to the next round or not but then Robbie scored his goal which was the decisive factor.

Although I didn't get to all the matches when we were back in Europe I know many people who did and they all spent a small fortune! I can't describe the feelings of going to these matches but it is fantastic when the opportunity arises to go to them. Fingers crossed that I can have the chance to go back to some pre-season tours, so long as they can start around my holidays instead of when I have to work.

Stuttgart 1992–93 Champions League.

This was the second time that the Champions League was now organised as group stages. The first leg was to be played in Stuttgart on 16 September 1992. Leeds United had insisted that all the fans who wanted to travel to this match must go on the official coaches. This caused a lot of problems with some of our fans, for example; Mick Hewitt from the South Kirkby branch of the Leeds United Supporters Club had already booked a trip for many to fly to this one. Eventually the club relented a week before the match and issued tickets to the group. As Danielle was only a couple of months old Phillip went to this one with Ken Beal who travelled with us to matches and my nephew Mark. They booked onto the many coaches that were put on from Elland Road to take fans to the match. My bottom lip came out when I dropped them off at Elland Road to get the coaches as I wanted to go to the match too; although I knew I couldn't go my heart still said yes!

The coach journey was very long, over 20 hours in fact so the trip wasn't for the faint hearted! It also wasn't good for the toilets on board either for such a long journey. There were a few stops along the way and one of the funniest things was having the coppers waiting for the coaches at the services. They went to the driver's side to stop everyone getting off the coach but unfortunately for them, they forgot they were English coaches. All the lads jumped out of the door at the other side of the coach and ran off before they could be stopped! The other thing was everyone using the roadside as a toilet but obviously that was no good for the few females on board! Leeds were up against it from the start of the match and lost the first leg 3–0 which meant that Leeds had a big hurdle to overcome in the second leg, if they were to proceed further in the competition.

The return leg took place at Elland Road on 13 September and in a thrilling comeback Leeds won the match 4–1 with goals from Speed, McAllister, Cantona and Chapman. This meant on aggregate the tie was 4–4 but Stuttgart were going through to the next round on the away goals rule. It was a shame we had lost so heavily in the away leg as Leeds deserved to go through on this performance. At the end of the match we started hearing rumours about Stuttgart playing an illegible player and a further replay was ordered to be played after awarding the second leg to Leeds 3–0. This meant that the tie was a draw overall and no away goals counted for the result.

As money was tight Phillip initially couldn't afford to go to the replay that had been organised at the Nou Camp in Barcelona. We were very grateful that he had the opportunity to go to the replay in the end when Ken offered to lend Phillip the money to go. This time they flew out to Spain and didn't have to endure a nightmare trip by coach. Again I was very jealous of the fact that I couldn't go but he couldn't turn down the opportunity. I had already been to the Nou Camp in 1975 to the European Cup semi-final which saw Leeds qualify for the Final, whereas this would be Phillip's first visit. A memorable night ensued when Carl Shutt scored late on for Leeds to send us through to the next round.

Karl Shepherd – Stuttgart trip!

We were an official supporters club, the Germany Whites, and the hassle we had to go through to get to this match was immense! The club were INSISTENT that we had to get on the official coaches from Elland Road, which would have meant us travelling from Germany to Leeds, to get on the official transport to go back to Germany, then BACK to Leeds after the match, and for us, back to Germany again!!!! They finally relented a WEEK before the match, but with strict instructions no alcohol was allowed (unheard of on a GW trip!) A couple of lads from my Regiment (Man City fans believe it or not), were saying they were going to make the trip down as well by car and somehow no amount of attempting to tell them it was pointless because they didn't have club cards or tickets was getting through, they were determined.

We eventually set off, on a dry sodding coach! Got to the service station and were immediately surrounded by around a hundred GCP (German Civil Police) and 20 RMPs (Royal Military Police). No searches were carried out and as soon as the RMPs found out we were forces, they backed the GCP off us and gave us the run of the place. We were allowed to wander wherever we wanted; good job really as we were there for over an hour before the rest turned up, but on entering the service station we found we were allowed to buy as much beer as we wanted!!!!! After about an hour and suitably p****d, the rest of the coaches turned up. Even in the car park it was an impressive sight! Without much hassle we were away again, with a full GCP escort. As I said earlier, we were the first coach in the convoy and with the rolling autobahns, it gave us a chance to see the rest of the convoy. Remember when coaches used to have those yellow skylight things instead of air conditioning? We had removed them and were stuck out of the holes with flags the lot, taking photos of the rest of the convoy (sadly lost in time). As I said earlier, we counted 64 now that was a sight you could only get from our coach or whichever unfortunate one was at the back! Amazing is the only word I can use to describe it. Whizzing through Stuttgart with a full GCP escort, red lights meant nowt!

And then the kicker. They stopped the coaches about half a mile from the ground, kicked us out and just pointed in the direction of the ground, no escort, nothing! Plenty of pubs to choose from and of course, we chose!!!! Eventually staggered to the ground and as soon as we were through the gates, there is a pallet of programmes in front of us. Now we're not used to free stuff and everyone was avoiding them thinking they'd get nicked for theft if they took 'em, so all of us grabbed a massive armful and proceeded to play at programme sellers, knocking them out at two Marks each!!! Yeah yeah I know, shouldn't have been conning fellow Leeds fans, but two Marks was only about 50p and we made a sodding fortune!!!!! We were on an open terrace, even further from the pitch than Brighton's old ground and the first people I bumped in to were the two lads from my Regiment! They had travelled as they said they would, by car and paid cash on the gate! What a fookin' joke!!!! As we know, the team never turned up and we got hammered. Leaving the ground via a tiny walkway with no obvious exits, a few lads started to rip the chain-link fence down. Immediately the GCP were all over us, battering any Leeds fan in sight. They then suddenly backed off and someone chucked a bucket of water at us. Only it wasn't water, it was liquid Mace, Pain? Wow!!! Eventually found the coaches, went home and thought it was all over. If only we knew! I still count the return leg at Elland Road as the greatest atmosphere I have ever witnessed!!!

Leeds v Stuttgart at the Nou Camp Barcelona 9.10.92

AS Monaco v Leeds 12.9.95

Nice, Monaco away leg 12.9.95

Nice, Monaco away leg 12.9.95

Left: Steve, Carol, Graham (Darlington) Phillip and Heidi Monaco 12.9.95
Right: Heidi Munich 1860 v Leeds 23.8.2000

Munich 1860 v Leeds 23.8.2000

Deportivo v Leeds 17.4.2001 Sonya, Karen, Heidi,
Sue and friend who joined us

Deportivo v Leeds 17.4.2001 Heidi, Karen, Sue and Sonya

Left: Deportivo v Leeds 17.4.2001 Robert (left) and Sonya
Right: Carole, Heidi, Sue, Emily and Danielle at Troyes 1.11.2001

Left: Sue, Emily, Heidi and Danielle at Troyes 1.11.2001
Right: Chris and Kev shrine at Elland Road

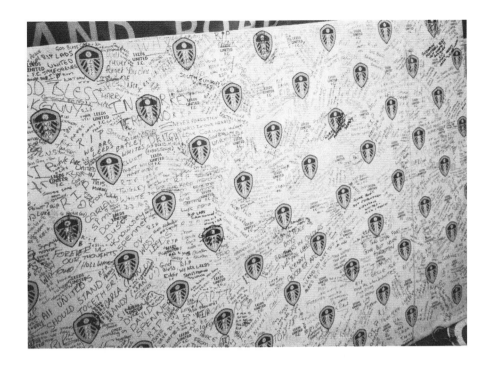

Chris and Kev wall at Elland Road

Chapter 10

The Leeds United Supporters Club – Selby branch

I had been a member of the Supporters Club for as long as I can remember. I originally started out in the Postal branch and joined Fullerton Park or Griffin branch at some point in the seventies as far as I can remember. I had started going to some away matches again in the eighties and one of these was to Oxford away and I had been travelling from Leeds with the Griffin branch. At this time I went with my friend Karen who used to go with us in the seventies, along with her two young children Kelly and Wayne. Around 1984 my sister Erica told me that she had seen an advert in the Selby paper about some lads trying to set up a Supporters Club in the district and that there would be a meeting in Selby. We both attended this and found out this had been instigated by Steve Benton and Paul Culkin from Sherburn. Eric Carlile and Ray Fell were there from the Supporters Club executive and told us of the requirements to set up a branch. There was to be a Chairman, a Secretary and a Treasurer; Steve Benton volunteered to be Chairman and Shaun Livsey from Hambleton the Treasurer, but no one wanted to become the Secretary. At the thought of this not getting off the ground I volunteered to become Secretary and thus the Leeds United Supporters Club – Selby branch was formed. I vowed to ensure that anyone who wanted to go to matches would have the opportunity to go to them, even if it meant that I would drive them to it myself. This meant that I had another seven years of not missing a match home or away. The branch covered a wide area and the coach picked up from Goole, through Carlton to Selby and onto Sherburn. There were many lads and a few lasses who travelled with us every week and it ended up being a very successful branch. We had loyal fans who travelled to every match including some from Hornsea and Old Goole as well as the other places mentioned above.

We needed 40 members to make the branch viable so we set to and organised meetings in Goole, Selby and Sherburn, where we managed to get the required number of members to set the wheels in motion. Once the branch had been set up we had to go to the Executive meeting at Fullerton Park in Leeds to be authorised by all the other Branches of the Leeds United Supporters Club. All the executives from each branch had to vote for the Selby Branch to start up officially. We had to remain in the other room until the voting had been done. Once we were given approval, we were invited into the other room to take part in the meeting and walked in to a round of applause. Collar shouted out that if he had known I was involved they would have voted no! It's a good job that he was joking. As it was, I knew the majority of people in the room as they were fans I had travelled all over the country with in the seventies. After this inauguration, we had to attend fortnightly meetings and once again I was indebted to my parents for lending me their car to get to the meetings and once again I am grateful for this.

In the early days of the Selby branch forming there were not many fans travelling to the away matches so I often drove a mini bus. Later, I heard that Collar from the Kippax branch had started using Voyager International, a coach company based in Selby, so I got quotes from the coach company too. I asked for the cost of a coach to every away match for the whole season so I was able to plan and work out travel costs to them all, by knowing in advance the total costs involved. Once the branch membership increased, we started travelling regularly with Voyager coaches. It also meant that many times we travelled on luxury coaches for up to 70 people and had toilets on the coach. After having different drivers for a while, we ended up having a regular driver called Ben who was brilliant. He often brought his friend Charlie along for the ride and we always had a fantastic rapport with them. I often did the map reading giving directions to get us to the grounds, although sometimes I did get things wrong. This happened on the way to Southampton when I missed the turn off so we ended up getting there right on kick-off. I also ensured that the supply of coffee for the driver was plentiful during the trip. We also arranged for a collection to be done for the drivers on the way back from the matches and my son Jamie loved doing this. Michelle also loved going around with my beret to collect the money too.

If we didn't have enough people for a mini bus or car then I would arrange for us to travel with The Kippax branch as we were able to get on the coach in Selby. One match standing out in my mind was travelling to Millwall for the Simod cup match on 8 December 1987 which Leeds lost 2–0. There was no way I was driving to this one so we joined with The Kippax and travelled down with them. When we arrived by coach, the first Millwall fans we saw were stood on the street corners and pretending to slit their throats. Obviously nice people, I don't think so! It was also a freezing cold night night, with a temperature of minus six degrees and approximately 500 Leeds fans were gathered together in the corner behind fences topped with barbed wire. We didn't have any trouble although it was a good show from the Leeds fans, as not many away fans would travel to the Old Den as far as I am aware.

Another time I was driving the mini bus and we were approaching a large roundabout on the outskirts of Derby. I saw a group of people crossing the road on the opposite side of the carriageway and realised that they were Newcastle fans. Luckily for us the traffic was moving and I was able to put my foot down on the accelerator and get away as they tried attacking the mini bus. They had seen the Leeds scarves hanging out of the back windows and managed to steal one and started banging on the sides. It was a split second decision seeing the situation unfold and I reacted to it, but that didn't stop me from shaking like a leaf once again as my nerves got the better of me!

We were given an escort on our way back from Peterborough in a mini bus. We had been travelling for a while until the coppers caught up with us and made us join the escort. They wouldn't let anyone break away when all we wanted to do was get home as it was a night match and late. Unfortunately the coppers kept us at lower speeds in the escort making it a very frustrating journey. Eventually we got to a roundabout near Doncaster where I tried pulling off to drop our RAF lads Dave Morris and Steve Waterhouse off at the Finningley site. The coppers tried to stop us and make us go in the direction of Leeds. I had to pull over and explain that I was dropping some of our lads off and it was only when the lads showed their RAF ID cards that I was allowed to drive in a different direction. The coppers obviously thought that Leeds fans only come from the city and wanted us to go there, what a mistake! It was nice to get away from their shackles and I managed to drop everyone off in the right places.

On our return from Southampton on a Voyager International coach the coppers escorted all the coaches from Southampton until Coventry! This was also the wrong direction for most of us to get back to Leeds and caused everyone to get very frustrated as they kept us at approximately 50 mph the whole way. Eventually we were allowed to go on our way even though we had challenged the coppers earlier to let us go on our way alone. They were trying to prevent any Leeds fans from stopping anywhere along the way, but most of us just wanted to get home after the match and all it did was wind us all up. They certainly managed to raise the blood pressure of a few of us and as I was pregnant, unfortunately after this my blood pressure stayed high for weeks!!

When Leeds got to the semi-final of the FA Cup v Coventry at Hillsborough on 12 April 1987 I had three coaches running to this. Steve and Shaun ran two of them for me and I ran the other one. After I had got on the coach the driver told me that he had just come back from abroad and had brought a crate of beer for the lads. I couldn't believe it! Of all the matches he could have done it, it was this one. No alcohol was allowed on the coaches in the first place and there were going to be so many checks by the coppers before we were allowed anywhere near the place that I knew what had to be done. The lads all drank the beer at the earliest opportunity and we stopped the coach along the way to get rid of the evidence prior to meeting the coppers at the check point. It was a good job because they even checked the boot of the coach for any signs of booze. The fact it was an early kick-off was to prevent the Leeds fans getting too much to drink before the match as well! When we got off the coaches near the ground we were stopped and had our tickets checked again, they weren't letting anyone near the ground without a ticket! Due to all the checking of tickets and stopping of coaches the kick-off was delayed for 15 minutes to allow everyone to get into the match on time. We eventually got into our seats in the upper tier of the stand. There was a fantastic atmosphere during the first half, especially when Leeds took the lead through a David Rennie header. We were ecstatic and there were fantastic celebrations in the stands including numerous Mexican waves. At half-time we were all talking in the ladies and agreed unanimously that we wished the half-time score was the score at the end of the match! Things had all been going really well until Brendan Ormsby made a mistake on the goalline by hanging on to the ball instead of clearing it. He was robbed of the ball by the Coventry player and they went on to score. They took the lead and we thought that would be it until one of our subs Keith Edwards headed an equaliser to force the match into extra-time. Unfortunately for us Coventry took the lead in extra-time so they went through to the final at Wembley.

The season didn't end there though as we got through to the Play-off Final against Charlton. They had stopped playing at The Valley and were ground sharing with Crystal Palace at Selhurst Park. Travelling down to Palace to play the first leg was a horrendous time for us. Ben was the driver of our coach to this one and we had only just joined the M1 near Sheffield when I saw something up ahead. I told Ben to slow down and it was a good job he did. There was a car parked in the middle lane of the motorway and they were retrieving their luggage from the road! We stopped at Leicester Forest and picked my friend Carole up whilst waiting for our second coach to arrive. We waited longer than we should have done but when it didn't come, we carried on down the motorway. Unfortunately with the delay, we ended up behind a crash and the traffic ground to a halt on the motorway for nearly two hours. What we didn't know at the time was that some Leeds fans in a car had crashed into the back of one of the Leeds coaches and had been killed. When the traffic started moving we carried on and when we were on the M25 there were even more crashes all over the place. We eventually arrived at Crystal Palace just before half-time. I had such a migraine by the time we arrived that I couldn't have cared less about the match as I felt so ill and didn't enjoy it at all. The reason why our other coach didn't turn up at the services was because they had gone down the A1 instead! This was in the days before mobile phones were invented!!

Another time on our way back from West Bromwich, the coach was on the A1 near Eggborough Power Station and not far from home. We neared an entrance to the A1 where an approaching car slowed down seemingly to wait for us to go past. At the last minute the car pulled out right in front of the coach and although Ben braked there was nothing he could do to avoid the crash and we hit the car from behind. As soon as both vehicles had stopped, I got out of the coach and ran to the car where I found an elderly couple in the back seats who had been injured. We called an ambulance and the coppers turned up too and breathalysed Ben which proved negative. The old couple were taken to hospital and later I gave a statement to the coppers. It wasn't a nice end to the day but hopefully the old couple were not too seriously hurt.

Whilst running the branch I met my husband Phillip at the fortnightly executive meetings, as he was running the Halifax Branch of the Supporters Club, having met previously at a pre-season friendly in Belgium in 1977. Although I moved to Halifax, I returned to Carlton every away match to run the coach. We got together after Leeds had played at Grimsby and their coach came back to Carlton for a pub stop and food at the Wheatsheaf pub. All was fine until Nidge Berry started a food fight!! Phillip and I were caught snogging just as they were getting ready to go and one of the Halifax lads ran onto the coach to tell the rest of them. It was whilst I was living in Halifax after getting married in 1988, that I received a telephone call at my home from the coppers. There was a lot of football violence during the eighties and they wanted to know whether I had any service crew members in my branch? I didn't have a clue and couldn't help them at all!

Whilst at Ayresome Park, Middlesbrough all the Leeds fans were stood waiting to be let out of the ground at the end of the match. We had been taken by the coppers to the opposite corner where we normally stood and everyone was just standing there waiting patiently. The next moment came a massive bang to the left of us, together with a load of dust rising upwards. I think it was a toilet block that had suddenly collapsed due to the pressure of the amount of fans stood there. Luckily no one was killed although some lads escaped with minor injuries, but it could have been a lot worse. The powers that be tried to blame Leeds fans for it but there was no rioting or anything and they didn't do anything wrong.

The Supporters Club in general has been slated over the years by some fans due to personal grievances. What I would say, is that all the people running these branches are volunteers doing their best for their members and getting them to matches. I have every respect for them as I know the input each and every one has to put in to ensure their branch members are looked after. This was often at a personal cost to them. As a Supporters Club, we would hold our annual dinner and dance and have had players in attendance such as Peter Swan, Russell Doig and Peter Haddock. I gave up running the branch at the end of our title winning season in 1992 just before my daughter Danielle was born so I went out on a high. Unfortunately, although the branch was taken over by others and ran for at least a couple more years, it eventually folded. They had eventually joined up with the York branch, but the coaches had stopped picking up from Goole and Selby which meant some loyal fans had to find other means of travelling to matches. I feel this had a detrimental impact on the branch folding, but also know the input that was needed on a personal basis, which could also have had an effect.

I will always be indebted to the Supporters Club Executive members who arranged for my eldest two children Jamie and Michelle to go into the players' lounge prior to a home match. After their sister Charlotte had died, we had great support from everyone and this was a great gesture. I went in to the lounge with them and we have got some photos from this time and they got plenty of autographs too. When we won the league in 1992 Phillip, Jamie, Michelle and I were invited to the Town Hall to celebrate along with the team. There were thousands of fans on the street outside but we were actually inside the building rubbing shoulders with the players. The biggest mistake I made was forgetting to take my camera to such a monumental occasion. I know some others got some photos of Jamie and Michelle and hopefully in time I can locate these.

Once away matches became all ticket affairs, this meant that as well as organising transport I had also to organise the number of tickets. Payment for the coach was always made as we arrived at the grounds as I didn't want to be carrying so much cash on me, but it also ensured the coach company received their money on time. Payment for the tickets had to be made after the matches and normally at the executive meetings. Where tickets were in short supply I always ensured that they were given to the members of our branch who had attended the most matches. This meant that the most loyal fans did not miss out. To ensure that there were funds to cover the trips and make them viable, we had a rule that if anyone booked their travel and ticket they had to pay even if they didn't turn up. This worked very well for our branch as a whole. If we ended up with any tickets spare due to non-attendees, there were always plenty of lads looking for tickets when we arrived at the grounds. These were always sold at face value and we never ripped any Leeds fans off.

The Supporters Club as a whole always held an annual dinner and dance for members as well as individual branches doing their own. These were also attended by the players and were always packed out. There was also an award for the player of the year. These events were great as the players mingled with the supporters and often we had a player who sat with us on our table. I can remember David Rocastle (who unfortunately later died of cancer) being sat on our table and at another event we had the pleasure of Glynn Snodin and his wife being on our table. Long after Don Revie's death, his wife Elsie would always give up time to attend these events before she herself died. Having photos taken with the players at these occasions were always a highlight of the event.

Steve Waterhouse, one of our former members has given his memories from his time as a Selby White below. Although his memories are blurred, he has come up with a few nostalgic things that he remembers from the 'Voyager' coach days.

- Steve said: "did you remember when we got lost going to Palace and you stopped the coach to ask a copper for directions? I've even enclosed the picture!"

- During a visit to Highbury for a night match we stopped at a pub in north London which was full of Arsenal fans but we had a good drink with them. When it was time to leave one Gunners fan we got on well with had lost track of time and would have missed kick-off, so we let him on our coach to the ground. We stopped right outside their end and he jumped off much to the amazement of hundreds of Arsenal fans.

- The all night drinking sessions in the Pot O' Four pub in Halifax before our visits to Millwall for 11.30 am kick-offs, with fans sleeping on the floor of the pub and snooker table!

- Stopping at Hillsborough to lay flowers/scarves before heading off to play Chelsea.

- The pub in Northampton that used to do us a nice breakfast before our trips to London matches.

- We were once chased by hundreds of disgruntled Irishmen celebrating St Patrick's Day outside a pub in north London. Our coach had stopped at lights outside the pub and one of our lot opened the roof window and shouted something that obviously touched a nerve, because glasses were thrown at our coach as they gave chase. Dave the driver had to put his foot down sharpish.

- A great memory for me personally is recruiting all my RAF mates to the branch between the years of 1984–89. Dave Morris, Paul 'Langy' Langham, Skid, Jock, Fordy, Big Brian, Tim, Ken Parkes, Robbo as well as me, who were all recruited from RAF Church Fenton and Finningley.

Recollections from Selby White – Mark Dovey

- On my 18th birthday we were all playing cards downstairs on the coach and were all wearing silly hats that someone had made.
- Our coach once caught fire or was full of smoke on the way back from Birmingham in winter which meant we had to stop at a pub just off the A1 until the problem was sorted.
- Don't you remember me getting John Sheridan's shirt away at Birmingham last match of the season and someone else got Neil Aspin's shorts.
- Plymouth away on a Sunday morning with a 12 o'clock kick-off. I think we got picked up at The Black Bull at approximately 2.00 am, we must have been mad eh!
- The all-nighter at the Pot O' Four Halifax and then getting coppers escorting us out of it at 5.00 am!!
- The things we forget then come flooding back like Telford in the FA cup. We didn't know if the match was on and we had to be half way there to find out. Waiting by a telephone kiosk and Heidi ringing up to see whether we should set off or not!

Following on from Steve and Mark's memories of the lock-ins at the Pot O' Four, the best part was coming out at 5 o'clock in the morning. We were trying to be quiet but the coppers were already waiting to escort us to the coach! Captain, who was running the Halifax branch of The Leeds United Supporters Club at that time, came down on our coach to Millwall and was the only one of his branch to get there as the Halifax coach broke down! The Red Lion pub at Northampton was also a regular stop off point and we often shared the stop with opposition fans as well as Leeds fans. Luckily nothing ever kicked off with the rival fans but this was more than likely to happen when stopping at the services along the motorway.

I really enjoyed running the branch including attending the fortnightly meetings at Elland Road. Even though I had stopped drinking alcohol, I always made sure that the lads and lasses had a pub stop along the way. I remember being sat in a pub and I went round to see everyone saying they had five minutes to drink up. Once that time was over I told them it was time to go and everyone got up en masse and returned to the coach. They were a good bunch and showed me a lot of respect which was greatly appreciated. One of the lads from Sherburn, Chris, started bringing sandwiches onto the coach to sell. If he wasn't travelling then I would prepare them all and sell them myself on the coach.

Recently on a blog with a review of my first book *Follow Me and Leeds United* by Rob Atkinson, I have seen a comment from one of the lads who travelled with us and is shown below:

"Counte Of Monte Fisto"

I travelled with Heidi during the late 80s and into the 90s with the Selby Whites. She was totally unique, I remember one game (Port Vale away, I think 0–0 was the score) we were all sat on a packed double decker and there were some 'lads' on that bus. Another supporters club bus came by us on the motorway & you could see from the televisions they were watching shall we say films of men's interests. We however were watching cartoons because there were a couple of kids on the bus and no one grumbled to Heidi's face.

Heidi was a woman who was held in massive respect by those who knew her, if for no other reason than she held the tickets. Everyone recognised how much personal time she gave to the club and supporters, a great character. I went to Halifax to collect my Bournemouth tickets from her house because she trusted us to go down outside the bus. A totally different era to now and missed in some ways, but not others. "MOT."

Left: Courtesy of Mark Dovey with Selby Whites
Right: Mark Dovey and Chris Newcastle away lost 5–2
courtesy of Mark Dovey

Left: Fordy, Jock, Shaun and Dave Millwall 1988 photo
courtesy of Steve Waterhouse
Right: Selby Whites Dinner Dance Neil Aspin

*Selby Whites Dinner Dance Peter Swan, Erica,
Ronnie Sinclair, Heidi and Russell Doig*

Selby Whites Dinner Dance Russell Doig, Captain and Ronnie Sinclair

Selby Whites Dinner Dance Russell Doig, Peter Swan
and Ronnie Sinclair

Skid, Langy, Steve, Dave and Heidi, WBA 1988 photo
courtesy of Steve Waterhouse

Leeds United Supporters Club Dinner Dance Mark, Shaun,
Billy Bremner, Mark's girlfriend

Leeds United Supporters Club Dinner and Dance. Selby Whites Erica, Heidi,
Glynn, his wife, Shez and Shaun

Chapter 11

Memories by Leeds fan Phil Beeton

Supporter of the Year at the Football League Awards 2014.

I met up with Phil and his wife Chris in Billy's bar to reminisce about our times of following Leeds and his memories are told below.

The first match of my 2,000 consecutive league run was in March 1967 against Manchester City at Elland Road and ended at Bournemouth on 25 March 2014. It was around the time of my birthday that my dad took me to Elland Road for my first match at the age of five, when Leeds played West Bromwich Albion at Elland Road in 1957. I can remember watching the whole of the 1961–62 season home matches with my dad who got me into football and am proud to say that I was at Elland Road for Don Revie's first match as manager against Sheffield United. My dad spoke very highly of Don Revie and said that he could be a good manager for us as he had played in an FA Cup Final, meaning he had a cup pedigree. Dad got us season tickets in 1964–65 to save messing about, as you had to get into the ground at 1.00 pm to make sure you would get in. This means it is coming up to my fiftieth year of having a season ticket at Elland Road too. Leeds won the Second Division in 1964 gaining promotion to the First Division along with Sunderland who were runners up. We originally stood in the Lowfields corner next to the Kop when I used to stand on a milk crate to enable me to see the match. The old boys' pen used to be in there which was separated from the rest of the Kop by a wooden fence. You would get a ticket from school if you played for the school team which was for this area in a pen behind the goal. I attended all the home matches during the 1960 to1963 seasons and went to see Hunslet rugby with my next door neighbour when Leeds played away from home, although I did attend the odd local away match at Sheffield United or Burnley with them being nearby.

I met my wife Chris whilst travelling to away matches with Wallace Arnold coaches. The first time I really chatted to her intensely was at the 1973 FA Cup second replay against Norwich at Villa Park which Leeds won 5–0. The author of this book Heidi, can also remember us getting together and holding hands on the coach. Heidi also attended our wedding with her friend Sue and I can remember going to visit her at the farm she lived at in Mill Lane, Carlton and seeing the little calves. Chris added that Richard Binns a mutual friend stood on her dress at the wedding and ripped it! I also have an embarrassing picture of Heidi on Chris's sofa at Kentmere Avenue, Seacroft. She was spark out with a ladder in her tights all the way up to her thigh, plus there is another picture of her with Chris's dog Kim.

Chris's first match was the 1969 Charity Shield against Manchester City at Elland Road on 2 August 1969. Leeds won the match 2–1 with goals from Gray and Charlton to win the Shield. It was also the debut of Allan Clarke who Leeds bought from Leicester City for a record £165,000 during the close season. Chris was first introduced to football by a girl she met at work who asked her to go to the match with her so she did. Chris's dad went to a match only once and after a police horse bit his ear he never went again. Chris also threw chewing gum to Gary Sprake the Leeds goalkeeper at every match.

My memories of following Leeds are of having to battle the numerous referees who always seemed to have it in for us as a club, with dubious refereeing decisions and also player-power which has been evident in later years. There have been plenty of players who haven't played to their potential numerous times for whatever reasons.

When Eric Carlile, secretary of the Leeds United Supporters Club became a board member, he used to cover the Central League matches. I used to go with Eric as his chauffeur and attended most of them alongside him. We would go in the boardrooms of the opposition clubs and that's when I met Bob Paisley, manager of Liverpool when we were invited into the board room there. Bob was the loveliest person and was telling us about his exploits during the

Second World War. You could tell there was a bond from the Don Revie and Bill Shankly era, because although Leeds and Liverpool were fierce rivals there was still mutual respect between the two clubs.

Other memories are being at Anfield the home of Liverpool when Leeds won the 1969 First Division title. Leeds only needed a point to win the title so I knew that if we drew or won they were the champions. Leeds did this by getting a 0–0 draw which was easy for them in those days and at the end of the match all the players were in each other's arms celebrating. Don came out of the dugout and gestured to Billy to take the lads to the Kop. Billy looked aghast at what he was being asked to do and Don told him to do it. The team got as far as the edge of the box and someone in the Kop shouted Champions and then the rest of the Kop joined in singing it. I was in tears and very emotional, but for an away crowd to do that, is something that I will never forget. My other favourite matches are the 7–0 defeat of Southampton at Elland Road and the showboating from Johnny Giles, trapping the ball and flicking it over his head was breathtaking. I have memories of a commentator saying that it was so perfect it was almost cruel! Another memory is Stuttgart where Cantona was taken off and Shutt brought on. I was just in the middle of saying "what is he doing?" and in the same breath said "what a fantastic goal" when the ball hit the back of the net!

The thing about following Leeds which most fans can connect with is the sacrifices made to follow your team. My moment of extreme sacrifices was during a holiday to Tenerife in 1987. We had no chance of making the play-offs so we had booked a holiday to my uncle's apartment in Tenerife, with my mum and Chris's mum and dad. But as we got nearer to the date of the holiday Leeds started winning again and we did the impossible, when we played Oldham in the semi-finals! Leeds went through on away goals when Edwards scored a goal within a minute of going onto the pitch which made the score level on aggregate. After extra-time this was still the score so Leeds went through on aggregate. We went on holiday and I was cursing, as it meant Leeds were to play Charlton in the Final of the play-offs and people were saying that my run of consecutive matches was ended. I couldn't settle and was like a bear with a sore head. Chris said that she knew what it meant to me and to just go!

I went to the airport on the morning of the Saturday we were playing Charlton at Crystal Palace's ground. I went to see a guy who was running the airport in Tenerife who took me into his office. I told him that I needed to get back to the UK preferably London as I had a really ill grandma, so he got me on a flight. He physically typed the flight coupon out for the return plane ticket and took 50 quid off me. There were no travel agents so he could have been anyone! I caught the flight into Gatwick then a train to Selhurst, got out of the station and looked around, thinking which way is it to Selhurst Park. I didn't have a clue so stood for a few minutes and then asked someone. It was a 10 –15 minute walk and I got to the ground for 11.30 am. Also there early was Terje Hansen from Stavanger who had flown in from Norway then a few minutes later Robert Gralle from Cologne. We had just been having a chat there for about half an hour when Robert made some quip that his wife didn't know he was there as she thought he'd taken the dog out for a walk! There was a fish shop at the end of the ground so we had fish and chips to get some food into us and also to kill time. We then waited at the corner of the ground where the away coaches would arrive. I was waiting for the Griffin Branch of the Leeds United Supporters Club to arrive as Simon was bringing me a ticket just in case I could make it.

Unfortunately there had been a massive accident on the M1 and the coach got there right on kick-off. All the members on the coach had been talking about me and saying this would be the first match I had missed in years, when Simon shouted to everyone that I was there on the street corner. I had to wait for him to get off the coach before we could get in for the match. Leeds lost the match 1–0 and I went back to Leeds with the coach and came home for the Saturday night. I had a relaxing day on Sunday before the second leg to be played at Leeds the next day (Monday) which I had stayed in England for. This time Ormsby scored for Leeds in the 1–0 win making it a 1–1 score on aggregate and meant a third replay would be played. I was in the players' lounge after the match and Taffy the night watchman came in to the lounge. I said: "what am I going to tell Chris now we have got a replay?" Taffy replied that she knows what's what as she had already rung up the ground to find out and knows the tie wasn't settled.

I returned to London as I flew back to Tenerife on the Tuesday and got the return flight from Gatwick that took all day. It had been a disastrous holiday so far with Chris looking after our parents for three days on her own and she was fed up whilst I was gallivanting all over Spain and the UK. On the Friday morning of the Final to be played at St. Andrews, Birmingham I was sent packing once again. When I got to Tenerife airport I saw the same guy as before and said my grandma's condition had worsened and I needed to return to the UK. It cost me another 50 quid return but he said that he was sorry as there were no spaces on any flights to any UK airport up to 6.00 pm! I asked if there were any standbys and I was put on a list and given card number five or six. There was one plane flying into Stockport International airport and they announced before lunch for the standbys to go to the desk. They took the first four on the list and I was one of the next ones, but when I went to the desk to enquire if there would be any more chances, they said no the flight was completely full. I went back to the car and drove back to the complex and was really down as I couldn't do it. Chris saw how miserable I was and said have I tried everything and to go back to the airport and stick it out.

I went back and found there were spaces on a flight leaving at 2.00 pm and it was Paramount airline flying into Bristol. I could use the ticket I had got but would have to return via Heathrow which was no problem as I just wanted to get there. The thing I can remember is that it was a no smoking flight, which was unusual as normally the last five or six rows were allocated to smokers, not that it affected me though as I didn't smoke. I got on the flight and flew back to Bristol airport arriving at 6.00 pm with a carrier bag containing a razor, toothbrush, toothpaste, a change of clothes and some money. I came straight out having no baggage to collect and needed a car. All the car hires were closed and they were just pulling the shutters down on the last one Hertz, so I shouted out to hang on as I needed a car. I signed up and asked whereabouts we were in relation to Bristol and the M5. My heart sank when I was told we were south of the city and it was going to take an hour to get past Bristol.

I drove like an idiot up the M5 and M6 to Birmingham which today would have got me banned for life and headed for St. Andrews which I knew was near the centre of Birmingham. When I got near the ground it was packed with approximately 15,000 Leeds fans and I couldn't park for love nor money. I decided to abandon the car on some grass and thought it wouldn't be there when I got back. I ran the half mile to the ground (in the days that I could run!) and the match had just kicked off, but luckily I had only missed a few minutes. Alec Hudson the Council member on the Leeds United board had left a ticket at reception on the off chance I could make the match. I picked it up and a chap took me to my seat which turned out to be in the directors' box. What a sight I must have looked, a scruffy sweating chap sat there with his carrier bag! I managed to see the match but after all my efforts our dreams were shattered when Leeds were beaten.

I had got all night till the flight the following morning, so I took time to let the traffic clear and returned to the car to see it was still there, unclamped and in one piece ready to drive. At 11.00 pm I drove steadily through the night and left the car at Heathrow just having a couple of stops along the way. I went for my return flight which was an Iberia scheduled flight via Bilbao. It was on time and still in with the 50 quid cost of the return ticket. There had been no problems with the flight and as we were coming down to land in Bilbao, the people travelling on to Tenerife were told to stay on the plane. We had just landed on the runway when the plane started veering all over the place and bumping about. I thought we had crashed and some Spanish people were shouting and waving rosary beads around. It was very scary and there was no time to think as I braced myself for the crash. I thought the plane would turn over and it was the worst thing that has ever happened to me, I thought I was going to die and for a few split seconds I thought this was the end. Then the pilot came on the tannoy and explained what had happened, that the plane had burst a tyre on landing and he had lost control of it. We pulled off the side of the runway where fire engines, the police and ambulances were waiting. Although nobody was hurt that I knew of, many were near to collapse. The pilot apologised and said that there would be a delay and we would have to go into the terminal. Once I knew we were safe I wanted to call Chris and tell her what had happened but there were no mobile phones in those days. I was worried as there was going to be a four hour delay and I couldn't get in touch with Chris. In the terminal building we were offered a glass of dilute orange together with a ham and cheese sandwich that was stale and hard. When eventually I got back on the same plane, there were lots of empty seats but I wasn't sure whether the passengers wouldn't get back on it or were getting off in Bilbao anyway.

I really wanted to contact Chris as I knew she would be upset and irate (in reality she was past caring at this point). After landing four hours late I got in the car and headed for the complex. I would tell her the truth but thought I'll be having the frying pan heading my way. When I saw Chris I said to her before you say anything, I'm lucky to be here. She didn't believe me and said to tell her another one. Once Chris realised I wasn't having her on it was a relief to know I was okay. The phone in the complex was in the office and I couldn't ring it as nobody was there, so they were completely in the dark at all times. Chris knew the score from the match as she had rung the ground and she said I don't know what's worse, when you don't know where they are or just the fact that you are waiting for someone to arrive! We had three days left of our holiday so I settled down with a couple of beers and got back on good terms with my mum who called me an idiot for doing it twice. Chris knew how it was though and she would have come back herself given the opportunity. Also as neither of us had a grandma I didn't feel bad about saying she was really ill to get the flights back to England. The irony of it all is that I got there quicker than the rest of the support who travelled from Leeds!

An insight on a trip abroad to Universitatea Craiova v Leeds United in Romania on 24 October 1979.

Leeds lost 2–0 on a trip behind the Iron Curtain. We were only allowed to change five pounds in sterling and we thought that we wouldn't be able to buy anything with that. We had to spend it all, as we weren't allowed to bring any of the currency out of the country. On our way there at the passport checks we were told it could take up to five or six hours to go through as we were met by armed guards. Eric Carlile had travelled with us and had a suitcase with him with a load of Leeds badges in it. They made him open his case, saw the badges and took a few badges out for their friends. This 'present' obviously worked and we found ourselves quickly on our way! Further on when we were stopped again, the guards went straight to Eric for some badges and meant we got through quickly again. It was obvious that someone had got in touch with them to tell them who to approach for the badges!

Our coach driver drove for 20 hours and nearly killed us going up a mountain when we found a tanker across the road in front of us. Some of the lads were singing for Stavros the driver to give them a wave; he duly obliged by standing up at the wheel and turned round to wave to them! One of our lads threw a sandwich out of the back window which landed on the mud track that we were travelling on. Seeing kids fighting over the sandwich was truly humbling. When we stopped we went round a supermarket which had rats running around it and the meat was covered with flies. We found we couldn't actually spend all the money we had with us and bought sunflower seeds and ice cream. Everyone was eating sunflower seeds and spitting out the kernels as the road was covered in them. Even the locals don't buy the vodka as they couldn't drink it. A driver on a train in the siding spat it out as it was 98 percent pure. Whilst at the match you could see the entire crowd being brought in from a power station when they were all snaking their way downhill. All the adults were wearing the same grey-blue uniform and all the kids wore the same dark blue uniforms and they had to go to the match. Afterwards they were all walking back to the power station. I still had change out of my fiver and brought 100 programmes back with the rest of the money. Others gave their change to some women who were in tears as they were so grateful, thanking them for giving them money. Memories are of the housing on show, the mines in the distance, running over dogs and chickens, dirt tracks and a dodgy driver.

Metallurg Zaporizha v Leeds United 3 October 2002 a 1–1 draw with Nick Barmby scoring for Leeds.

This was a nightmare trip and was certainly something you would never have done back in England, but because we were following Leeds, we just went and did it! For this trip we had joined up with Mick Hewitt and the Leeds United Supporters Club South Kirkby Branch to travel to the match in the Ukraine. We had been told that under no circumstances were we to travel by train as we would be going into bandit country. The trains would often be held up and valuables like watches and jewellery taken off the passengers. Because of this Mick hired a plane to Kiev for the group of us but when we saw the plane, there was lots of nervous laughter! The good thing about the plane was that it was white with a blue and yellow stripe down the side; the bad thing is that you would never ever have got on the plane in the first place under normal circumstances! I don't know how much Mick had paid for the flight and it showed. It was horrific, you had to enter through the end of the plane and climb up three steps to find your seat. The seat belts weren't adjustable and the seats were like deck chairs, the ports holes had net curtains hanging from them that were held on with drawing pins and there was a piece of leather dividing the Leeds fans from the pilot. To cap it all one of the tyres was bald and the air hostess had to sit on the toilet for both take-off and landing as there were no spare seats available! Our refreshments consisted of an out of date cake bar and orange juice plus the cabin was full of dead flies! Would we have got on a plane like this in our country? Not on your life!! The co-pilot had a Metallurg cap on and was smiling and nodding in front of us. The actual plane trip wasn't too bad as it was smooth, we didn't go very high and once we got used to it were saying "keep going lad" as we followed the river all the way down. There was scared laughter from the adults and we were glad to get down and off the flight. We didn't have the same plane for the return trip as someone gazumped Mick with a higher offer, so they took the plane to Minsk instead. We had to wait for a different plane but that wasn't as scary. In the airport all the police were crooked, had machine guns and were very aggressive trying to take beer and spirits off the group. In fact it was a pretty scary situation to be in.

Bournemouth 25 March 2014 lost 4–1 with McCormack getting the Leeds goal.

My 2,000 consecutive Leeds match was at Bournemouth and the last 34 miles to the ground were spent in a cop car. Chris and I had been invited to the boardroom by the Chairman for the match but the coach had to wait at Rainham Services for the copper escort. We had been given a time to arrive at the ground but the Police commander wouldn't let the Griffin coach get into Bournemouth earlier than the rest of the coaches. Because of this Bryn Stokes from West Yorkshire Police said he would get us there by picking us up at the coach rendezvous point. I had wanted to do the match by travelling in with my mates and people in the branch on the coach, thus keeping everything as normal as possible. We had a cop car waiting for us at the services as we got off the coach and there I am in a suit and tie. You can count on one finger the times I have attended a match dressed in this way. Chris Mozzer from the branch got one picture of me going into the car as Bryn got the handcuffs out and threatened to put them on me. What I found very poignant was when we started driving away in the cop car. All the coaches were in a long line at the services including a couple from Fourways, some others and the Griffin and everyone applauded us. That was a fantastic sight and brought a lump to my throat. A member of the Bournemouth constabulary was driving and despite a bit of traffic they got us down there on time. I kept getting telephone calls from cameramen from Sky TV saying are you nearly here?

We had to report to reception on arrival and the Sky cameraman wanted to have a picture walking towards me. I said they could do one take as we were late and then going straight in which we did. At the reception they knew who we were as we had got a film crew with us and we were given our passes. I was then missing for half an hour whilst they did an interview for Sky and one for the Football League. I had met Jeff Mostyn the chairman of Bournemouth at the football awards dinner. He introduced himself to me and said he had heard my 2,000 match was at their place and he formally invited me there and then to join them for a meal. That was a fantastic gesture. When we went to the boardroom Jeff Mostyn, a lovely chap, signed a programme and gave Chris a kiss. We were part of five Bournemouth personnel as their guests with Peter Lorimer, Dominic Matteo and David Haigh as the Leeds guests and we had names plates for the eight of us. Jeff asked Chris what the score would be and she said Leeds were going to win 4–0. Unfortunately that score line was spectacularly wrong for Leeds and he said to her at half time, "what did you say the score would be?" Jeff also presented me with an autographed shirt from when Wise was there as it would mean more to me than him. I also received a Man of the Match ball from Sky which the lads had signed in a silver pen plus I got a limited edition medallion from Bournemouth to commemorate their centenary year. Bournemouth were superb and fantastic hosts.

The following Saturday at Elland Road, David Haigh took us into the Harewood suite. There were three massive tables and 35 people in there with dozens from Doncaster with their wives. I was very honoured to meet the Countess of Harewood and Leslie Silver a previous Leeds Chairman was in there too. At half-time a car was at the East Stand reception to take me to the West Stand Banqueting Suite to meet Paul Dews. I knew I was getting presented with a five year season ticket and also received a framed shirt with my name on it and the number 2000. I received a goodie bag on my seat in the boardroom which was a posh Leeds United carrier bag containing a tie, scarf and cuff links. David Haigh was the perfect host and as soon as I went to the West Stand at half-time he moved to sit with Chris to check she was alright as he knew she struggles with her eyesight. He asked if she needed a hand and was very kind. Throughout the awards dinner David Haigh was texting me all the time saying good luck, hope you do okay and congratulations. I feel that he was a genuine person when he resigned from GFH. We are very grateful for the way he and the club treated us and took the trouble to look after us. Matteo and Lorimer also had a lot to do with things and were very kind to us too.

My memories of the 1965 FA Cup Final are that my aunty had just died and her funeral was coming up. Dad asked my mum whether we should still go to the Cup Final even though we had tickets for the match and the train down there. My mum said that it was a one off and probably wouldn't happen again and we should still go. So I went down to Wembley with my dad as a 12-year-old and he told me that when we were singing the hymn 'Abide with me' to think of my aunty Doris. Whenever I hear that hymn now, it goes through me and I always get emotional as we were quite close. Coming out of the ground after extra-time, we were walking down the long steps with some Liverpool fans alongside us and I had my rattle and my Leeds scarf on. A scouser with a red and white beanie hat put his arm round my shoulders and said: "never mind son, you've got a good team here and will be back here soon". He was right too, as we returned over the next few years for the League Cup Final 1968 v Arsenal and 1996 v Aston Villa, FA Cup Finals in 1970 v Chelsea, 1972 v Arsenal, 1973 v Sunderland and 1974 and 1992 Charity Shield matches v Liverpool and that comment sticks in my memory.

I can remember going in the Roker end at Sunderland where I was hit by a dart. I was wearing my jacket with my diary in the inside pocket. Al my best mate who married Chris's friend Colleen said: "are you alright?" I hadn't seen the dart hit me as luckily it got stuck in my diary next to my heart. I kept that diary for months with the holes still in it! I was lucky, as other fans were coming out with darts stuck in their heads. Another time I was at the Anfield Road end at Liverpool and Colleen saw us on the road and shouted: "how have you got here?" when another bottle went flying past you, as you were trying to pretend you weren't a Leeds fan! We saw one lad running in and out of cars in the car park who got battered by a large group of Liverpool fans. We saw him roll up into a ball as there were that many of them. Two other memories are Cardiff which stands out when this beast of a Cardiff fan pulled the car park diamond chains off their posts, swung it round his head and put it straight through the coach window. Hibernian when the coach driver had his arm out of the window when we were stuck in traffic and one Hibs fan held his arm back whilst the other took his watch.

Leeds fans have definitely suffered over the years for supporting the best football club with everyone being jealous. We were lucky to have been brought up around that time and it has been a privilege to see them. Bobby Collins who had a terrible injury that put paid to his career, was the catalyst of getting Revie's team going in my opinion. Even in later years seeing Yeboah and Cantona we saw some great players. My dad drooled over John Charles and would tell me the finest half-back line number 4 Willis Edwards, number 5 Ernie Hart and number 6 Wilf Copping along with John Charles were the best he had ever seen. Revie's team just rolled off the tongue for us.

The other thing that is fantastic about being a Leeds fan are the great people you meet over the years that you never forget and who still come. People like Terje Hansen from Norway who has a season ticket and it costs a fortune to come and Fotis from Greece who started supporting Leeds after his dad went to the European Cup Winners Cup Final in Salonika in 1973, who stays with us twice a year. When Leeds returned to Salonika for a second time, this time in a friendly match, Blackwell who was the manager at the time came up to see all the fans.

The Leeds United Supporters Club has been a big part of my life since 1979 when I started running the Griffin branch and regard it as my family. Everyone knows each other and there are a hard core of 25 who don't miss a match and others who cannot go every week. Some are students and I respect the fact that they can't get to every match. One of our oldest members died recently Ellen, who never missed a match and was as good as gold. She will be remembered for having her rosary beads in her hands and waving them at the referee. We have lost some good people along the way, some got married and had families, some lost jobs or can't afford it and some have sadly died. We lost one member aged 60 who only joined recently to travel with his lad aged 40 who had been with us a lot longer. He got on the coach to say his dad can't go to Forest on Boxing Day as he died yesterday, there were hundreds of people at his funeral. You have got your overall family of Leeds fans including the away support and then your little family that you travel with.

Chapter 12

Football Recollections by Andy Johnson

My earliest emotions of Leeds was the p****d off feeling I had after we had got beaten by Everton in the FA Cup semi-final at Old Trafford on April 27 1967 – I was seven years old, our kid had gone to the match and he'd been building up to it all week. I tuned in to the radio commentary and routed for us. The desolation I felt after the 1–0 defeat was one that I would become used to over the next 45 years.

I think it was this year that our old man bought us a Subbuteo for Christmas – a bit like a joint present. It comprised of two teams and a pitch – plastic square goal posts with brown nets and a shiny brown plastic ball which was nearly as big as the players – one team was red and white the other blue and white – Scum and Everton. Indignant, our kid went out and bought a little tinlet of white Humbrol paint from the local model shop and soon Everton became Leeds – we now had a Leeds v Scum Subbuteo set.

When we played, our kid always had to be Leeds – he would take great delight in putting 10 or 12 goals past me and if I ever had the audacity to score, he would jump up and run round the pitch singing "YOUR GONNA GET YOUR F*****G HEADS KICKED IN" then chin me. I would copy and try doing the same whenever he scored. He would pretend to back off into the hallway and up the landing steps – he'd get to the top – and as I ran up he'd charge down and steam into me – terrace style – giving it "AG – AGR - AGRO-AGRO" – and "GELDERD AGRO HELLO HELLO" it was just fun and he never hurt me. I got to learn all the latest terrace songs through Subbuteo before I'd even started going to matches properly. I was still playing with the remnants of it ten years afterwards – there were players with no heads and no arms, with bobbles of rubberised Bostik and Evo Stick from where they'd been repaired. Even to this day I've still got various bits of 40 odd year old Subbuteo in the loft and now and again I get them out for a laugh.

My first match was Crystal Palace at home in April 1970 – the season we were chasing the lot and finished with nothing. I'd been nagging my old man for about two years to take me – we won 2–0 with Jones getting both – the second a fantastic diving header which I still visualise. I've still got the 15 shillings ticket stub from the Lowfields Road seats where we sat. My old man took me out of duty though, rather than enthusiasm – he was a rugby man – "Nancy over paid Prima Donnas" he called them (ring any bells today?) He only ever took me to two other matches after that – it wasn't his sport and he never really encouraged me. The encouragement came from our kid – David. He was the right age at the right time for Revie's emerging giants and everything he sucked in from that team – that era – the music, the fashion – everything – rubbed off on to me. When he died tragically aged only 30 in 1984 it was the saddest day of my life – I still miss him.

I was 16 when I first went away; I went with our kid – seven years older than me and his best mate Gregg, who soon became a good mate of mine. 8 October 1977 v Bristol City, we lost 3–2 and Big Norm who was by now playing for them, scored a cracker. It's the only thing I actually remember about the match and although we lost, the whole spine tingling feeling of the day out and everything associated with it – from meeting early doors at the train station – smuggling six cans of McEwen's Export on to the train – the banter and crack of like-minded fans – the coppers escort before – with all their lads following – waiting for an opportunity – then repeating it all again on the way back – to actually getting home in one piece – is what still sticks in my mind – I was hooked there on in and soon doing regular away days. I was growing up and soon making new mates through Football – finding all sorts of ways to hook up together and get to matches – Cars – Van Hire – Wally Arnolds – Football Specials. I'd started to lose touch with most of my old school mates who originally I'd gone to home matches with only a couple of years earlier and was doing matches instead with our kid who knocked around town on match days. I was soon mixing with an older crowd of town lads – people like Pete Dillon – Dave Scobie and Gregg – they would go to the bar for me when it was my round to make sure I wasn't kicked out of the pub because I was under age – but also to make sure I paid my turn.

Towards the back end of the 70s after a couple of nightmare trips on the Special and Wally Arnolds we joined The Three Legs Supporters Club (now the Vine) then run by Tony Lazenby. The 'Legs' based on the Headrow was a massive 'Leeds' pub that drew support on match days from all over the area – we went to a few matches with them, but soon mixed with others who were going with a different Supporters Club Branch – one that had more of an edge to it. That Branch was the Kippax Branch!

Spurs 1981 – Away.

I have just been looking at some old scrap book clippings and it got me reminiscing about Spurs in the Cup 1981–82 which was a very lively day out. I went as usual with The Kippax and we had a right turn out (four coach loads). They were all lads and everyone wanting it because of the lad who had sadly lost his life down there the season before.

We stopped off at the services first (I can't remember which) and we were about 15 minutes behind the other three coaches as we pulled in. They left to continue their journey onwards before us and as we started to go back to our coach we still had a few minutes to kill before leaving. That's when four coach loads of West Brom pulled in on their way to Gillingham. The last two or three of our lot – including our kid, (who was wearing a silly leather patched Beret – which apparently cost him a fortune) were making their way back across the coach park to us when they were sussed and suddenly about 150 Baggies charged them! I never saw our kid run as fast and as his younger brother naively thought he was a soft twat for running and not standing. Our driver was already on to it and had got the coach mobile and started to move off, gradually picking up speed. Our kid was chasing after the coach with 150 chasing after him and was the last man as we hauled him on, drip white and sweating like a twat. His 'don't I look cool beret' now draped lopsided over his perspiring brow – desperately trying to regain his composure. As we sped off we all collapsed laughing.

Once at Tottenham we walked from the coaches down the High Street towards the ground – a good 20 minute walk with just a small copper escort, and as we passed The Bricklayers Arms it emptied and the Spurs fans in the pub came to have it out with us. There were too many of us though and we stuck together and held our own, putting them on the back foot. Then as we neared the corner towards the ground the service lot arrived and we had them in a pincer. This was the first season Leeds really started to travel in numbers to the big London clubs and it felt great at last, to take it back to them in their own back yard. Seeing us all together behind the goal making the noise we made was class – we must have taken about 7,000 fans.

Afterwards, getting back to the coaches though was a different matter; we came out all mob handed at first, but in the winter darkness we started to get disjointed and our recognised numbers began to dwindle. We started to get picked off by hit teams who had mingled in with us – they were older blokes, mid 30s to 40s and were smashing into us – sniper like with hit and run tactics. Suddenly no f****r knew who to trust, as many now had taken off their own colours for protection and before you knew it, paranoia had set in. I remember quite clearly, one Leeds lad being put through a shop window front – which was ironically a Funeral Directors! Eventually as we neared our coaches we got it back together and launched our own attacks, but we'd taken some casualties alright.

I'd been to the match the previous season when one of our fans sadly lost his life – we took maybe 1,800 tops. It was hostile and intimidating with talk of Leeds lads getting blades pulled on them underneath the stands when they ventured for a p**s, but it was nothing like the scale of what awaited us after this match. Consensus amongst us all as we travelled back up the motorway, was it was more than just Spurs out for Leeds that day, more like a 'London United' firm with big Gangster geezer types co-ordinating the attacks. We played them again a few weeks later in the League and expected the same but nothing really happened.

Match Recollections.

Match recollections and games to single out, or incidents, where do you start? Most of it has been documented and written about already anyway.

For me it started on The Clock Work Corner as a twelve-year-old around 1972–73, watching the older kids taunt the away fans in the Shed and then a couple of years later as you graduated to the Kop. The in-fights of Leeds on Leeds when 14 and 15 year old youths would battle and sort out their territorial estate wars down the Gelderd End terracing. As it neared 3 o' clock the bigger lads who'd been drinking downstairs or in town, would come up into the stands and kick you out of the prime viewing perch you thought you'd secured by getting in early. The European Cup semi-final v Barcelona at Elland Road in 1975 still sends a tingle down my spine whenever I see the highlights. City in the FA Cup matches of 77 and 78, all the Scum games at ER in the mid 70s culminating in the mass battles of 3 May 1980 when they failed gloriously to win the League in our backyard and licked their wounds all the way back to Manchester via Zulu Hill. There are loads that stand out, the early 80 pre-season tours of Denmark and Scotland, the London trips to Spurs and Arsenal when at first we hardly showed, only to swamp them within 12 months with our numbers. Chelsea in 82 and the trashed Scoreboard of 84. Millwall – the first time, when the entire crowd spent the whole 90 minutes checking each other out and nobody would leave the ground at the end. Then the season after when we broke down after the match and were stuck in the car park for two hours. God knows how many windows went through, freezing our b******s off all the way back up the M1 – laughing ourselves silly at how we escaped home in one piece. Then of course the horror of Birmingham and the all so near glory of Hillsborough and Charlton at St Andrews until at last, the final glory of Bournemouth in 1990. How can you ever fully describe the force that took over you during this decade? These were our times and our days, we were the right age in the right place and as an away force-fan wise; we were at our absolute peak! Winning the Division One Championship two years later was great but the 1989–90 season was THE season that finally saw the rebirth of our Club.

After '92 I stopped going, things were changing for me and I'd met Karen, who I would eventually marry. We settled down, bought a flat and made a home together and then our Cherie came along, so now we were supporting something even more precious than Leeds United. I still managed the odd match and followed everything though the media. Circumstances took over though when we started to implode and by 2004 the pull became too much, I ended a 12 year exile. We were drowning and the need to support Leeds again drew me back in. I was compelled to go back; I knew then that Leeds United never ever leaves you. One of the first thing I noticed was how much the dynamic of our fan base had changed, from the 'Nitty Gritty' lad culture to the 'Happy Clappy' new wavetype of football fan that all clubs now seemed to have attracted since the Taylor Report and false Ritz and glamour of Sky TV. There were still plenty of old faces about but the grounds and atmosphere had become far more sanitised and sterile.

Match Highlights – Bristol City.

I reckon the most emotional match I've been to at Elland Road since the 1975 Barcelona match was the Bristol Rovers match of 8 May 2010, when we needed to win on the last day of the season to ensure promotion from League One.

How many that day realised it was the first time since the Inter City Fairs Cup Final against Juventus in 1971 that we had actually 'Won' something on Elland Road soil? I didn't, I'd forgotten and it was Pete Dillon who reminded me later that night whilst we were celebrating back in Leeds town centre. Is it any wonder then, why the ground went so f*****g crazy at the end? I can still hear Ben Fry's desperate and futile pleas over his microphone as full-time approached and thousands began to encroach towards the cinder track: "please keep off the pitch at the final whistle. Anyone trespassing faces a lifetime ban from Elland Road" – "Leeds United Football Club will pursue vigorously and prosecute all offenders". Yeah, Yeah too f*****g right Ben...now f**k off!!

The sense of anticipation had been building all week – through Facebook I'd managed to hook up with a few old compatriots I'd not seen for years, so come Saturday morning the hairs on the back of my neck were doing overtime. We met in town about 11.00 am – Tom, Paul and me and the pubs were already packed with our support, instantly reminding me of the big matches of yesteryear and adding to the sense of occasion. The Horse and Trumpet, Northern Monkey, Slug and Lettuce, Becketts and finally Spencers, all spilling over; everyone was out for this one, Priestley, Slugger, Terry Ford, Dave Green, Hazey and loads of others I hadn't seen for years talking and catching up again. The atmosphere and sense of camaraderie was just the same as it has always been, electric!

We're inside the ground for about 2.40 pm, C22 West Stand Lower Paddock, in the queue for the £3.75 freezing p**s that Ken Bates dares to call lager and for the umpteenth time argue the scenarios and permutations of promotion. I look around and take in how crammed it is with lads you know wouldn't normally choose this part of the ground but like us, are just desperate to be in any part of it today, the first seeds of doubt set in as I ask myself: "are we going to turn up today?"

We build some early pressure, play in their half and make a couple of half chances, but before we know it, Bristol have survived the 20 minute mark and are comfortable. The heavy fog of nerves and fear swirling through the stands begin to tumble down the terrace and onto the pitch. Passes go astray and Bristol grow into the match – lungs and legs get heavy with the burden of expectation and the fear of failure, not for the first time in these pressure cooker situations, we start to toil. Beckford well offside, half-heartedly puts the ball in the net and the ref rightly disallows the goal and then... GRADEL!! WHAT THE F**K AREYOU DOING YOU STUPID TWAT? Seemingly from nothing, Max Gradel has lost it completely with Jones the Bristol full-back who is man marking him. As our players usher him away he goes berserk with everyone who goes anywhere near him for fully five minutes, giving the ref no option but to send him off! It eventually takes the intervention of two stewards to get him off the pitch.

I turn to Tom and Paul, who like me look on in disbelief and anger at the way Gradel has let down his club at the most crucial time. Déjà Vu envelopes me at the realisation the script is starting to be written and another season is about to go t**s up again. I look towards the pitch but I'm not really watching the match anymore – thoughts turning instead to the previous forty odd years, and how injustice has followed us everywhere. Bent officials and dodgy decisions, jealous media and an inner tendency to self implode at crucial times always conspire to rob us.

I list them in my mind's eye, it's engrained in our DNA – Lorimer's goal at Villa Park 67 ruled out by Ken Burns as Chelsea progress to Wembley: Sprake's calamity clanger the year after at Old Trafford at the same stage gifting Everton this time, a passage to the Final; The epic campaign of 1969–70, shortened due to an impending Mexico World Cup. Chasing the unprecedented and impossible Domestic and European Cup Treble with a squad of 16 players, eventually crashing in the very final stages as fixture congestion and fatigue tore into the threadbare resources of Revie's Lions. Burned out and self destructing we finish with nothing, but become immortalised for a new generation of fans. 71 and Tinkler 'The Twat' ... 72 and Molineux – 48 hours after the Cup Final needing a draw for the Double, 'thanks Mr Hardarker' ... 73 and that b*****d Stokoe, then off to Salonika for the most corrupt Final in the Cup Winners Cup history...

"We off down for a pint?"

"Eh," My thoughts are disturbed by Paul's question.

"It's almost half time – we going down for one?"

"Yeah we need one."

We get a pint and discuss the events.

"If Gradel was here now I'd crack him right in the f*****g mouth, does he know what's at stake?" says Tom.

"Well I hope Grayson makes sure he never pulls on a f*****g white shirt again," agrees Paul.

I start ranting, "It's going t**s up again boys and you can read the f*****g script, seen it too many times and I can't be arsed with this anymore. As soon as them gates are open, I'm off, I'm not f*****g sitting through another one of these again.

"No-No-No we'll still win this," counters Tom.

We argue all the way back to the stands as the teams come back out.

The second half is under way but I'm soon drifting again … 74 and the calamity own goal of Clough's appointment over John Giles – Don's obvious choice of continuity for the Club and dynasty he built. 1975 and the Parc des Princes – events that burned and scar deep into the soul forever. Is it any wonder so many of us over a certain age became such bitter and twisted b******s throughout the 70s and 80s? Our capacity to fuck up and freeze at vital stages is more breathtaking and iconic than our successes – it's part of our genetic fibre, it's what makes us Leeds. The three seasons on the bounce 77, 78 and 79 with more heartache in the cups as we fail to turn up for domestic Semis. Now it's the air of expectancy and the burden of our history that weighs us down whenever we get a sniff of a pending achievement. 2006 in Cardiff and 2008 at Wembley against the football might of Watford and Doncaster the recent examples. Now it's happening again as a break down the left by Bristol results in a cross by Jones to the far post – the balls hooked back into the box and Duffy cuts in, losing his marker to make it 0-1.

"B*****D, S**T AND F*****G DISASTER – F**k this," I get up and head for the exits, down the steps and towards the gates, only they aren't open yet. Pondering for a few minutes, watching Sky Sports News updates and weighing up the likely play-off matches – I go for a p**s instead, before eventually making my way back to my seat.

"I thought you'd gone," says Paul half laughing.

"Bottled it – you never know" I reply sheepishly – shrugging my shoulders

"Well its s**t or bust now – someone out there's got to take this by the scruff of the neck."

"That's part of problem though mate we don't have enough natural leaders out there do we?"

And that's when Johnny Howson announced his credentials and took the match by the scruff of the neck and showed he could lead. Bradley Johnson's miskick somehow finds Becchio – who back to goal lays it sweetly onto Howson's right boot and…

WHOOOSH 1–1, "KIN GET IN YER B*****D".

Our legs & arms embrace into a threesome man hug that would look decidedly gay in any other situation had it not been a goal celebration. We go tumbling and crashing forward over two rows of seats and join 38,000 others doing exactly the same. The whole mood of the ground changes in an instant – Bristol visibly wilt and shrink – United – given a kiss of life – blossom and bloom back into ascendency – heaved onward by 38,000 togetherness, we are now unstoppable! Five minutes later and the now atmospheric Elland Road suck the ball into net for the winner – Beckford capitalising on a clearly intimidated goalkeeper's weak clearance.

Celebrating long into the night in Leeds town centre with old mates and bumping into faces I've not seen for years Sharpy, Barney, Ian 'Blackpool' Hewitson, Steph Robinson, Paul Matthews, Pete Dillon. Everyone from years back seems to be out in town – a throwback to the good old times.

I wake Sunday morning with the expected hangover and that anti climatic feeling you always get on the morning after such a fantastic day before. I played back the day's events in my head and knew that now we were actually up. You wouldn't have wanted it any other way – *THIS* was the best way we could have got Promotion!

Chapter 13

Memories from Leeds fans

Ashley Tabony, Hayden Evans, Neale Sheldon, Lee Hession,
Andrew Butterwick, Dave Cocker, Terje On Tour Hansen,
Arnie Pirie and Keith Gaunt

Recollections by Ashley Tabony.

It took three years before I finally convinced my dad to take me on the ultimate pilgrimage, to Elland Road. As an early 10th birthday present we set off for Yorkshire in September 1976 for the match against Newcastle. We dropped mum off with some relatives and headed for Leeds. I remember we parked up at the old dog track and when I got out of the car, there they were, those floodlights I'd read about, the biggest AND BEST in the world. There was also that wonderful view of the West Stand across Fullerton Park. This was where I belonged, it just felt right, and I was deeply in love by now.

I think we were quite late into the ground, but there was a problem with our tickets and for a while I found myself stood by the tunnel, next to the pitch, while dad sorted it. The players were warming up and I was stood looking at them, this close and utterly star struck. In the end we were nestled on the front row, down towards the south stand, dad had his flask and hipflask out; all was good with the world. I don't remember much about the match, it was 2–2 and I do remember my dad disappointing me by suggesting Carl Harris was no Eddie Gray replacement, but once again the result was secondary to the visit.

By this time I had become an autograph hunter, so we came out of the West Stand and I went a-hunting. I can look at my autograph book from that day now and remember the mayhem, chasing Newcastle players like Nattrass and Craig first, then our boys. Jordan signed as he got into his car, these blokes were real, and this was just incredible. Eventually the car park is all but clear, just me, dad and the steward on the door of the players' lounge. It is 6 pm and dad wants to head home, but I need two autographs, THE two autographs, Billy Bremner and Allan Clarke. Dad took my book off me and went and asked the guy at the door to take it in and get it signed, the bloke didn't take the book and I felt sick. Dad said: "he says if you want the autographs that badly, go and get them yourself".

I walked on air to the door, opened it and walked in. Billy looked round and said "what can we do for you son?" I explained and in a flash he and Sniffer had a stool for me in between them both and a glass of coke. They signed my book and spoke to me kindly, talked of where I lived and how I was to stay loyal to Leeds United forever because they always would. Just magical, I can remember to this day what it felt like, just bloody magical. I came out 20 minutes later and to this day my dad maintains the look on my face at that moment was the purest joy he has ever witnessed. Thanks Billy and Sniffer, you gave me and my dad one of our greatest memories, just by giving a bit of your time. I got home from school early that week to find Billy had been sold to Hull, I guess this was why he and his mate Sniffer had been talking and yet he still had time for a little Brummie in a snorkel parka armed with a Bic biro. Billy and Sniffer, my greatest Leeds United heroes.

Memories.

As a Midlands based 'Revie child', two memories stand out more than any others, my first match and my first home match.

My first match was just before my seventh birthday, 13 October 1973. My Dad told me that morning he and my Grandad (my other hero then and now) were going to take me to my first match. I had the paper in front of me and looked down the fixtures. Grandad was a Villa fan, but they weren't at home. Birmingham were at home to Wolves. But wait, Leeds were away at Leicester … where on earth was Leicester relative to Pype Hayes in Birmingham? There was only one thing for it; I've got to ask, "Dad, are we going to Leicester?" I said, trying not to sound too hopeful. "Don't be silly Ashley, that's miles away". I remember sitting there, trying not to be too disappointed and consoling myself with the thought "at least I'll get to see Derek Dougan".

So we get in the car and off we go. Now I didn't really watch where we went, head into Shoot magazine, but then I looked up and we were on the motorway. Now even at seven I knew you only went down the Birmingham Road and along the Expressway to get into the City Centre, and this little candle of hope lit in my mind.

Then I saw it. The sign pointing to Leicester, and we turned and followed its direction. I remember I wanted to burst with excitement, but didn't dare. Before long the truth was out. I leapt out of the car and Grandad bought me a scarf and a pennant from the fella at the roadside, I still have them today. We went into the ground, we had grand seats in the upper tier of the main stand, I walked up the steps, and ... Oh lordy lordy, nothing prepared me for this. The pitch, the crowd, the noise, this was me, this was everything I ever want, or need. Not true of course but at that moment, for a young boy, that was just incredible, I wanted to live that moment forever. Then they came out. My heroes, the images I treasured as soccer cards and Shoot posters, there they were, waving to me, as they did the Leeds wave. All of us must have this moment, I'll never forget it, it was a moment of complete commitment and you are MY TEAM, FOREVER.

The match itself probably sums up the next 40 years really, promised much but a bit disappointing, we led 2–0 early on, my King Billy scored and raced across to salute me (the fact we were sat just behind Don is irrelevant!!) however Leeds blew it and it finished 2–2. But to be honest and this will sound odd to anyone not smitten by a football club, but sensible to anyone who is, it didn't matter. I'd consummated my relationship with Leeds United, the sweet smell of victory could wait for another day, we had taken our vows, for better or worse, richer or poorer. I am so glad that day happened, Leeds United Football

Club has made me laugh, smile, frown and cry, but I wouldn't have missed a day of it since that day.

Memories – Hayden Evans.

Memories I have include travelling to Roker Park to see Leeds at Sunderland. Although things have changed in recent years, like every other fan that went with their mates to matches, there were some hairy moments. I still carry an injury to this day with a replacement ankle after the trouble I had on the day Leeds had beaten Sunderland 1–0. It had been naughty outside the ground before the match, but as we turned up from work we went to get our tickets that had been left by the players for us. When they were given to us we saw that they were for the clock stand, a Sunderland stronghold so we said there was no way that we could go in there. The response to us was that we were told to either go in there or f**k off! We said it would be a disaster for us but decided that we would go in the allocated seats. As it was, things had been okay for most of the match only to turn nasty towards the end. Macca's dad who was with us, had waved to him on the pitch when he had spotted him, but unfortunately this had pointed us out to the Sunderland fans looking for trouble. The Sunderland fans gathered around us and Macca's dad got attacked. Two of the lads with us went to help and stand up for him but they too got battered. I was thrown over the top tier wall and landed on the terraces below. I was taken to Sunderland General hospital and was out of action for six months. The Leeds United team found out where I was and got me out of Sunderland, but it took a long time for me to overcome the injuries and put an end to going to matches at that time.

I also have some fond memories of the era where Batts, Speedo and Vinnie who lived up Shadwell way were in the team. There were some great times and Speedo would join us as we would leave Elland Road to go to the Red Lion tap room. We would have gammon, egg and chips and be just in time to watch Cilla's Blind Date which Speedo loved. We did that for every home match for a couple of seasons. They were good times and have given me some lovely memories, especially as Speedo is not here anymore.

One of my best memories was travelling to Barcelona's ground to see Leeds take on Stuttgart.

With the usual celebration drinks and chants of "We are the Champions, Champions of Europe" everyone headed for Los Ramblas. A good friend of mine, James Brown was there with us that night and had a moment of inspiration in the lap dancing bar, "it doesn't get any better than this, beer, women and Leeds United! We should re-live this through a Mag!!"

His magazine "*Loaded*" went on to outsell all the lifestyle magazines at the time, becoming one of the most successful lad's magazines of all time ... all after a night out watching Leeds!

Memories – Neale Sheldon, Stoke Whites.

I was fortunate enough to be allowed access behind the scenes at Reserve and Youth fixtures during the 1980–93 era by coach Peter Gumby.

I did some scouting reports during our first FA Youth Cup success, even sneaking a video camera into a couple of matches. Video cameras weren't small things back in the 80s and early 90s either. As well as getting film footage of opponents such as Stoke and QPR, I managed to get into Norwich's training ground to watch them go through various free kick and corner routines, until their coach suddenly realised I was taking too much of a keen interest and promptly stopped the training session. He sent the players indoors and accused me of being a b*****d spy from Leeds! He did his nut down at Carrow Road later that evening after he saw me going into the victorious Leeds dressing room after the match.

Back in the 80s we had a good crew of supporters and parents that followed the youth team and I'd like to mention two in particular that got to a good whack of Reserve and Youth matches. Julian Barker from Sheffield did a lot of match reports for the Leeds match day programmes and the late Howard

Sheldon who was a long-time member of the Griffin Supporters Club Branch, who at one time must have held the record for the amount of Leeds First Team, Reserve and Youth team matches attended whether they were League, Cup or Friendly based. Howard was a collar and tie man who worked at Leeds University as an accountant. I can remember him standing on the touchline at a Youth fixture in Rotherham with his feet up to the ankles in deep mud soaked wet through.

Peter Gumby used to look after us regulars who watched the Youth Team and he'd send out a player with cups of tea from the dressing room. On one occasion Simon Grayson who was Youth team captain, was sent out with some tea and he was too busy chatting to us to notice that all the players had gone in for the pre-match team talk. "Oh s**t" he said, "I think I've missed the team talk and I'm supposed to be leading the lads out," with that Grayson sneaked back into the dressing room!

Billy Bremner was also a lovely guy who appreciated folks supporting the youth and reserves. I spent many an hour in his office before midweek reserve fixtures, supping tea and talking football, or even nipping across the road to the paper shop to get Billy 20 Bensons. The apprentices loved Billy; he would be out on Fullerton Park in a suit and shoes having a knock about with them.

One of my first conversations with Billy was about a nasty little sod playing at right-back for the youth team; he had an edge to him. Billy said he thought he was going to be something special, it was non-other than a young David Batty.

Howard Wilkinson was a different kettle of fish, he was very hard to work out and one minute he would be thanking you for your support for turning up to an away reserve fixture on a dark, rain soaked night in places such as Newcastle, Grimsby or Birmingham. He thought some of us were totally mad, he just didn't get the fact that Leeds for me wasn't just the first team, it was all the Leeds teams, it was the camaraderie with players, grounds staff or anyone associated with our great club.

On other occasions Wilkinson was quite angry at times that one or two of us found out about private practice matches and behind closed doors friendlies. Good old Peter Gumby sometimes tipped us off about matches, "don't tell the gaffer", he would say. One particular match springs to mind, a hastily arranged Reserve XI match took place on the afternoon before a mid-week first team match. After morning training, Peter Gumby whispered to me; follow the team coach from the West Stand car park at 2.30 pm. The match was more of a fitness match for the likes of Mike Whitlow who had just joined us from non-league Witton Albion.

Just after half time, Gumby was getting anxious as Dick Bate, one of Wilko's coaches hadn't turned up to watch the match. Instead of going on the team coach Dick Bate had decided to drive himself to some College grounds where the match was being played. Anyway Mike Whitlow instead of taking it easy and getting in some match fitness, had gone in for a robust tackle taking the ball, two attackers and the referee out in one lunging slide tackle. Whitlow had taken a knock, and Gumby had helped a hobbling Whitlow to the dressing room after shouting to me to keep an eye on things. Here is me shouting at players from the touchline, apparently in charge, when Dick Bate saunters up, no Peter Gumby in sight. I had been taking notes of scorers etc, so that pacified Dick Bate somewhat, but he was baffled as to how I knew about the match, saying Howard wouldn't be pleased as it was a private match.

The funny thing is, Wilko was laughing about me being there next time I saw him. I think Wilko gave it up as a bad job trying to keep Leeds fans away, however, his brain plan of Thorp Arch went someway to stopping fans from watching training, Wilko hated fans watching training at Elland Road. John Reynolds the grounds man was another lovely bloke, who would let you through the groundsman's entrance between the West Stand and The Gelderd End and he let you wander inside the ground as long as you behaved yourself. Again Wilko wasn't amused when he spotted me in the Lowfield seats watching a behind doors match. John Reynolds had kindly let me in and I'd sneaked into the Lowfields via the bar areas of the Gelderd. Wilko caught me in the car park after the match and gloomily said, "I suppose you will be doing a match report!"

The Batty family; you could write a book on them alone! I was fortunate enough to be on friendly terms with David Batty's parents, Alan and Mary, a lovely down to earth, Yorkshire couple.

I had a couple of near escapes down at Chelsea and Millwall. At Chelsea there were about 20 of us in the complimentary seats behind the dugouts at Stamford Bridge; we all knew the score and we didn't communicate except for the odd nod and wink. Just before the match started, in breezes Mary Batty with a Leeds scarf round her neck and promptly sits amongst us. I don't know who was more surprised us or the ugly Chelsea lot who were gawping at the brazen lady in the Leeds scarf.

Anyway, I managed to whisper to Mary, that it may be a good idea to hide the scarf and to keep quiet. Unfortunately, Leeds scored early on in the match, the Leeds fans behind the goal were going mad and so was the lone Mary Batty celebrating behind the Chelsea dugout. Luckily the coppers stepped in to stop a few Chelsea scumbags from having a go at Mary.

The next hairy moment came at Millwall on a weekday evening before a Full Members Mickey Mouse Cup match. I'd got to London early and had just come out of New Cross Gate tube station; there were loads of useful Millwall supporters hanging around just waiting for Leeds to come. I was minding my own business walking down to the ground when, an old Rover car pulled up on the opposite side of the road, "Hey Stokie, which way t'ground?" boomed a nice West Yorkshire accent from Alan Batty in the Rover car. Quick as a flash, I'd run across the road, jumped in the back of the car and shouted for f***s sake drive quickly. Alan Batty sped off, not before a couple of bricks and a bottle had been thrown at his car, looking through the back window there were several Millwall running after the car!

Memories – Lee Hession.

15 October 1977 was the date my father announced to me aged around eight, that we were to go to Elland Road as Leeds United were taking on the mighty Liverpool.

I had never visited Elland Road before and with the introduction of the Premier League a vast dream away, all I can recollect about football was watching either Leeds or Sheffield United on the television on a Sunday. (Martin Tyler's voice still takes me back 38 years to those days of Ray Hankin (Leeds) and Alan Woodward (blunts)). Dare I say it, but I did not know then that a supporter only supported one team back then, as far as I knew only us and the blunts existed. So we set off from home in search of an elderly gentleman by the name of Harold who lived near 'Sheila's café', who as a friend to the players, was a ticket tout and so had our tickets for the West Stand.

We entered the West Stand to a crescendo of noise in what is now the area B4. The crowd was over forty-five thousand and very busy with Leeds fans mulling around the bar area. Being eight years old I was starting to get quite nervous as I had never been anywhere as busy before, I then followed my old man up the few stairs to the seating area. Our seats where positioned high up in the West and I remember feeling nervous of the occasion as the higher we climbed the stairs the more frightened I became. Heights were never my thing and I became scared, I told my father that I could not go any further as I felt the higher I went the chance of falling became greater so I said that I would go back to the bar area and stay there where I felt safe.

Upstairs in the stands my dad must have been well cheesed off having paid probably two to three pounds for a ticket for his son who was not even watching the match. I am not sure how long I was stood around listening to the chanting and singing, for after a while my father found me and said that I could sit with someone else on their knee about half way up where it was less scary.

I sat on the knee of this portly gentleman as I tried to take in the match, the atmosphere was immense and most of the crowd cheered as Gwyn Thomas scored a goal for Leeds. I was totally in awe of the ten men wearing the white admiral shirt with the blue admiral logos down the sleeves, David Harvey was either wearing a Blue or green shirt, the blue being my favourite as it did not conform to the traditional green.

When I was fifteen years old, I stood on the Kop for the first time with some friends who I had met in Morley. We paid our pre Bates pittance and walked up the stairs to see the Gelderd End slowly filling up. I remember the Kop being packed, but what surprised and shocked me the most, was that seven years after my first visit to Elland Road I realised that the Kop was all standing whereas when it was packed out in 1977 I thought everyone, like us, were all seated.

It was not until sometime after the Liverpool match that my dad had said to me, "remember that man whose knee you were sat on for the Liverpool match? He was non-other than Paul Luty, the actor who played *Nobby* the barman in the TV comedy *Love thy neighbour*".

Looking back, I did not fall in love with Leeds United at that match, it was the subsequent matches over the next few years versus Spurs, WBA, Arsenal and Southampton (Frank Worthington's debut) that I fell in love with Leeds United. Now aged 44, I guess Leeds United is part of my family now and wherever I go, my Leeds United shadow 'HAS' to follow!

Andrew Butterwick – Travels of a Leeds fan at http://leedsfan.blogspot.co.uk/
My first MATCH was in 1972. My Grandma and Grandad lived in Beeston near Cross Flats park. On a Saturday, we would visit them and Dad would go to the match and afterwards have tea, which always consisted of tinned Pilchards, a boiled egg and salad followed by tinned peaches and carnation milk. Dad would pick up a *'Green Un'* on the way back from the match and I would devour the detail from front to back whilst listening to *Sports Report* on Grandad's crackly wireless. Then the time came when I was allowed to go to a real match and not just listen to the roar of the crowd from the top of Beeston

hill. We were playing man utd, who at the time were just starting a decline that would see them relegated to what was then Division Two. Their team was still sprinkled with stars the press adored Charlton, Best, Stepney, Kidd et al and Dirty Leeds were at their footballing peak destroying teams with a brand of football that has never been repeated.

I remember the walk to the ground as if it was yesterday. There was the hustle and bustle of the river of people flowing down the hill to the ground. The underlying threat of violence around each corner, this was also the peak of hooliganism and man utd had earned a fearsome reputation that Leeds United were more than happy to match. As we got nearer the ground the excitement grew along with the intensity of the smell of burger and onions. Clutching a programme, I entered the ground through the Lowfields Stand turnstiles. The terrace was packed and not all were Leeds fans. I wriggled to the front to get a better view as the first half flew by. It was 0–0 at half-time. The second half would stick with me for an eternity. Leeds destroyed the old enemy 5–1 and by the end were toying with the hated man utd by playing keep ball to the joyous Ole's from a packed crowd. I remember Eddie Gray and Peter Lorimer taunting the reds at a corner. Eddie with his elbow resting on the corner flag waiting for a defender to tackle him before shimmying round the flailing attempted tackle. After the match, I remember been dragged quickly through the streams of crowds leaving Elland Road as sporadic fights broke out between rival fans, only stopping to buy a paper from the man shouting "Greeeeeeeeeeeeen Un". The Pilchards and Peaches tasted particularly sweet that evening. I was hooked on the most addictive drug in the world ... Leeds United!

Dave Cocker.

I have been pleased to have been able to help out my old mate Rob Collins, Bobby's son. I have recently managed to reunite him with Bobby Collins 1965 FA Cup Final Shirt which has been 'recovered' after being 'missing' for 40 years. The shirt was recently handed over to Rob at Elland Road with a few celebration drinks before and after the match! There has not been too much good news about Leeds United recently, so it is nice to have a story that warms the heart.

Terje 'On Tour' Hansen from Norway.

I am a regular visitor from Norway having seen 473 live matches during my time of supporting Leeds and five seasons as a season ticket holder. I have not missed a league match at Elland Road since 14 March 2009, with last season being my best ever on tour by attending 32 out of 55 matches Leeds played. That is an excellent achievement for me as I don't live in the UK and have to travel so far to every match.

I first came over to Leeds in the early seventies and was introduced to Eric Carlile who was part of the Leeds United Supporters Club. Initially I stayed with Eric when I came over from 12–17 May 1978 as well as eight or nine trips after that. Since then I have stayed in bed and breakfast accommodation and cheap hotels. I was in Sweden in 1984 for an indoor friendly v Djurgaarden and the first match I attended was Viking Stavanger against Leeds in 1976. I have travelled to Europe to Barcelona in the Champions League and Spartak Moscow in 1999 for a UEFA Cup match. Although the results of the play-off finals were not good for Leeds in the end, I went to both Cardiff against Watford and Wembley against Doncaster. Other disappointments were the League Cup Final at Wembley in 1996 against Aston Villa and Hillsborough in 1987 for the FA Cup semi-final v Coventry. However, one thing that I am proud of is the fact that I have seen all four goals that David Batty scored live!

Highlights for me include being at Bournemouth when Leeds got promoted back to the First Division in 1990 and also for being at Elland Road when we played Norwich for the last match of the season, when we won the First Division title in 1992. At the start of the 1995–96 season on 21 August, I was at Elland Road to see Leeds take on Liverpool. This was the day that

Yeboah scored a screamer of a goal that ended up being voted goal of the year and also meant that Leeds won the match 1–0.

Cup matches included the 4–3 win over Liverpool in the Charity Shield at Wembley in 1992 which included a hat trick from Eric Cantona. The famous January Third, remember the date, match in 2010 at Old Trafford in the FA Cup Third Round, when Leeds beat man utd on their home turf with a goal by Jermaine Beckford. Some other special moments include all the cup matches against Premiership teams when Leeds were in League One which had some very good nights amongst them. I also managed to attend most of the Champions League home matches too.

When I travel to Elland Road for a weekend home match, even if only attending one, I endure a long 20 hours of waiting/travelling time. By the end of next season, I am hoping to have attended over 500 matches including attending some away ones which will be a remarkable achievement for me! I have mentioned some of the big matches I have attended already in this recount of my memories, but another of my favourite moments was the promotion day from League One in 2010 which was great. Also to be able to watch so many matches in the Champions League holds special memories for me.

A record I also have was travelling through four countries in one day! After Barcelona away I travelled to Amsterdam, then Stavanger where I met my mum at the airport for some clean clothes. I then checked in to fly to Newcastle, got the train to Leeds for a league match on the Saturday, then a Champions League match on the Tuesday.

Heidi's comments are: "This is dedication and Terje is an absolutely fantastic role model of a Leeds United fan and shows why they are special!"

Arnie Pirie from Meanwood now lives in Aberdeen but went round with us in the seventies.

We went in your mini once to Liverpool with Bob Vasey and Sue or Karen I think. I remember my dad saying that the car wouldn't make it over the M62, but it managed it both ways with no problems. I got two tickets to see Leeds and Rangers at Elland Road. We flew down to Manchester airport in the morning and were returning to Glasgow the next day. On the return trip we found ourselves on the plane with the whole Rangers team including McCoist, Walter Smith and Hateley. In later years I was in Peter Lorimer's bar and ordered a taxi to take us to Meanwood. I couldn't believe it when the driver thought I was from Aberdeen and hadn't been to Leeds before, when he tried charging us £30 for a fare that should have been £6.50 max! He got short shrift from me and shouldn't have done a detour!

Keith Gaunt – memories.

I can always remember the first match I attended in 1964 at Derby away, because the coach went over a hump backed bridge and I promptly threw up. The bridge is still there in the middle of a roundabout in Derby to this day.

I drove to Sunderland when we had only been given 500 tickets for the match in 1989–90. I was trying to get some more tickets for some of my mates so set off from Surrey straight after work on a Friday evening, carried on past Leeds until I got to Sunderland. On arrival, I kept asking Sunderland fans if they had memberships as the tickets were only on sale to Bronze, Silver and Gold memberships. It also would have meant them not wanting a ticket for the match as they were only allowed one ticket each, but this proved impossible. What I didn't know was that I was on CCTV until the coppers turned up to ask me what I was doing? I said I was buying tickets as we had only been given 500. I was told our tickets had already been sent to Leeds and I replied yes, 500 but we need 5,000! The coppers told me to leave and then escorted me out of Sunderland with a cop car in front of me and one behind me, to ensure I did indeed leave!

When we were banned from Carlisle, we were due to play someone at home on a Saturday morning prior to the match. I got up at 6.00 am and drove up to Carlisle to be there for the ticket office opening at 9.00 am. I bought some tickets and then drove back to Elland Road where I arrived back in time for the match.

Leeds were due to play Hapoel Tel Aviv of Israel in a UEFA cup match in 2002 but because of troubles in Israel, the match was switched to Florence, Italy. I came out of this one with the match ball. Prior to the match I'd been for a steak dinner and had a couple bottles of Chianti before going into the ground. During the match Wilcox kicked the ball high up into the stand and the ball landed next to me. It was a long time before I even realised the ball was there, so at the end of the match when it was still there I took it with me. John Reynolds got this autographed by the team for me.

We had played PSV Eindhoven in a couple of pre-season matches before we were drawn against them in a UEFA Cup match in 2002. We had been in town before everyone was put on buses to go to the ground. Spud and I decided we wanted to go to a bar so walked back as I knew where we were going as I'd been three times before. We found that we were only allowed a jug of Heineken if we bought a pizza, so did this. As we had already eaten we drank the beer but left the pizza before going back to the ground.

I travelled to Toronto in 1981 for a four team tournament so we had two matches to play not one. I was going up to the ticket office for tickets when Maxwell Holmes, a Leeds United director saw me there. He said if I had come all this way, then I would be a guest of the club and go in directors' box for the two matches. At the first match I met the Canadian chairman, an ex-Bolton Wanderer's official who asked for a favour, as he had a guest from Benfica and could I look after him. I couldn't believe it when I was introduced to Eusébio who was considered as one of the greatest footballers of all time. Unfortunately the language barriers meant I couldn't talk to him as he was Portuguese and couldn't speak English and I couldn't speak his language. It was still a fantastic opportunity of meeting with the great man though. When the tournament finished the Canadian chairman asked me to come and look at a plastic pitch, as they were considering getting one as QPR in England had one and he wanted my opinion. After running around it the next day in football boots, I told him it was sub-standard and he said thank you we won't buy it then! When I was leaving the chairman said if Canada qualified for the World Cup in 1982, we would be their guests for the whole tournament, but unfortunately they lost in the play-off.

I travelled to Tokyo with Mick Hewitt and others. Mick met Fotherby, a Leeds United director when he was going for some tickets, so Mick asked him for some. Fotherby said that if we had a current premier card we could have them. Unfortunately we had set off on 31 July and they'd been issued on 1 August and it was now the 3! We didn't get any tickets which wasn't very charitable after travelling all this way to watch Leeds United, so Mick had to go and buy them.

Leeds played a match in Johannesburg I think it was 1995. Joan Armatrading a singer was staying in the same hotel and gave us some free tickets for her concert. The match was around the time when Lucas Radebe joined the club. I remember the nightmare of getting picked up by the coach at the airport and of the coach driver Noel driving down the road with his feet on the steering wheel whilst smoking wacky baccy. Whilst in South Africa, Mick Garner and I got a taxi driver for the day which cost 50p and he took us to his football match, Soweto Swifts in Cape Town, which was televised all over South Africa. We were the only two white faces in the ground and the cameras kept panning in at us two because of this. When we saw the Leeds United players a couple of days later, Radebe said how fantastic it was to see white faces at a South African football match.

 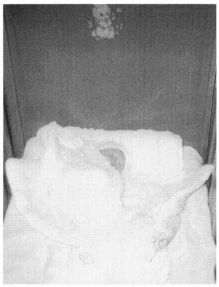

Left: Jamie mascot v Luton 2 Nov 1988 v Luton Littlewoods Cup
Right: Charlotte 6 days old – youngest Leeds fan in the crèche
at Elland Road v Crystal Palace 23.3.91

Left: Michelle, Lee Chapman and Jamie 1991 after Charlotte died
Right: Michelle and Jamie 1992

Danielle mascot v Charlton

Chapter 14

Loyal Supporters

Leeds United have always had a hard core of loyal fans who travelled all over the country and world to see them. In the seventies, many of us had something in common which was to follow our team and keep out of trouble at away matches. The fans never all stood together at away matches unless there were great numbers there. You just paid to go onto the terraces and once through the turnstiles, found a place to stand where you had a good view. If there was chanting and singing from our fans in a group, you could go and join them if there were many of us in attendance. If there were only a few Leeds fans and you wanted to stay anonymous or not attract any attention, you would stay away from groups of Leeds fans and instead stand in isolated pockets all over the terraces. You could be wearing your colours and suddenly find yourself surrounded by opposition fans. You certainly became adept at hiding your colours, by whipping your scarf off from round your neck and stuffing it up your jumper or down your trousers. You had to be quick as well. Fans who were regularly involved in fighting never used to wear their colours which enabled them to mingle easily. The only reason they knew their own fans was by recognising faces or they knew them as mates or by name. Even though hiding scarves down trousers was a good idea, sometimes our lads were spotted by the opposition fans when their scarves worked their way down the trouser leg. The ends of the tassels could be seen coming out of the trouser leg and ended up with the lads getting attacked and in some cases getting a severe beating.

It didn't matter where I went; I didn't want trouble or looked for any but always seemed to be in the thick of it, probably because I wore my colours. Even though I was scared, I was proud to be a Leeds fan and wanted to show who I supported, but obviously by wearing my colours this highlighted the fact that I was a Leeds fan. I was very hot headed about the fact that I wanted to be able to wear my colours to away matches, because at Elland Road it seemed away fans could walk around the ground without any bother. Away from the ground may not have been so easy for them, but it irritated me that we weren't allowed the same courtesy at their ground.

There were times though when I did hide my colours because you had to continuously assess the situation. Even then it didn't matter how hard you tried to hide who you supported, but you could be sussed out very easily. At Anfield one year, it may have been that we had been spotted wearing our colours before the match or maybe it was just a fluke. After the match I had hidden my scarves only for a Liverpool fan to pat me on the head and say: "hard luck, better luck next year!" after we had just been beaten 2–0.

At a different match at Anfield, one of our supporters was chased by some Liverpool fans before the match had even kicked off! He ran into someone's house and straight up the stairs to get away from them but it didn't stop them. They just ran into the house after him and kicked the hell out of him on the landing. Luckily the house owner came and stopped it, but what a shock they must have had! Another story of the good and bad at Anfield was about a Leeds fan who was attacked in the car park by Liverpool fans as he tried to get back to the coaches. He was kicked unconscious and it was only because of a Liverpool fan dragging him into the back of his van that he escaped. The Good Samaritan then drove him to the coach and dropped him off when he came round. Anfield was also a bad place for another Leeds fan when he was kicked in the face by a copper's horse. Having the imprint of the horseshoe on his face showed the seriousness of it and as far as I'm aware this did have an impact on his life in later years.

Whilst travelling by train to one match we met some Liverpool and man utd fans who said we should wear the horrid colours of red and white, no way! It is because of them and trouble from their fans that we hated the colour so much and still do. When I look back at things, the hatred of red came about because of all the trouble we encountered during the seventies from opposition fans who wore those colours. We had trouble at Middlesbrough, Arsenal, Forest, Stoke City, Sunderland as well as the two teams just mentioned above who all played in red, so it is no wonder the hatred is there! Red is therefore, also a swear word in our family and nothing we own is that dreadful colour and even the children have been raised to hate it! This hatred of red is also a bond with many other Leeds fans who travelled to matches around this time.

The Leeds coaches often came under attack from other fans both before and after matches. At one match at Chelsea one coach had some windows put through on arriving at the ground. As well as putting the windows through, the Chelsea fans threw a pram and a dustbin on to the coach!! To make matters worse the same coach was attacked after the match but by Tottenham fans and ended up with some more windows put through. At another match in the capital some of the coaches were attacked by Millwall fans after Leeds had been playing at Charlton. The funny thing was they got the shock of their lives as Leeds fans jumped out of the broken windows after them before the coach had even stopped. They certainly ran away quickly!! Despite trouble that did occur, the one thing that became a bond with our supporters, was to get together at the next match and talk about the experiences that we have had. The empathy that Leeds fans showed each other was because many of us had either seen, or become involved in violence, through no fault of our own.

When travelling by the special trains, we would always have a welcoming committee of opposition fans as they knew when you would be arriving at the station. You had to keep your wits about you even if there was an escort by the coppers, as often these escorts were infiltrated by the opposition fans but it was fine if everyone stayed in a large group. When the special trains stopped running to football matches due to all the damage that was caused to them by football fans in general, we started travelling by coaches. This meant that we still often had a welcoming committee of the opposition fans when we arrived. It depended on which ground we had gone to and also what time we actually arrived there. More often than not we arrived over two hours prior to kick-off and there was nowhere for you to go until they opened the turnstiles. If we managed to go to a ground where the fans weren't waiting for us to cause trouble, we would go to the pub, but this didn't happen very often. As the opposition had an idea of the times we would be arriving and also where the coaches would be parked, it was very hard to avoid coming into contact with them.

Later when it got really bad with attacks and damage to the coaches from other fans throwing bricks at them, some of the coach companies stopped travelling to matches for a while. We knew it wasn't our fault, because the majority of times it was only as the windows were put through that you knew the first thing about it. The cost of replacing the broken windows though meant that it wasn't worthwhile for the coach companies to run to football matches. Although this stopped happening in later years, recently some Leeds coaches had a window put through at Millwall and I have also heard that a Hull City coach was attacked at Liverpool. I certainly hope this kind of incident doesn't start coming back as it should stay in the past.

In 1975 we travelled to a match at Stoke City. After we arrived at their ground, we went round to the Stoke end and were buying programmes when a gang of Stoke fans arrived. We felt sure that they could have attacked the Leeds fans, as there weren't many of us outside the ground, but they just went by probably as they had no bricks to chuck at us this time, as they had in the past. I was talking to some lads from Bradford who asked if I had a picture of their banner from Ipswich and said they were famous as well when I said I had. We were all mad when we lost the match and after the final whistle had blown the Leeds fans set off for the coach park, which meant we had to go past their end. We didn't get far before seeing all the Stoke fans ahead of us who were coming out of the Bootham end. All of a sudden they started throwing bricks at us so we got out of the way and ran back into the ground. We made our way further up the terraces and came out again to find the Stoke fans had disappeared with the Leeds fans in pursuit. When we got back to the coach a Leeds man was going mad because they had gone for his little lad.

Our coach was the last to leave Stoke and our driver took a wrong turning and we ended up going to Preston. By the time we arrived at Birch Services on the M62 we found we had missed the entire rumpus with Chelsea fans. Loads of Leeds coaches had pulled into the services only to find a welcoming committee of Chelsea fans who were on their way home from their away match. They had come across the bridge to our side of the motorway to fight our fans but they got more than they bargained for. They thought they could have a go at our fans, but bit off more than they could chew when Leeds fans put up a good fight and soon returned the Chelsea fans to the other side of the motorway.

You can't ban us!

Following trouble at Millwall in 1985, Leeds fans were banned from away matches at Carlisle, Wimbledon and Hull City. Well that certainly put the cat amongst the pigeons, because Leeds fans en masse who went to all the matches would not be put off that easily. For the first match at Carlisle loads of Leeds fans including myself made the trip to Carlisle to get tickets. I took my daughter in her pushchair on the train and just headed up there to buy some tickets. I noted the train stopped at Appleby so made a mental note of the place in case I was asked for my address.

When I arrived at Carlisle and made my way to the ground I found that there was a queue of fans buying tickets. When it was my turn I was asked who I was buying my eight tickets for so I said my family. They asked for my address so I gave them the first line of my address together with Appleby which they accepted. It's a good job they didn't ask for a postcode as that would have blown my cover well and truly. I came away with my eight tickets and was very happy on the way home. I wasn't the only Leeds fan in the queue either!

On the day of the match I travelled up with Mick from Tadcaster and some others in two cars. We weren't wearing any colours for once because we had been told that the coppers would be stopping any Leeds fan getting near the ground. Well that didn't work did it, because when we had parked up and gone up to the ground, we found out that they had been sending Leeds fans to one end of the ground to keep us all in the same place! The best one was when they asked a lad where he was from and he replied 'Donny'. It was lovely to see the amount of Leeds fans who had turned up to watch the match despite the ban!

In the meantime, Leeds fans had also been getting their tickets for both the Wimbledon and Hull matches. It was funny to hear that the Halifax lads had got their tickets through a Chelsea fan. He had gone to see Chelsea play in London and made a trip to Wimbledon's ground to get them a load of tickets. Leeds fans all over the country were helping each other to get tickets and once again we had got ours. Wimbledon had a big shock on the day of the match when all the Leeds fans who had gotten tickets turned up en masse, but we were allowed into the ground without any problems. By the time it came for the Hull City match, the coppers had heard that Leeds fans had got tickets all over the ground already, so the ban for us attending away matches was lifted prior to it!

Luton Town also banned all away supporters after trouble with Millwall in March 1985. They had only been playing for 14 minutes when play was held up, although it eventually restarted. Lots of seats were smashed and although it was nothing to do with us, we had to suffer. This match meant that some of the southern based Leeds fans helped us out with tickets. Phillip and I received two membership cards for the Luton Town end so we were able to go. I thought I would give the game away whilst going through the turnstiles, because I put the card in upside down!! What an idiot, but at least I got in. This was a match where you had to keep a low profile though and not let on you were a Leeds fan.

We reciprocated the generosity of our southern based Leeds fans by getting tickets for them when Bradford had a low allocation of tickets for Valley Parade. We knew at the start of the season that there wouldn't be many tickets available when we played them, so many Leeds fans had already bought membership cards from Bradford at the start of the season. When tickets went on sale I drove through to Bradford to buy them, but as usual I got lost trying to find the ground. Once I had parked up I found lots of other Leeds fans in the queue buying tickets. I still have the ID card somewhere too! Where there's a will there's a way!

After relegation at West Bromwich Albion in the old First Division in 1982, Leeds United fans had restrictions imposed upon them for away matches. As behaviour had improved when Leeds were due to play Bradford City at Odsal, the powers that be refused to listen to Leeds' concerns about lifting the restrictions in time for the match. It was as if they wanted something to kick-off because it seemed like the whole of Yorkshire had turned up for the match. The club's predictions were right as trouble did indeed kick-off all over the place as mentioned previously. After this in 1986 the red U card was brought in for all Leeds fans travelling to away matches. This was an ID card to ensure you were eligible to buy tickets and you had to show it to get into the grounds. Leeds fans still have all ticket matches wherever they play to this day, with membership cards in place to buy match tickets.

The resilience of Leeds supporters over the years has been fantastic despite obstacles being put in place to thwart their loyalty and wherever we have been, they would turn up in their thousands. When Leeds played Doncaster Rovers at the new Wembley stadium in the Play-off Finals in 2008 in front of over 75,000 fans, the official number of Leeds fans in attendance was 43,700. The funny thing though was seeing a group of fans appear in the Doncaster Rovers end and once everyone realised they were Leeds fans, the group just got bigger and bigger with fans getting out of their seats amongst the Doncaster fans and joining the Leeds fans.

Leeds United's fan base is second to none. Despite all the traumas and tribulations that have happened over the years, it remains a fact that the supporters have stuck with them through thick and thin. We were relegated into the Third Division (League One), the lowest point in their history but that season was one of the best supporting Leeds. We were docked 15 points as mentioned earlier in the book, but all this did was ensure the Leeds fans were united in their stance and the camaraderie grew and grew.

Our support away from home during this last season 2013–14 has been fantastic especially since there has been such a lack of football on the pitch. Despite the turmoil going on at the club, the fans still go to the matches with the view of having a good time. This consists of singing, throwing beer around (must have too much money if they can afford to throw it away), dressing up in fancy dress and last year at Birmingham we had a lad doing a belly slide along the floor stripped to his underpants! The more "normal" of us enjoy the company of our fans, the pub stops, the getting together with others and can enjoy ourselves that way. Whichever way our supporters want to go to matches, they are still the best fans in the world for their loyalty!

Karl Shepherd.

Remember 'The Club Show' on Sky Sports on a Saturday morning? They followed a group of fans from a different club every week. When it came to Leeds, Sky sent a camera crew out to Germany to come with us. The amount of s**t we got in for that from the Military was amazing! We had it sussed, with us all being forces, we got what were called fuel vouchers, which meant that we got a discount on already cheap fuel, it literally cost us around 30p a litre!

We stockpiled them and with the (again) discounted mini bus hire, filled RAF fuel containers (some of the Germany Whites were RAF for their sins lol), which we sat in the back of the minibus. Illegal as hell, but it was cheap!! Because we had a mini bus coming back from Germany every week, we also got frequent traveller discounts on the P&O Dover-Calais ferry and yes I know we're going back to the late 80s early 90s, but it cost us a grand total of around £35 each for travel from Germany–Leeds–Germany!!! The best of it is, we had an 'Agreement' with a certain pub in London that we used to drop duty-frees off with them every week. Everyone had a separate thing, mine was King Edward Cigars, I'd buy a few boxes of 50 cigars for 33 marks (just over a tenner) and flog them to the pub for £80. Profit every trip!

The amount of beer we got through on trips was legendary and one of the lads (who shall remain nameless) was known for supping Carlsberg Elephant beer as though it was going out of fashion. Anyway, due to careful editing, in one shot he's trolleyed on CEB and literally in the next shot he's driving the mini bus on the last leg into Leeds! The fact he'd been off the beer for over 12 hours wasn't mentioned!

The main reason for all the s**t we got dropped in was because as Military, in those days the threat from the IRA was very real, which meant you had to be unpredictable, vary your routes, check your vehicles for bombs etc. There we are, all forces, telling this Sky camera crew EXACTLY what route we take every week, giving out all sorts of personal details as well as the odd state secret, while p****d out of our brains in a mini bus loaded with illegal fuel and duty frees!! I personally got fined £300.

Brian Austin memories.

Zurich pre-season friendly in August 1980.

Tez Overend and I set off from Halifax and I parked my car in an industrial estate where I used to deliver goods to (I couldn't do that now) and then went to Heathrow airport for the flight to Zurich. We flew for an hour with the pilot and it was fantastic seeing the Matterhorn, a landmark mountain in Switzerland that is also a symbol of the country, getting bigger as we were coming nearer. We landed in Zurich and all the Halifax lads were there waiting for us including Soggy, Dallas, Captain and Arbuck who were all steaming. We met some man utd fans in the train station who'd had some trouble themselves, who told us not to go into town as there were 300 of their fans there. We told them they'd better go away fast, as we were expecting another four Leeds fans to arrive and you'll get chased some more! Tez, Glyn Brand and me had booked into a hotel and then all the Halifax lads sneaked into the hotel and shared the room, but no one dared to nick my bed!

We met Brod and Gary Edwards and loads of others and we were stuck for two days without anything to do, so we went to a travel agent and booked a trip up the mountain for 24 of us where a James Bond film had been filmed two weeks previously. The guide on the bus was trying to speak English and be funny saying: "in these villages where they make holes for the cheese" and "if you look at the kerb edge they are high up so little people can jump in front of a bus to commit suicide!!" Everyone had a great time throwing snowballs at each other; it was just something that happened. We started descending the mountain in a cable car that held 50 people and had other tourists on. I was stood right at the front near the window and as the car went over a pylon I grabbed the bar to hold on, thinking I was going to fall over. Soggy looked at me and said: "we are 8,000 feet up in the air, what good will holding onto the bar do you?" On another night we were in a bar and these lads from Featherstone rugby were in too. There had previously been some run ins in Halifax between the two sets of fans and it ended up with them having a set to with each other. In another bar we were singing the *Alouette* song and were told to keep it down by the barman, so everyone went down on their knees so he gave up! We had a good time in Zurich.

Malaga.

Johnny Reggie and I went on our own and stopped in Benalmadena next to a pub called the Red Lion. I met an Irish bird and we went to the Torremolinos nightclub which had bouncers with guns and was the best one I'd ever been in. It had a swimming pool downstairs and in the middle of the pool with a six feet stage around him sat the DJ. At night time they had a competition with the winner being King of the castle, where competitors threw everyone off the stage until the last one was left on to become the King. They also did it with females too who became Queen of the castle. It was in a posh area where the jet set lived, that we played the two teams in the tournament. We hadn't met other Leeds fans at this time as everyone was scattered all over and not together. It was the middle of summer and we went to the first match by train. At the ground we met Gary Edwards and others who had come by coach and we went back with them on it. They got a lad drunk who had just got married, made him sing on the coach and he nearly fell out with his wife over this. We had a good time and spent a week there, a lot of time in a pub called the Winston Churchill.

After the European Cup Final in Paris in 1975 we had to spend a lot of time in Calais as there was a strike on, delaying the ferries to return home. We stayed in one bar all night and only later found out that things had been going on all over town according to the Police. They came to the bar where we were and arrested us all saying we'd been smashing windows all night. A woman in the bar said no we had been there all night, but we were still taken away in the back of a cop van. This was later shown on BBC television and in the documentary I can be clearly seen in the back of the van being taken away! The BBC wouldn't let us say that we had done nothing wrong either and still showed the clip. Later on, the same woman who had stuck up for us earlier in the bar came to the cop station to say that they had got the wrong ones. We were then let go as we had done nothing wrong.

In Werder Bremen one of the Bradford lads was arrested for stabbing a lad and taken away. The coppers questioned him and a woman witness came to look at him, then said in German that it wasn't him. The coppers turned round and told the lad that the woman had identified him as the one who had done the stabbing. He replied in perfect German, that he knew exactly what she had said and he hadn't done it! They had to let him go then as he hadn't done anything wrong!

Going to PSV Eindhoven we ended up in a campsite next door to the PSV training ground which had a big bar. On that night there was a private do on and they let us all in and got everyone drunk. When the bar shut we took crates of beer with us and had these Dutch fans singing songs with us. The second time we played PSV we were going past their supporters club. Two blokes and a woman came running out to see us and said number 13 come in. There was a giant photo of when the ground was first opened on the wall and there at the front was Tez Overend with no shirt on and me with my number 13 yellow Leeds shirt on! You could see us both as plain as day with no one else near us, so I've no idea what we were doing. The photo had been taken from one of the floodlights of all round the ground in one shot. The last time we played there I went to try and find it again, but as it was in an old building that was now derelict I couldn't find it. I met a lad from Germany called Kurt who threatened to shoot someone with a starting pistol. We got a load of tickets for the match off an English lad who now played for PSV, who had previously played for Carlisle or Workington Town.

At Deportivo there was a bar on the beach which had a big glass case with a cup locked in it. They locked all the doors so no one could get in or out and got the cup out and put it on the table. It was so heavy that it took two men to lift it. They let everyone have 10 minutes to have their photos taken with it and then put it back in the locked case. I wish I'd had my camera with me but unfortunately didn't, but it was a fantastic opportunity. They then opened the bar doors again and found loads of people had been trying to get in.

A few years ago in 1995 I went to Chelsea with Carl from Halifax who is a Chelsea fan, Claire and Flapper. We were sat in the open end with the Chelsea fans; we had been sat there for a while when a copper came up to me and said excuse me but are you are a Leeds fan, when I was sat there with my Leeds shirt on! I got kicked out then as Claire was saying that's my dad and even the Chelsea fans were saying leave him he's alright!! On my way out the copper said his wife came from Leeds and my life won't be worth living if I tell her I've kicked a Leeds fan out! Once we were away from everyone he then took me into the main stand told me to put my jumper back on, cover my shirt up and don't say a bloody word!! I obviously met the only decent copper in London!! Leeds beat them with McAllister and Yeboah (2) scoring in a 3–0 win so I'm glad that I managed to stay in and see the match!

Ill health stops me going to matches now, but I will always follow Leeds United. The one thing that stands out in my mind is that no matter where you went, it was surprising how many people you would meet up with who you knew for years.

Marc Bracha – author of Bairdy's Gonna Get Ya!

My first match was in 1977–78 at home to Birmingham. Although I was very young at the time to remember too much about it, Leeds won 1–0 with a goal from Ray Hankin and it went from there. My dad took me to the home matches but after getting beaten at Elland Road 5–0 by Arsenal, I told my dad that I didn't want to go again as I was getting stick from the kids at school for following Leeds. I went to Norton Junior School in Doncaster and it was full of Spurs fans as they had won the FA Cup two years running, which has made me hate Spurs more than man utd over the years. My dad turned to me and said: "you will follow this club through thick and thin and through whatever is thrown at you". My dad understood what being Leeds is all about having seen the great Don Revie side play. My school books were full of me watching Leeds and I cried at school when Leeds were relegated at West Bromwich Albion in 1982, especially when we were getting hammered all the time.

Dad had brought me up on his own with help from my grandma so we couldn't go to every match as he had to work too. The Second Division days include memories of Eddie Gray and Billy Bremner managing Leeds and watching players who were my idols like Arthur Graham, Carl Harris, Ian Snodin, John Sheridan and Ian Baird. For some reason I didn't like Andy Linighan and if Leeds were beaten I would always blame him and wouldn't watch us on Grandstand. If Leeds won, as well as reading the paper that we had delivered, I would always go to the shop and buy a different one and read that match report too. It was after Paul Madeley's last match for Leeds that I began to understand what being Leeds was all about. When I was 15, with all the crowd trouble that was around at the time, my dad wasn't keen on me going to the matches on my own, but I started going by train. Wilko came along and put some glory back into watching Leeds and the rest is history.

My favourite season was 1989–90 when we were promoted from the Second Division. When we won the First Division in 1991–92 I took it for granted that we would have success for a long time, especially after my dad told me many stories about Revie's time at Leeds. I had started drinking alcohol by this time and I didn't fully appreciate the successful football that we had at that time. After this we had the Premiership, then came a few lean years. I have had Season Tickets in different parts of the ground. In the late eighties I was in Lowfields and then moved to the South Stand, West Stand Paddock before moving into the Kop when it became all seated and I kept the same seat for many years.

I moved down to Norwich in 2002 and wanted to settle down there. I got a job at Ladbrokes at a weekend for nine months which meant I couldn't attend matches as I was working Saturday and Sunday. Things changed when I got a job at Norwich Union and then later at Aviva when I started working Monday to Friday. In our relegation season in 2006–07 I missed a few matches at the start of the season but started travelling regularly to matches again and have only missed a handful since. I got to know a few of the lads when travelling by train and meeting up with others in pubs. Now I travel to home matches by car with my mates Shaun Powley and Paul Benson and I love the banter, because no matter how bad things are, I still go to matches thinking Leeds will win. Even if that doesn't work out, the banter is still there on the way home and I wouldn't change anything apart from the score obviously! The longer trips are great.

Marching on Together; I don't think there is any other club song where the words mean so much. "We've been through it all together and we've had our ups and downs, we're going to stay with you forever, at least until the world stops going round". The best atmosphere with this song blaring out from the Leeds fans was Leicester at home in April 1990 when we won 2–1. McAllister had equalised for Leicester after Leeds had been given the lead with a goal by Sterland. Time was running out when Strachan scored in the last few minutes to ensure Leeds got the three points to remain in the top two and keep our promotion hopes alive. I can remember looking across at the bedlam in the South Stand as the ball hit the back of the net and the crowd erupting in euphoria. The scenes and celebrations are something that will stay with me forever. In one sense you can't describe them, but anyone who was there that day will know what I mean. This is the bond that Leeds fans have and means so much to us all. I had sat in the West Stand for this one as my mate, who played for Leeds schoolboys, had got some tickets and my dad was over in Lowfields Road.

Disappointments for me include the FA Cup Fifth round at Aston Villa in January 2000 when Leeds lost their 2–0 lead through Harte and Bakke goals to lose 3–2 with a Carbone hat trick. I thought we were destined to win the cup that year but it wasn't to be. The same reason was the FA Cup Sixth round defeat at Wolves in March 1998 when Hasselbaink missed a penalty late on, so near yet so far! I've been lucky to see Leeds get promotion from the Second Division, win the First Division title, seen them in Europe but now I am 41, I am desperate to see them win the FA Cup. The 2006–07 season when we knew that relegation was coming as early as October, after the heavy 4–0 defeat at Elland Road by Stoke. We had had a terrible start to the season losing nine out of the first 13 matches. The following year with Denis Wise as manager during the - 15 points season was a fantastic time to be a Leeds fan. There is no doubt in my mind that Gordon Strachan was my best player and my all-time hero was John Sheridan. McAllister could also count as one of the best players on his day.

Now you have email and mobile phones so you can arrange to meet people. I've made some fantastic friendships over the years including big Mick

Hewitt, Gary Edwards, Shaun who has lived down here all his life, the lads and lasses who accompany me on trips from here and many others. On our return from Rochdale last season after our defeat of 2–0, no one spoke in the car all the way home. Shaun dropped Karen off, then Deano who has travelled with us for six or seven seasons. Deano said that was him done and I replied that I was looking forward to the next match at Hillsborough. That turned out well as we lost 6–0!! There is nothing like Leeds United for affecting your emotions. Away from home when Leeds are winning, there is no better place to be. MOT!

Gary Sleat

Shropshire Whites have been arranging travel to matches since 1969. We are a pretty vocal bunch with never a dull moment! Some of our memorable events include having an extra pub stop whilst waiting for Boris to be released from A&E following his swallow dive from the south stand upper to the lower tier. Mr Ash accompanying Huddersfield constabulary to their after match 'coffee session', we had to wait for him in the pub over the road from their headquarters. We have had dancing on London Bridge following one of the many trips to Millwall. We have to thank Mr Humph who drives the mini bus for us for putting up with our antics and eventually getting us back home.

Danielle left and Emily right

*Emily (left) –
Laura, Emily,
Hannah (right)*

*Danielle and Emily
at Elland Road*

*SLI Don Revie
Statue 21 May
2011 Paul Reaney,
Emily, Heidi and
Allan Clarke, photo
courtesy of Alex
Handley*

Rob, Alan Green, Lawrence and Connor Snodin at Charlton 9.11.13

Daz Norwich White at Charlton

Leeds salute Hannah, Alexis and Laura

Danielle, Emily, Hannah and Laura Christmas 2012
– photograph courtesy of Peter Howarth Photography

Chapter 15

Fun times

In later years my eldest daughter Michelle, her friend Claire and Brian Austin (number 13) a good friend of ours and my daughter's Godfather, all started travelling to away matches with the Halifax lads on the fun bus.

Michelle Kite – Leicester 1-0 Leeds on 28 September 1996

I had just turned 14 when I went to a match at Leicester with the Halifax branch of the Leeds United Supporters Club. I got my ticket for the match through the Halifax branch whereas, Brian and Claire had gotten theirs separately. Claire was visiting her Dad that weekend so was getting dropped off at the ground. Unfortunately, he dropped her off at the rugby ground by mistake, so Claire had to wander around the streets to find the ground. Brian went into the ground before me, but when I got to turnstile I was told I was in the wrong section. I then went around to the other entrance whilst Brian was going mad with the bloke on the turnstile because he had turned me away. Luckily I was sat with the rest of the Halifax branch. After losing the match, trouble began in our side of the stand. Some of the Halifax lads grabbed me and kept me out of harm's way. We managed to get to an exit that was about three people wide when the coppers decided to bring a horse down towards us. Roly had his foot trodden on by the horse and was threatened with being arrested when we complained about it.

Pre-season friendly against Celtic, 24 July 1999.

Leeds won the match 2-1 with a goal from Smith and an own goal from Tebily in front of a crowd of just under 53,000. An excellent attendance for a pre-season friendly with the Leeds team being Martyn, Mills, Harte, Batty, Radebe, Woodgate, Hopkin, Smith, Hasselbaink, Kewell and Bowyer with subs Bakke, Kelly, Haaland, McPhail, Robinson and Jones.

When I was 16, I travelled with Brian to Glasgow and stayed in a hotel room for the weekend. Sonya my cousin came up on the Saturday morning to join us and slept on the floor of the room that night. Brian is a horrible snorer so he woke up in the morning covered in anything that I could throw at him overnight, including his clothes that had been neatly folded at the end of his bed and his shoes. Before the match we went to meet some of the Halifax branch who had caught the train up that morning. We went to go in one of the pubs but the bouncer wasn't going to let me in because I had a Leeds shirt on. He said that if I turned it inside out I could come in. Andy Bates went mad and gave me his jacket and said I was not going to turn it inside out. I also remember Andy Bates having only a toothbrush in his pocket for his luggage which was confiscated by the stewards at the match.

When we went into the ground, me, Brian and Sonya had tickets in the Celtic end. We walked round to the Leeds side and climbed over the barrier into our fans. After the match we went back to the pub for an hour before me, Brian and Sonya headed off to get changed and grab a bite to eat before meeting back up with the Halifax lot a bit later. About five minutes after we left, trouble started and bottles were thrown. Andy Bates ended up in hospital not long after with a broken leg. The following morning when we went to visit him, we found out he had discharged himself and jumped back on the train to go home. That evening, before heading home the next day, the bouncers looked at me and Brian a bit peculiarly when we went to a club. They said Brian was too f*****g old and I was too f*****g young so we could go in and ended up having a great time!

Message Board Life by Slicks.
It was back in the 1999–00 season when I was an award winning FFL team manager in the works two tier FFL league system, that I found myself idly flicking through this fairly new-fangled internet malarkey for team news. Friday lunchtimes were spent trawling newspapers, and then on the net with

Team Talk, News Now and PhysioRoom.com for snippets of who may or may not be playing at the weekend. As my team were largely made up of Leeds United players and the odd show pony (JJ Okocha & Freddie Kanoute spring to mind), I typed in 'Leeds United News' into the search engine and clicked on the links that it returned. One of these was for a Leeds United message board under the Old Rivals network. I idly clicked on the link and then spent my lunch break laughing out loud at the tales and goings on of the assortment of LUFC fans that gathered there from quite literally all around the world. Not only that, folk from other clubs had their own message boards under the Rivals umbrella and often popped onto the Leeds board to swap insults and vice versa. I silently looked in for weeks not feeling brave enough to add my twopenn'orth until one Friday afternoon when the temptation became too much. The Leeds fans would start a 'WACCOE' thread on Saturdays opposing team's board. One poster would start "We are the Champions" and the next would follow "Champions of Europe". These threads got bigger and bigger and this particular Friday as was the norm, incurred the wrath of the opposing fans who frothed at the mouth at our claims at being The Champions of Europe (you all know the story behind that one). I could hold back no longer and registered my FFL team name as my username. *leedsRslickers* was then let loose on the internet and I found myself joining in with the best of them.

It actually came as quite a surprise to me to find out how far and wide our fan base stretched. I would go to matches usually alone and not realise that so many folk stood around me had travelled the length and breadth of the country and from overseas to be there. On the Rivals board, there was HarryofOz, AndyCA, Kloggen who lived in Denmark and Sigmund in Sweden not to mention the others from all points of the UK and Ireland. There was a whole branch of 'That London' Whites usually led by Nighthawk and Mikey. Before I knew it, I was logging in every lunchtime and passing the time of day with these folk. The humour was second to none and rarely a day went by without me laughing out loud at my desk. That was right up until we lost Chris and Kev in April 2000. The message board moderator was having problems of his own and not looking in very often. The absolute worst of internet trolls would come onto our board and I'm not going to even give them the dishonour of going over their behaviour but enough was enough. And to think other clubs call US scum!

One of our posters VerryTerribles set up a home fans only message board to get rid of the trolls and named it WATCOE (presumably named after our Friday afternoon goings-on) which had teething problems so Fieldy (residing up in Edinburgh) took it over, turned it yellow and renamed it WACCOE. Somebody else hosts it now, but to this day it is, I believe, the biggest and busiest Leeds United message board on the internet. Sadly Rivals got left behind and we lost many good posters along the way who never made the transition. BillyisGod tried to get Rivals up and running again but there had been too much water under the bridge and everybody had jumped ship for WACCOE. Sky took Rivals over before eventually pulling the plug.

WACCOE meet ups began happening. In those days you could take your own beer into the Peacock beer garden and that's where we would all meet pre match and friendships that crossed over from cyber life to real life were made. It's where I have come across Heidi (or as we know her – Billy04MyHero) the author of this book as well as many others who have become close friends. In fact, some are like family to me and we have been to various families 'do's' along the years. HarryofOz became firm friends with a number of us and every few years, comes across to the UK from Sydney for several weeks staying at one or another of our homes and taking in every Leeds match home and away along the way.

Friendships have been made from the Rivals days with fans from other clubs too (I use the word 'friends' loosely here as I risk getting lynched for this and may have to go and get my Father's gun to defend myself). Somewhere kicking about the internet is a photo of SheffWhite and BillyisGod with two of the Chelsea dudes (Noeyebrows and UptheChelsk) taken in the Peacock beer garden when Chelski came to town. Noeyebrows and I are firm friends to this day. I have a soft spot for fans of Sheffield Wednesday, even though they hate everything that is Leeds United and we have had many an online 'row' about various issues. They are mostly top folk and I've had the pleasure of meeting a number of them too along the way.

So from very small beginnings, message board life has changed my whole football experience. I have been with these online to real life friends the day we got relegated to League One, then the unforgettable day that saw us promoted back to the Championship (four years to the day as I write this in fact) and then most recently … the day we stood shoulder to shoulder for Gary Speed. I have stood like a rose between the two thorns that are ClearlySighted and Elland1919 as they bickered on about something or other whilst Blackpool were hammering us at home one cold midweek night. I've proudly worn the magnificent Dr Who-esque type LUFC scarf that NELWhites Mum knitted for me (I had a severe attack of Scarf envy when he turned up in one) and I've rejoiced in a karaoke curry house in Southampton with Lou, Gloria, SimonB and others after we came back from 0–3 down at half time to win 4–3.

I can't write about football in the 80s and message boards as the world wide web was but a twinkle in Bill Gates eye back then but man; have I had some fun along the way since the first time I stumbled across the Rivals network. There are of course many more LUFC message boards out there, some of which I've dabbled in and I'm fairly sure each one hosts its own little community of LUFC fans from all corners of the globe. These days I look in on WACCOE and watch the next generation of Leeds fans having their say on all things Leeds United and beyond (including favourite flavour crisps/cheese etc etc) and sometimes have a little comment. However, I do miss those Friday afternoons childishly WACCOE-ing the opposition on Rivals and am really grateful to message board life for bringing me together with some of the finest LUFC fans I could ever have met.

MOT.

My own recent highlight.

It is only in recent years that I have managed to return to some away matches but straight away the bug of watching matches has returned. Although I don't drink alcohol anymore, I am happy to have a pub stop for a couple of hours (I stopped drinking 25 years ago as it was a waste of time due to it never agreeing with me!) This season in particular, the one match that stands out for me is Charlton away:

Charlton v Leeds Saturday 9 November 2013, 3.00 pm kick-off Leeds won 4–2 Ross McCormack (4 goals).

I wasn't looking forward to the early morning start today at 5.30 am although I was looking forward to the match. Turned out that I was still wide awake at 2.00 am so had just over three hours sleep. At least going on the coach from Leeds meant I could go to sleep on the way there and back. Just before I set off from home the heavens had opened and there was a right downpour. Got to Elland Road and went for a hot chocolate at McDonalds before parking up outside the East Stand and going for the coach.

Luckily once on the coach I did get some sleep and a bit later I put my headphones on and listened to music on my ipod. As usual when listening to music I automatically started singing, the only thing was no one else could hear the music, only my singing! It caused a lot of amusement on the coach with everyone laughing at me and trying to take the mickey. As it was, I said it was better to be happy than miserable and shows that I will always sing at football matches too. I felt in a really happy mood so didn't take offence at the teasing.

We stopped off at Tower Bridge for a couple of hours and I took a few photos. On our way to the pub the heavens opened again with torrential rain. I sat with a group of at least 12 of the Fullerton Park branch who I travelled down with. Lewis and his granddad had come to join us when I came back to the table with my latte. They said that he had only seen one victory so far and we said it would be two today. I had said that I wanted three points today and I didn't care how we did it but we had to win!

Just as we were going out of the pub to the coach, we started talking to three lads who had been talking to a few off our coach. I thought they were Chelsea fans but they were WBA fans on their way to Chelsea to watch their team. I showed them my book and said that WBA were mentioned in it from when we went to Johnny Giles's testimonial there and had a horrendous time from some of their fans. They thought the book was for Leeds fans but I said no it could be of interest to others and said that if they knew anyone who went in the seventies or female fans to pass the word round. It was nice to have a chat with opposition fans without any nastiness too.

As we set off we got stuck in traffic so the driver turned round and we went the other way which was fine. I fell asleep only to wake up at the ground and heard someone say there was a pitch inspection and the match could be called off in the next 10 minutes! I said in dismay that there was no way I was setting off at 5.30 in the morning for the match to be called off! They also said kick-off had been delayed until 3.30 pm. I decided to get off the coach and go and wait by the entrances and stood with Julie from Fullerton Park and Phillip 'thumbsup' Cresswell. I decided today that I was going to get photos of more people I knew rather than just random crowd photos. It had been tweeted that if it rained again within the next 10 minutes the match would be called off. We stood there as the rain stopped and a bit of blue sky came through so we were relieved when they said the match was on. A couple of weeks ago the match against Barnsley had to be abandoned just after half-time due to a waterlogged pitch, so they weren't going to let us in until a decision had been made.

As soon as I got in the ground, Jo Entwhistle came to see me to say hello with the three people she had travelled with. She said she wants me to sign my book *Follow Me and Leeds United* that she had bought and I said anytime. I also had to show it to one of the lads and told him about it. Another three lads stood next to us and one of them was singing WACCOE – We are the

Champions, Champions of Europe. I said to try and sing it slower as it was awesome when done like that. I think I mentioned to them about it being done properly in Paris in 1975 at the European Cup Final. That's when one of them said he was only born then. He said he had two wishes, one that I would have been his mum and secondly he wasn't telling me what it was!

Whilst I was stood there I saw Tony from Kippax who bought one of my books at the Viking Fest recently. He told me he'd read the book and thought what I'd had to put up with was sinister at times. He said it was really bad as well, what had happened, with the abuse I had got from lads both verbally and sexually. We had a bit of a laugh over it though when he mentioned the t**s word! I also have an ambition regarding the fans recording many of the old songs that we have sung at matches over the years. This has support from Tony, Gary Edwards and Mick Hewitt who have wanted to record the old songs too. As many of these songs haven't been aired for years, many of our fans are unaware of them. It would be nice to do this so that they can be shared with our fans and ensure we can recreate the atmospheres of the past at Elland Road once again.

As I went into the stand I was looking for my seat thinking it didn't exist and I had got the number wrong. I was nearly sent flying down the stand and looked round to see it was Douggie from Bacup who had knocked into me on purpose. Then I saw Daz from Norwich and he said he hadn't forgotten about my book and would be getting it. As I carried on I got shouted at and saw it was Andy who I got engaged to in 1975 and he said hello so I took a photo of him for old time's sake.

I ended up sat with a good crowd and was next to Mitch and some of the Fullerton Park branch. I was behind Rowley Birkin and The Bawlbag from WACCOE, with Mick Hewitt and also Alan Green nearby. I had a good talk with Rowley as I have followed his lead to take photos at the matches and post them on WACCOE. Personally, I also post them on Facebook, Twitter, LinkedIn and my website, sharing the photos with our worldwide fan base. As we were more or less at the same place in the stand it would be interesting to see who took what.

When the teams came out onto the pitch, it was then that I noticed the state of the pitch, with standing water meaning the ball wasn't running. We started off by attacking the goal towards us. I had my camera out videoing the Leeds fans trying to do a proper WACCOE chant and just turned it back towards the pitch as Ross McCormack put the ball into the net. McDermott had brought back Danny Pugh and Michael Brown into squad and Mowatt was out injured. They started off a little bit slow but to be honest they both put a decent shift in. Apparently they both have a great attitude in training and off the field so although initially I was a little bit dubious, it turned out to be a good decision. We had been playing okay despite the conditions and it was only then that I realised it was raining heavily again! We started time wasting towards the end of the first half, I thought it was because Wootton was injured. It wasn't the right decision for Leeds because it meant they took the foot off the pedal and let Charlton back into the match getting an equaliser just before half time.

On my way back into the stand I saw Daz again and he bought one of my books from me. I then went further down the stand to get a photo of Alan Green and Lawrence and a few others got in the photo including Rob who my niece Sonya sits next to. Also Mick Hewitt was in the background and he asked me if this was for my next book, definitely!

We managed to get a penalty which Ross McCormack duly scored from to send us into the lead once again. Unfortunately we let one of theirs into the penalty area and they managed to equalise again. This wasn't the end though, as Ross got onto the end of a cross to volley Leeds back into the lead again and give him his first hat trick. The match culminated in a 4–2 victory for Leeds when Ross got the fourth goal direct from a free-kick he took.

It was a well-earned victory and three points. It was one of those fantastic days of being a Leeds fan and having to be there. We had non-stop singing and got our atmosphere back. Loved it!! This was also our first back to back win this season having beaten Yeovil 2–0 at Elland Road both scored by McCormack too, so we have to move onwards and upwards.

Leeds Memorabilia.

Another big thing about Leeds fans is the memorabilia they have collected over the years. When I moved house 11 years ago, I decided that I would sell most of my Leeds United memorabilia that I had in my possession from my many years of following them. I have found in recent times though that I have become very nostalgic about all the things I had. I did get a telling off from Mick Hewitt for putting a pin hole through my European Cup Winners Cup programme from Salonika in 1973. I had pinned it to my wall to have on display but by doing this, had reduced the valuation of it somewhat. The things that I wouldn't sell though were my badges, mirrors and mug collections along with some pennants. Recently I have managed to replace some things that I had sold in the past by bidding for them on eBay. This includes some scarves, a Leeds T-shirt with the team pictured on it plus some Leeds shirts from earlier years.

I started collecting my badges in the late sixties/early seventies and kept them all on a scarf at home which was on my wall. Eventually they have been framed and now take pride of place in my dining room with 275 Leeds badges on show. There are a few Scotland, Rangers, Celtic, Yorkshire and England badges amongst them too. In my early days of supporting Leeds, it was easy to remember which badges you had and you were able to spot a new one straight away. In recent years this has become harder because the same badge was being brought out in so many different colours together with some for every match. I only buy certain ones now that catch my eye!

My mirrors include a European Cup Final 1975 and a Geared to Success one and hold special memories for me as I have had them such a long time. They are also links to the years where I followed the best team in the world.

My Leeds United mug collection have been bought over the years and every time I see a new one, I try and buy it, having got approximately 75 different ones collected over the years, I keep most of them in boxes with only a few on display to prevent them getting broken. My Billy Bremner and Marching on Together mugs take pride of place at work. The pennants again are mostly from the seventies.

In the seventies I also taped the Kop at Leeds by taking my cassette recorder onto the terraces. This has now been kindly converted into a digital version by Chris @LeedsFanzines for me and can be viewed on my website www.followmeandleedsunited.co.uk under the YouTube link but beware, they contain swearing!! Obviously if anyone is easily offended then they shouldn't view them but as they are authentic, they show what it was like at the time. Sue has also found her cassette tapes and when they are converted they too will be published on my website.

In my earlier days of following Leeds there wasn't as much memorabilia available although there was a souvenir shop at Elland Road, plus a small portacabin. My friends and I spent hours in the shop over the years. We also said that they should bring out things like wallpaper, bedding, rugs and many more items in Leeds United colours. It looks like we were marketing stalwarts in the making, as these things are now available to buy. I still wear my Leeds colours wherever I go, flying the flag as a Leeds fan. I have found that strangers often come up to me and talk about Leeds and many times found out that we support the same club. The name of Leeds is spread far and wide and encourages communication between people.

Finally, my support of Leeds United will continue with my family brought up in the correct manner. I have done my part in keeping the memories of following Leeds in the seventies and later years alive. I feel it is important for our fans to know what it was like to follow the best team of the era in Don Revie's team and also having success at the same time. Lots of our fans have never experienced the good times only the bad, so it is important to share these memories. There are many more Leeds fans who are able to talk about the matches in more detail, whereas my experiences come from a fan's perspective. My grateful thanks to all our fans who have shared their memories for this book, because it doesn't matter if you attended the same matches or not, each and every one of us see things through our own eyes. I will never stop loving the reminiscing about where we have travelled to support Leeds United and long may it continue.

Marching on Together. We all love Leeds!!